T0035672

PRAISE FOR *THE GENIUS ZONE*

"The inner intelligence of the body is the ultimate and supreme genius. Gay shows how to connect with this inner intelligence and discover the secrets to healing, love, intuition, and insight."

   —**Deepak Chopra**

"Imagine sitting down with the coaching legend, Gay Hendricks, as he works his transformational magic with you! Reading his new book, *The Genius Zone*, is just like that. He's truly a genius at giving us the tools to unleash our own genius."

   —**Arielle Ford, author of *The Soulmate Secret***

"Hendricks provides some helpful ideas about creativity. . . . There's plenty to recommend in this practical workbook."

   —***Publishers Weekly***

PRAISE FOR *CONSCIOUS LUCK*

"Those intrigued by how mental visualization and intentionality can lead to a 'more abundant' life will love this."

   —***Publishers Weekly***

"Inherently fascinating, thoughtful and thought-provoking, insightful, practical, and thoroughly 'reader friendly' in organization and presentation, *Conscious Luck* is a unique and extraordinary addition to community and academic library Self-Help/Self-Improvement collections."

   —***Midwest Book Review***

"*Conscious Luck* is a toolkit for writing your own happy ending."

   —**Debbie Macomber, #1 *New York Times* bestselling author**

"Luck isn't as random as you might think. The secrets in *Conscious Luck* will accelerate your journey from where you are to where you want to be."

—Jack Canfield, coauthor, #1 *New York Times* bestselling
Chicken Soup for the Soul® series and *The Success Principles*™

"This is an engaging, mind-blowing, and ultimately practical guide to creating more luck in your life. I highly recommend it!"

—Marci Shimoff, #1 *New York Times* bestselling author of
Happy for No Reason and *Chicken Soup for the Woman's Soul*

"*Conscious Luck* is as unique as it is powerful. It approaches luck from many different angles—somatically, psychologically, spiritually, and behaviorally—and uses true, inspiring stories to illustrate the principles."

—John Gray, #1 *New York Times* bestselling author of *Men Are from Mars, Women Are from Venus*

Your Big
Leap Year

ALSO BY GAY HENDRICKS

The Big Leap
Conscious Loving
Five Wishes
Conscious Living
The Corporate Mystic
At the Speed of Life
Learning to Love Yourself
Conscious Luck
The Genius Zone

YOUR BIG LEAP YEAR

A Year to Manifest
Your Next-Level
Life . . . Starting Today!

Gay Hendricks

ST. MARTIN'S
ESSENTIALS
NEW YORK

First published in the United States by St. Martin's Essentials, an
imprint of St. Martin's Publishing Group

YOUR BIG LEAP YEAR. Copyright © 2024 by The Hendricks Institute, Inc.
All rights reserved. Printed in the United States of America. For information,
address St. Martin's Publishing Group, 120 Broadway, New York, NY 10271.

www.stmartins.com

The Library of Congress Cataloging-in-Publication Data is available upon request.

ISBN 978-1-250-29279-7 (trade paperback)
ISBN 978-1-250-29280-3 (ebook)

Our books may be purchased in bulk for promotional, educational, or business
use. Please contact your local bookseller or the Macmillan Corporate and
Premium Sales Department at 1-800-221-7945, extension 5442, or by
email at MacmillanSpecialMarkets@macmillan.com.

First Edition: 2024

10 9 8 7 6 5 4 3 2 1

*To my mate, best friend, and creative partner
for the past 44 years, Kathlyn Hendricks.*

CONTENTS

INTRODUCTION
Welcome to *Your Big Leap Year*!

First, take a moment to celebrate yourself for making a life-changing choice. You're beginning a year with unlimited possibilities for developing your highest potential. *Your Big Leap Year* offers you the opportunity to take 365 daily leaps forward to your genius—even if you only have a few minutes to invest.

You may have already read my book *The Big Leap,* the original inspiration for this daybook. If not, let me introduce you to the two big subjects at its heart. First, *The Big Leap* shows you how to eliminate your Upper Limit Problems, the ways you sabotage yourself when things start to go well. Then, it shows you how to live your daily life in the Genius Zone, where you're doing what you love to do and what makes your best contribution to the world. *Your Big Leap Year* gives you daily tools for accomplishing both of those goals; it's a yearlong sequence of the wisdom and skills I've found most essential for living a life of genius.

Your Big Leap Year *Begins When You Do*

Some daybooks are designed to start on January 1. This one isn't. It begins the day you decide to take the leap. Rather than following the calendar year, *Your Big Leap Year* is organized around key themes that build on each other as your year proceeds.

The Genius Spiral: Three Cycles

Think of your path to genius as an ascending spiral. As you go around and up the spiral, you discover an ascending set of concepts and skills, all of which build on each other. That's the way *Your Big Leap Year* is organized. The first cycle of the spiral contains leaps based on *The Big Leap* material in the order it appears in the book. For example, you begin the spiral with the commitments that give you a solid foundation for the journey to come. Later in the year, you will revisit the subject of commitment, as well as all the other Big Leap concepts, in a second and third cycle, as you go higher and higher up the spiral. By the end of *Your Big Leap Year*, you'll know everything I've found of value about how to live full-time in your Genius Zone.

What To Expect in Your Big Leap Year

There is nothing like the power of systematic daily practice to bring forth your genius. Even if you get wisdom in a dazzling flash of enlightenment, it's the daily practical use of it that makes a difference. *Your Big Leap Year* gives you an ideal step-at-a-time way to go on a journey to your genius.

Here's what a typical day of *Your Big Leap Year* looks like. First, you get a paragraph or two of essential wisdom on one of the key themes of *The Big Leap*.

Themes include:

- How to discover your genius
- Stories from my own quest
- The power of commitment
- Overcoming your Upper Limit Problems
- Getting from the Excellence Zone to the Genius Zone
- Breaking free of your limiting beliefs
- Living in your Genius Zone
- How to create the time you need for your genius
- Bringing forth the genius of your relationships

After the day's theme, you get a practical process to put the wisdom to work for you. Among the processes are transformational activities such as:

1. Commitments that invite specific aspects of your genius
2. Wonder questions that tap your deepest creative source
3. Affirmations to establish new positive ideas in your mind
4. Journaling and other tools for awareness and exploration

The book proceeds one day at a time through multiple rounds of the Genius Spiral, each theme and activity taking you higher and higher toward the full expression of your genius.

Keep in mind, sustainable change happens gradually. This journey is made up of focused, psychological shifts that might seem small at first—but if you commit to each Daily Leap, you will look up one day and find yourself miles ahead of where you once were.

Bonus Leaps

Every leap year, the number of days in a year changes—in the same way, each person's Big Leap Year will be unique. There may be days when you don't feel the day's leap applies to you or your situation. Or it may be that your Big Leap Year falls on a calendar leap year and you need one more Daily Leap. If that happens, I've provided Bonus Leaps for you to use. You can find them at the back of the Daily Leap section.

Getting Back on Track

None of us are perfect. We forget, we get busy, and sometimes we simply don't have enough energy. If you find that you've missed a day or two (or three or four . . .), that's okay! Take some time to think about why this journey is important to you, why you started it in the first place. Review the last few leaps leading up to your break and check in with yourself: Do you still have these phrases internalized? Do you still have answers to these questions? If yes, jump back into the next leap! If no, backtrack until you find where you are psychologically, and start from there.

Journaling

For those interested in journaling, I encourage you to add a writing component to each leap, whether it's writing down the phrase of the day, an answer to the day's question, or simply how you're feeling that day. Journaling can help you keep track of your progress and revisit your answers to important questions.

From My Heart to Yours

When I set out to write this book, I had one goal I'd never developed for any of my other books: I wanted to write the book I wish I'd had to guide me on my own journey. You'll be the ultimate judge of whether it's useful, but I can guarantee you this: every day of this book has ideas and tools that not only changed my life, they also sometimes took me years to figure out. If I can save you a year, or a month, or a second on your journey to genius, I've succeeded to my highest expectations.

One of my principles is to begin every new enterprise in a spirit of gratitude. As we begin this journey together, I'd like to express my sincere appreciation for you. You have my deepest respect for choosing to invest your time and energy in your genius. In my view, the world needs more genius. It needs *your* genius, your special contribution.

Your choice to embark on a journey to your genius is deeply moving and deeply personal to me. When I began my own journey, I chose a life purpose to guide me along the way. My chosen life purpose is to expand in love, abundance, and creativity every day while I inspire others to do the same. Every day you work on your genius, making your own dreams come true, you are also making *my* dream come true. It's a double blessing, and I'm very grateful for it. My best wishes to you as you set off on the adventure of a lifetime!

THE
DAILY LEAPS

THE
FIRST
CYCLE

– – – – – – – – – –

The mainspring of genius is curiosity.

—**Charles Baudelaire,**
French poet

DAY 1
Beginning *Your Big Leap Year*

It begins with a bold question for you:

Would you be willing to make this day the first in 365 days of positive leaps in your life?

With your willingness and commitment, you can transform this day and every day to come into a journey to your highest creative potential—what I call your "genius."

Over the course of the next 365 days, you will have the opportunity to clarify and manifest many goals of your own. As you bring your own chosen desires into reality, you will also get a thorough grounding in the meta-goal of this book: to assist you in making your whole life an expression of your genius.

Ready and willing? If so, today's leap sets your journey to genius in motion.

YOUR LEAP FOR TODAY

Use this comprehensive commitment to guide each day of your journey:

I commit to expanding my genius every day of my life.

Say it to yourself several times right now to get a feel for it. Going forward, say it in your mind and out loud throughout the day. You don't need to know what your genius is yet. You'll have many opportunities to map it out as we go along.

Committing to your genius first allows you to bring forth the details of your genius in the perfect time and place.

DAY 2
The Power of Heartfelt Commitment

Commitment is the key opening action in any program of transformation. With conscious, heartfelt commitment, you can achieve goals that seem miraculous.

The most important journey any of us will ever take is only twelve inches long: from the head to the heart. Including the heart in your commitment gives the journey passion and the promise of love.

YOUR LEAP FOR TODAY

Bring to mind that big commitment you made yesterday:

I commit to expanding my genius every day of my life.

Say it to yourself a few times in your mind, in your own tone of voice. Then, shift from thinking the commitment in your mind to feeling it in your body. Embrace the commitment and welcome it into your heart, just as you might embrace a dear friend.

As you go through your day, pause occasionally to say the commitment in your mind or out loud, then remember to savor it in your body. Make a genuine, heartfelt commitment to expanding your genius in every moment of your life.

DAY 3
Exploring Willingness and Commitment

Take a moment to feel the difference between willingness and commitment. Both are essential to your journey of transformation, but they serve different functions. Feel what it's like to be willing to do something. It means you're open to the possibilities.

Commitment feels different. When I tune in to what willingness feels like in my own body and mind, it's a benign space of openness. Commitment has intention. Willingness opens the space for something positive to occur; commitment takes you into action.

YOUR LEAP FOR TODAY

Say the following two statements out loud several times.

I'm willing to expand my genius every day.

I commit to expanding my genius every day.

Notice how essential yet how different they feel in your body: willingness opens the space; commitment aims you toward action.

In the days to come, you'll use your willingness and commitment as superpowers to claim your genius life.

DAY 4
The Force of Felt Intention

In yesterday's leap, you felt the difference between willingness, which opens you to action, and commitment, which has intention.

Intention moves you in a specific direction and changes your energy, preparing you for launch.

Want to physically experience what that means? Right now, sit down. Relax into the chair or surface you're sitting on. Now, have the intention to stand up—maybe even feel yourself straighten up a little—but don't actually stand. Remain sitting but notice what's happening in your body.

Your brain has sent a signal to your body to make standing up happen. Your nerves, your balance centers, and your muscles are all gearing up for the upward movement of your body. In the moments leading up to standing, before the physical motion begins, your whole energy shifts upward. Can you feel that?

Take a moment to anchor that experience in your body so you can access it for all of your Big Leap commitments.

YOUR LEAP FOR TODAY

Just as you'd direct yourself to stand up, direct yourself to expand your genius and to be able to easily experience more and more positive energy in your life.

Repeat the following statements:

I expand my genius.

I easily experience more and more positive energy in my life.

Say them first in your mind a few times and then out loud.

Feel the shifts in your energy as your whole being prepares to turn these internal intentions into actions. From now on, add the force of felt intention to your commitments.

DAY 5
The Power of Wonder

Wonder is a superpower in manifesting your goals and dreams. When you wonder, you open a direct relationship with the creative force in yourself. When you focus your wonder on something you really want to know, you create results that often feel like magic.

In *Your Big Leap Year*, you'll learn how to use the superpower of wonder through a technique I call "wonder questions." A wonder question is something you really don't know and really want to know. When you genuinely wonder about something, it creates an opening through which creative new ideas can pour forth.

YOUR LEAP FOR TODAY

Turn on your superpower of wonder with the following simple process. It's the first of many to come this year that assist you in harnessing the awesome power of wonder.

Ask this wonder question in your mind several times:

To live my very best life this year, what do I most need to learn?

As you go through your day, bring your wonder question to mind often. Focus on simply asking the question. Your mind will spontaneously come up with creative answers if you ask the question sincerely.

DAY 6
Using Your Superpower of Wonder

When you find the right wonder question, the results can be life-changing. Early in my career, a young medical doctor came to me because he had not been able to create a successful, lasting relationship. I assisted him in developing a wonder question that turned out to be transformational: "*Hmmm*, how can I get the love I most want and need?"

He focused on it every day, and six months later, he introduced me to a lovely woman he was seeing. When I last heard from them, more than twenty years later, they were still happily married.

Note the "*hmmm*" that began his question. Today's leap shows you why and how to use this simple tool to add power to your wonder questions.

- -
YOUR LEAP FOR TODAY
- -

When people genuinely wonder, they often say "*hmmm*," as in "*Hmmm*, what would I like for lunch?" Science tells us that when humans make a humming sound, we integrate the logical and emotional sides of the brain.

Wonder questions work best when you not only think them in your mind but also feel them in your body. If you begin your wonder question with a "*hmmm*," you bring whole-brain, whole-body power to your wondering.

Say the following wonder question in your mind three to five times, beginning each time with a mental "*hmmm*."

Hmmm, how can I get the most life-changing learning from my Big Leap Year?

Circulate the question through your mind several times today, each time beginning the question with a *Hmmm*.

DAY 7
Exploring the Upper Limit Problem

In *The Big Leap*, I described a problem that plagues even the most successful people. I call it the Upper Limit Problem, the tendency to sabotage ourselves when things are going well. We hit the upper limit of how much good feeling we can tolerate and unconsciously create an argument, accident, illness, or some other negative event to bring us back down.

In exploring your Upper Limit Problems, do your best not to criticize yourself for having them. My students nicknamed Upper Limit Problems "ULPs." Everybody has ULPs, just like everybody gets hiccups. No need to make yourself wrong for getting an ULP now and then. The important thing is to learn from your ULPs, and in your Big Leap Year, you'll have lots of input on this crucial subject.

YOUR LEAP FOR TODAY

Turn on your superpower again by wondering about Upper Limit Problems. Use this wonder question to open up a friendly inquiry into your own ULPs. Say it in your mind several times:

Hmmm, **how do I sabotage myself when things are going well?**

Float the question through your mind, including the *Hmmm,* several times throughout your day. Be friendly to yourself; notice if you're asking the question in a critical tone, and if necessary, shift to a friendly one.

DAY 8
Exploring Your Genius

The great benefit of learning about your ULPs is that you open more space for your genius to emerge. As you begin to spot your Upper Limit Problems, you have more opportunities to discover and bring forth your highest creative potential.

Think of your genius as a diamond with many facets that reflect your brilliance. The first and most important facet comes to light in today's leap.

YOUR LEAP FOR TODAY

When you're in the Genius Zone, you're doing things you love to do. You'll learn other ways to know you're in your Genius Zone, but doing what you most love to do is the best one.

Ask yourself this foundational wonder question several times in the quiet of your mind:

Hmmm, what do I most love to do?

Wonder questions work best when you ask them sincerely, with heartfelt intention. Aim for a tone of genuine wonder when you ask your question and you'll be rewarded with surprising answers from your deeper self.

DAY 9
The Power of Contribution

In fifty years of working with people in various formats—including individuals, couples, and executive coaching—I've asked literally thousands of questions.

On one memorable occasion, I asked a question that made my client burst into tears and say, "That's the best question I've ever heard in my life!" In today's leap I'll ask you the same question.

YOUR LEAP FOR TODAY

In *The Big Leap* I make the point that genius is at the intersection of creativity and contribution. In other words, our greatest leaps of genius come when we're focused on making positive contributions to the people and world around us.

With that in mind, float the following wonder question through your mind:

Hmmm, how can I spend the majority of my time doing what I most love to do while making my greatest contribution to the world?

In my years of working with people, here's something I've been surprised and delighted to discover: the happiest people are those who are expressing their genius and making contributions that benefit others as well as themselves.

DAY 10
Mapping New Territory

If a bald man finds a cure, he will surely use it on himself first.

—Turkish proverb

I first discovered the Upper Limit Problem in my own life by noticing how I sabotaged myself when things were going well. For the first year, I was my own (and only) client, mapping out the new territory of my ULPs and the fears that fueled them. As a result, my ULPs became fewer and my feelings of being "in the flow" became greater and greater.

I soon got a happy surprise—other problems in my life simply disappeared as I extended the time I spent in ease and flow. To my astonishment, I began to see how I created problems to block the flow of good feelings in my life. It was as if I had an allergy to feeling good for more than a few days at a time. Fortunately, there was a cure.

YOUR LEAP FOR TODAY

Willingness is a powerful tool of transformation. For something new and positive to happen in your life, you have to be willing for it to happen. Use the following statement of willingness to extend the flow of good feeling in your life:

I'm willing to enjoy the flow of good feeling for longer periods of time every day.

Circulate the statement in your mind several times. Tune in to your body and feel your willingness. Don't be surprised if you feel some doubt about whether it's actually possible. It's natural to encounter doubt when you begin to take more responsibility for your own well-being.

As you go about your day, circulate the willingness statement through your mind and body often.

DAY 11
Focus on Good Feeling

As I navigated through my ULPs, using the same ideas and tools you'll use in *Your Big Leap Year*, I enjoyed the flow of good feeling more and more.

This increased positive energy in my body led to a surprising awareness. I realized I had early programming that feeling good was not such a good idea. I remembered actual prohibitions against feeling too good.

Popular proverbs said by my mother and grandmother were "Don't count your chickens before they hatch," "Pride goeth before a fall," and "The only thing worse than not getting what you want is getting what you want."

They were probably trying to protect me from disappointment by tamping down my exuberance, but it left the adult aftereffect of feeling guilty about feeling good.

YOUR LEAP FOR TODAY

Willingness sets the stage for commitment. Once you're willing for something to happen, commitment is the step that propels you toward action. Make the following commitment in your mind and out loud several times:

I commit to enjoying the flow of good feeling more each day.

Notice if you feel twinges of guilt or doubt when you make the commitment. These feelings are natural and normal; most of us have old programming about not letting ourselves feel too good.

Making a sincere new commitment is the best way to clean those old prohibitions out of your mind.

DAY 12
Focusing on the Larger Flow of Life

For the last couple of days, you've been exploring the flow of good feeling inside yourself. That inner focus is crucial. How you feel inside affects every choice you make in the outer world of your relationships, your work, and your play.

To discover whether you're in the flow of good feeling, all you need to do is tune in to your inner world for a moment. The outer parts of your life also have a flow to them, but it's harder to detect because of the number of moving parts. Today's leap invites you to tune in to the larger flow of your whole life.

YOUR LEAP FOR TODAY

Take a few moments to reflect on this wonder question:

Hmmm, **to what extent do I feel a satisfying flow of ease and productivity in my whole life?**

Be honest with yourself, even if the answer is difficult to accept.

When I first asked myself that question, I had a sobering realization: I only felt a satisfying flow about 10 percent of the time. Although it depressed me at first, being honest about it gave me a strong motivation to increase my whole-life flow.

DAY 13
The Four Zones That Shape Our Lives

In *The Big Leap*, I describe four zones in which you live your daily life: Incompetence, Competence, Excellence, and Genius.

When you're in your Incompetence Zone, you're doing things you're not good at (and usually don't like to do).

In your Competence Zone, you're doing things you are okay at but that somebody else could do just as well.

When you're in your Excellence Zone, you're doing things you excel at. You're doing well, so well in fact that you fall prey to the trap that's built into this zone: burnout, and its close cousin, rust-out.

In your Genius Zone, you're doing what you love to do and making your most essential contribution to the world around you. You'll learn a lot about these zones in coming months, beginning with a clear-eyed look at your Incompetence Zone.

- -
YOUR LEAP FOR TODAY
- -

Almost all of us, even the most successful, spend a surprising amount of time doing things we aren't good at and don't like to do. Today, get honest with yourself and explore your Incompetence Zone.

A wonder question gets you under way:

Hmmm, **how much time each day am I doing things I'm not good at and don't enjoy doing?**

Float the question through your mind several times. Feel the wonder of it in your body.

As you go through your day, pay careful attention to your moment-by-moment experience. Note times when you're doing things you don't like to do or are not good at.

DAY 14
The Ho-Hum Zone

Today, we take a deeper look at the Competence Zone, the times when you're doing things another person could do just as well. My students call it the Ho-Hum Zone because people are often bored when they're in it.

What is your version of the Ho-Hum Zone like? When I finally took a fearless look at how I was spending my hours, I discovered that an uncomfortable number of them found me doing something I could do but someone else could do just as well. Today, you have an opportunity to take your own fearless look at this area of your life.

- -
YOUR LEAP FOR TODAY
- -

Take a few moments to turn your superpower of wonder on the Competence Zone.

Here's a wonder question to ponder throughout your day:

Hmmm, how many hours of the day do I spend doing things that someone else could do just as well?

Be easy on yourself as you make these inquiries. Sometimes there's a tendency to get critical when you see things that are costing you time, money, or love. Nobody ever got happier through faultfinding, so do your best to be friendly with yourself.

DAY 15
The Excellence Trap

Excellence is a good thing almost any way you think of it. When you're in your Excellence Zone, you're doing things you're really good at; you're also getting good feedback in the form of money, promotions, and plenty of approval.

However, there's also a downside to this zone: when you get stuck in it too long it can make you miserable. The reason is that your fourth zone, the Genius Zone, is beckoning.

If you heed its call, you can propel yourself to heights of success you may never have dreamed of. To get started, map out your Excellence Zone with today's process.

YOUR LEAP FOR TODAY

Reflect on the following two wonder questions, designed to illuminate your Excellence Zone:

Hmmm, what do I excel at?

Hmmm, what do I do that brings me the most approval from people around me?

Make a list of your responses to these questions. They will help you understand your Excellence Zone, which in turn will make your transition into the Genius Zone easier.

DAY 16
Tracking Your Genius

Today, I offer you a bold possibility, something I practice with great benefit. I found that my genius emerged faster when I tracked it.

At first, I tracked my genius in minutes, because I wasn't spending enough genius time every day to track it in hours. However, as I often tell my students, "Genius is addictive." Within a few months of tracking the minutes each day I was doing what I most loved to do, I found I was counting it in hours. Today's leap gives you a simple way to get started.

YOUR LEAP FOR TODAY

Look at your calendar for yesterday. Scan through the day and your activities, hour by hour. Count the number of minutes or hours you were doing what you most love to do.

When I first started doing this, I was surprised to find how few minutes I was actually in my genius. Tracking it became a motivational tool for me, as I hope it will be for you.

Going forward, note the minutes you spend in the flow of your genius, and watch them turn into hours.

DAY 17
Going All the Way

During *Your Big Leap Year,* you'll encounter one bold idea after another. Today is an opportunity to go very bold.

On prior days we discussed the idea of consciously expanding the amount of time you feel good each day. In the eighties, when I was formulating and testing the ideas in *The Big Leap,* I started tracking the amount of time I felt good in my body every day. This inspired me to change my eating habits, exercise more, and clear up many ULPs. Within a couple of years, I went from feeling good an hour or so a day up to averaging six hours.

That was great, but I found myself wondering, *"Hmmm,* if I can feel good six hours a day, can I feel good all the time?" Now I invite you to wonder about this same bold question.

YOUR LEAP FOR TODAY

Focus for a few moments on this wonder question:

Hmmm, am I willing to feel good all the time?

Run it through your mind several times. Be prepared to get back talk from your mind. As soon as I formed the question, my mind kicked in with "That's impossible" and "Nobody can feel good all the time."

It's a bold, unfamiliar idea that challenges us to expand our sense of what's possible.

DAY 18
From Willingness to Commitment

After I got willing to feel good all the time, my next bold step was to make a commitment to it. The commitment eventually paid off, even though it took me quite a few years of dedicated focus.

Other than a three-day bout of flu in 1996, a case of food poisoning in 2003, and five days of a Covid-induced stuffy nose in 2021, I've felt good all the time now for more than thirty years.

It feels strange to write such an outrageous thing, but I'm happy to be able to.

YOUR LEAP FOR TODAY

Circulate this bold commitment through your mind several times, then say it aloud several more:

I commit to feeling good all the time.

Tune in to your body; notice if you feel sincere with your commitment. Allow your mind to surface any resistance to this bold idea. Throughout your day, pause occasionally to refresh the commitment in your awareness.

DAY 19
Adjusting Your Inner Thermostat

Think of the Upper Limit Problem as an inner thermostat setting. Unconsciously, and often for long-ago reasons, our inner thermostat gets set at a certain point. Its job is to regulate how much positive energy you allow yourself to enjoy.

When that thermostat setting is exceeded, meaning that you're having more success, love, and good times than you're used to, the ULP kicks in and brings you back down to familiar territory.

YOUR LEAP FOR TODAY

Use this wonder question to illuminate your inner thermostat setting:

Hmmm, how much success, love, and good times am I letting myself have right now in my life?

Check in with yourself now and then throughout the day to ask this question again.

An honest appraisal of where you are gives you the possibility of upping your thermostat so you allow yourself maximum positive energy.

DAY 20
Savoring

If you have a favorite food, you probably savor each bite more than you would if you were eating something you feel "blah" about. For example, my wife, Katie, makes amazing deviled eggs. I love them, and when I eat them, I savor each bite mindfully.

When you're savoring, you focus your attention so you can enjoy the flavors more. The concept of savoring goes well beyond food into your moment-to-moment life. In daily life, savoring means to focus consciously on enjoying good feeling itself.

Savoring is a direct way to eliminate your Upper Limit Problems. If you learn to savor your good feeling for longer and longer periods of time, your ULPs will slowly recede and disappear.

YOUR LEAP FOR TODAY

Pause for a moment and rest your attention on the sensations and feelings of your whole body. Scan your inner body from your head down to your toes and back again.

As you appraise all your inner sensations, find an area of good feeling, some place large or small, where you feel good. Let your attention linger on the area of good feeling. Savor it by feeling it thoroughly.

Carry this practice into your day, returning your awareness often to savoring good feeling.

DAY 21
Taming the Ego

Resistance to feeling good for long periods of time can also come from fear. That was certainly true for me. I knew if I dissolved my Upper Limit Problem, it would free me to commit to my genius. And that would mean *really* going for it—which was terrifying.

What if I failed? The excuses I'd used up to that point for failing: "Yeah, I failed, but I didn't really try," "I wasn't feeling well," or "It wasn't really what I wanted," wouldn't cut it. I'd be left facing a more devastating sense of failure.

If this sounds familiar, you're probably up against your ego, the part of you that craves recognition and protects you from humiliation and ostracism. A threatened ego protects itself by filling your mind with fears about making the Big Leap. Suddenly you're imagining all the disasters that could befall you if you go for it. Your mind starts telling you that it's better to stay in your small, safe comfort zone than to risk venturing into the unknown.

When you live in your Genius Zone, you don't need recognition, and you don't fear being humiliated; you're too busy doing what you love to do. As your genius grows, your ego slowly goes into retirement.

YOUR LEAP FOR TODAY

The next time you feel fears coming up about changing your life for the better, stretching yourself, or coming up short if you go for it, remind yourself of how the ego tries to keep you in the comfort zone.

Ask yourself these questions to bring the power of your awareness to bear on your ego:

Are these fears just my ego trying to protect me?
If so, how?

Asking these questions interrupts the escalation of your fears and loosens their grip on you. You're then freer to feel compassion for your ego and take its dire predictions with a big grain of salt.

DAY 22
Why We Dim the Light of Our Genius

Have you ever wondered how your ULP setting was programmed?

In my many years of studying this subject, what I've discovered is that at some point in your early childhood, usually before you could think for yourself, a setting was established, limiting the level of positivity you allow yourself to feel.

This was usually the result of the child-you trying to take care of others' feelings—most often the feelings of a parent, a sibling, or a caregiver. Children are sensitive to the energy of the important others in their lives and are quick to adjust their behavior to avoid making those others feel bad. Today's leap takes you on an enlightening excursion into the past to resolve this ancient issue.

YOUR LEAP FOR TODAY

The events that caused your programming are often lost in the past. What remains are your upper limits. Over the course of this year, you're going to be exploring the patterns that hold your limits in place, and this increased awareness will go a long way to dissolving them.

Today, lightly scan your past for any instances of trying to protect others' feelings—at your own expense. For example, dimming your joy to avoid causing jealousy, hobbling your skills to let someone else win at a game, or not voicing an idea of yours so you don't make others look bad.

For today, simply notice if that behavior is a tendency of yours. It's part of a quest you'll be on in future days of your Big Leap Year as you dismantle the dimmer switch on the light of your genius.

DAY 23
Transforming Guilt, Enjoying Good Feeling

Guilt is one of the most effective ways of bringing down any good energy we may feel. When something positive happens to us, like getting a raise, or feeling loved, or having a creative breakthrough, our good feelings often collide with a negative belief we have about ourselves.

Perhaps we believe that we don't deserve to be happy because we're basically flawed, or that we must have cheated in some way to succeed, or that we did something in our past that disqualifies us. When our happiness crashes into our negative self-judgment, it creates a surge of guilt.

If the guilt prevails, we shut down our good feeling with a conscious or unconscious act of self-sabotage. This dispels the guilt—but strengthens our upper limits. If our good feelings prevail, we increase our capacity for positivity, bringing us another step forward in our journey to genius.

YOUR LEAP FOR TODAY

Enhance your progress by making this commitment:

I commit to consciously letting myself enjoy the positive things in my life each and every day.

Say it out loud a few times. Then close your eyes and let it sink into your deeper self by repeating it mentally another few times.

You can practice your commitment by thinking of one thing that's going right in your life right now. Consciously savor it until you feel a whole-body smile. Bask in that feeling for as long as you can.

DAY 24
The Power of Enjoying What You Have

In yesterday's leap, you committed to consciously enjoying the positive things in your life. This deceptively simple commitment is the foundation of the Big Leap. Consistently following through on it will immediately and immeasurably improve your life.

Practicing it also frees you from one of the most widespread delusions in the world: the conviction that feeling good comes *after* you accomplish all your goals and fulfill your desires.

Most people believe that when you finally make the money, find the right relationship, and fully develop your creative talents, then, and only then, do you sail off into the sunset, completely blissful.

What you'll find as you start to enjoy the money you already have, the connection you already feel, and the creativity you experience every day, is that your capacity for positivity expands. And when that happens, more and more good comes flooding into your life.

--- --- --- --- --- --- --- --- --- --- --- --- --- --- --- ---
YOUR LEAP FOR TODAY
--- --- --- --- --- --- --- --- --- --- --- --- --- --- --- ---

Revisit yesterday's leap and expand it to cover all the areas of your life.

Start by finding a place in yourself that feels good about whatever money you have right now. Unless you're truly destitute, you have enough money to keep yourself clothed, fed, and sheltered. Let the gift of your present wealth, however small or large, kindle a glow of gratitude and joy inside you. Stay with it for as long as you can, at least a minute or so.

When you feel complete, turn your attention to your relationships. Rather than focusing on what you don't have, find the place inside that feels good about the love you do have in your life—with your partner or friends or family. Giving your attention to that positive feeling is like blowing on a spark, making it bigger.

Repeat this same process for your work, your creative pursuits, and your health.

DAY 25
Looking Outward and Inward

Gratitude is happiness doubled by wonder.

—**G. K. Chesterton, British writer**

There are only two ways to live your life. One is as though nothing is a miracle. The other is as though everything is a miracle.

—**Albert Einstein, theoretical physicist**

Just as soon as I get comfortable with astronomers telling us there are millions of other galaxies out there, they come along and say it's actually billions.

Looking in the other direction (inward), I used to think the liver did 350 vital functions; now, it looks like it's closer to 500. While we're walking around blissfully oblivious of our liver, it's down there busily making immune factors, removing bacteria, clearing out bilirubin so our eyes don't look yellow, and hundreds of other things.

YOUR LEAP FOR TODAY

Pause for a moment or two during the day and send your gratitude in both the outer and the inner direction.

Appreciate the billions of galaxies and whatever is going on out there. Just appreciate the miracle of it.

Then go all the way inward: appreciate your liver and your other organs for the sheer miracle of them. All of them are amazing machines that took millions of years to get working right.

Appreciate yourself also for the consciousness you have and how you're applying it to owning your full genius.

DAY 26
New Beginnings

At the beginning of each year, I like to give thought to the things I want to manifest in the coming twelve months. On New Year's Day, Katie and I often go out to a spot near our home called Meditation Mount. There's a bench we sit on that overlooks the beautiful mountain valley where we live. We have a "manifestation meeting" while looking out over the expansive vistas. We also like to come up with an affirmation that captures the attitude we want to bring to the year. Here are a couple of ours from years past:

Wherever I go, may I learn and love as much as I can in every moment.
Wherever I am, may I be always open to inspiration and truth.

YOUR LEAP FOR TODAY

At this early stage of *Your Big Leap Year*, take some time today to reflect on what you want to create in the coming months. Be as specific or as general as you like but focus on things you could manifest in the course of this year.

Here are a few examples:

Get a new job.
Lose ten pounds and get in shape.
Get clear on what my genius really is.
Finish my organic chemistry class and apply to graduate school.

After you get a list you're satisfied with, work up an affirmation that expresses the attitude you want to bring to the year. If one doesn't come, feel free to use one of mine above.

DAY 27
The Three Kinds of Receptivity

You signed on for Your Big Leap Year because you're ready for positive change. Whether you're just becoming aware of your Upper Limit Problems or getting more and more comfortable in your Genius Zone, you're working through this book to make progress in your life.

Your receptivity to the information in these pages will determine how fast or slow that progress is. Three types of receptivity play a role in your progress.

The first is receiving through your mind. The mind runs all incoming information through the filters such as "Yes, I agree with this," or "No, I don't agree with this." Then, it manufactures thoughts.

The second is receiving through your heart—deep down in your body without any filter. This is the way most people receive music or beauty. You let the input flow over you as it's happening, but you don't try to think about it.

The third is a balance of the two—you're open to all the input, and you engage your mind to process the experience and learn from it.

YOUR LEAP FOR TODAY

As you go through the day, be aware of what type of receptivity you're using. If you find yourself receiving just through the mind, thinking your way through the day, switch on the powers of receptivity in your body.

Or if you notice you're in your feelings too much and not using your mind, engage your powers of thought to get back in balance.

Use this commitment to give yourself a good foundation to stand on:

I commit to using all my powers of receiving to expand my genius.

Circulate the commitment through your mind and feel the power of it in your body. As you move through your day, bring it into your awareness occasionally to celebrate the power of commitment.

DAY 28
Becoming Aware of Your Triggers

You dissolve your upper limits by increasing your awareness of them. The mechanics of Upper Limit Problems are basically very simple: when you experience success in your life, you unconsciously create problems, conflicts, and dramas of all kinds to keep yourself from enjoying that success.

The problems may arise in a different area of life than the one in which you had your success. For example, if you have a financial breakthrough, your upper limits may trigger a crisis in your relationship, or with your health.

If you fall in love, your upper limits could manifest as a career setback or an accident.

Your upper limits do whatever it takes to rain on your parade, bringing you back within the acceptable range of happiness you'll allow yourself to experience.

YOUR LEAP FOR TODAY

Explore your upper limits on the level of the microcosm, by bringing the laser beam of your awareness to the ups and downs of your day.

Anytime you feel your mood sink, pause for a moment, and look for any wins or moments of connection or lightness that occurred sometime before you noticed you were down. Then take a breath and point yourself back up toward the top edge of your happiness capacity.

When you have a moment of happiness today, consciously savor it, and be aware that your upper limits might try to bring you down. Notice if you have the urge to eat or drink too much, or get into an argument with someone, or simply start worrying. At this point, you don't have to do anything except notice. Just your awareness is a powerful step of growth.

DAY 29
Snap!

Resilience is one of our great gifts as human beings. We can snap back from challenges to emerge stronger than before. We can snap out of limiting beliefs in the wink of an eye.

Ironically, though, we can also stay stuck in old patterns and limiting beliefs for long and painful periods of time. In our favor is the power we have to replace old limiting beliefs with fresh, empowering ones.

YOUR LEAP FOR TODAY

What's a limiting belief you'd like to snap out of? Take a moment now to think of a specific limiting belief, such as "I can't find time to work on my genius" or "I don't know what my genius is." Once you have found one, turn it into a new commitment statement. For example:

I commit to finding time to express my genius, or **I commit to discovering all aspects of my genius.**

As you go through today, be on the lookout for limiting beliefs, even relatively trivial ones such as "I can't find a parking space."

When you become aware of them, turn them into positive commitment statements.

DAY 30
Ten-Second Savoring

The best way to start any journey is to first savor where you are.

—**Anonymous**

Take ten seconds right now to appreciate who you are and what you have created in your life.

1...2...3...4...5...6...7...8...9...10.

Then, focus toward the future with the leap below. It's something I've done at least once a year. I learned it from Katie forty years ago, who learned it from her mother. Find out if it works its magic in your life.

YOUR LEAP FOR TODAY

Build your future from the bottom up, so that every step you take is in love.

Contemplate each pair of shoes in your closet. Acknowledge each pair and ask the question, "Do I absolutely love to wear these?"

Collect the shoes that you don't absolutely love to wear and donate them. Don't be swayed by sentimentalities such as "I paid so much for these I can't possibly give them away."

Be ruthless in giving away shoes that don't make the grade; your feet will appreciate you for being encased in shoes you love.

DAY 31
Courage

Here's a conclusion I've reached through being with thousands of people as they worked to express their genius: those who have the courage to discover and bring forth their genius break through to unparalleled heights of productivity and life satisfaction.

It's a rare form of courage to stay dedicated to your genius throughout all the challenges of life. The Incompetence, Competence, and Excellence Zones are always beckoning us to spend our precious time in them. Only the courageous can fulfill their responsibilities while also creating time and space for their genius to emerge.

YOUR LEAP FOR TODAY

Take a few moments right now to embrace the idea of courage. Think of what courage means to you and feel how you experience courage in your body.

Use this affirmation to bring courage to life in your journey to genius:

I enjoy the courage to recover quickly from challenges and let go of my limiting beliefs.

Say the affirmation a few times in your mind and out loud. Get the feeling of it in your body. Bring it to life several times as you move through your day.

DAY 32
Expanding Your Comfort with Feeling Good

Trying to make the leap to your genius without identifying and dissolving your ULPs is frustrating, like driving a car with one foot on the brakes. You won't enjoy the ride as much.

When I first began my own journey to genius, I came into frequent contact with the scared part of me, the version of myself that wanted to play it safe. As much as I yearned to express my genius, there was a part of me that wanted to stay in my familiar comfort zone. Today's leap will give your comfort zone a gentle stretch.

YOUR LEAP FOR TODAY

Take a moment to remember a peak experience from your life—a moment of triumph, or intimacy, or of feeling supremely fortunate. A moment that lifts your heart just remembering it.

Check your clock to see what time it is and then close your eyes. While taking slow, deep breaths, feel the joy of that experience in every cell of your body. Be in that positive energy for as long as you have time for—or as long as you can without any negative energy like worry thoughts or bodily aches or pains interrupting you.

When you're finished, open your eyes and check the time. How long were you able to sustain feeling good? That's your baseline positivity tolerance for the present.

Today, and in the days to come, do this exercise again and watch as your tolerance increases. Bringing your awareness to the edge of your comfort zone naturally stretches that limit.

DAY 33
The Hidden Barriers

There are four hidden barriers to feeling good that are based on fear and on false beliefs we hold about ourselves—beliefs that seem true and real but *aren't*. That we take them to be real on an unconscious level is what makes them such big barriers.

When you shine the light of your awareness on these beliefs, you realize that they're not real. Then the barriers they've been holding in place melt away, leaving you free to feel good more and more of the time.

YOUR LEAP FOR TODAY

Everyone I've ever worked with has had one of the four hidden barriers; some have had two or three. To start, I want you to accept the possibility that you have at least one hidden barrier that's holding you back from having all the love, success, and abundance you're capable of experiencing.

To prepare yourself for the process of disappearing those barriers, take a few deep breaths and let this affirmation reverberate inside you:

I spot my limiting beliefs and no longer give them energy.

Repeat the sentence silently four or five more times, and then let it go. It will settle into the deeper levels of your mind and heart all by itself.

In the coming leaps, you'll start identifying which of the barriers you have.

DAY 34
How Hidden Barriers Come to Be

Your hidden barriers are formed in this way:

Situations in your early past create fears in you.

Those fears cause you to believe certain false negative things about yourself.

Those false negative beliefs create a misunderstanding about who you really are.

This distorted image of yourself does its most effective barrier work on an unconscious level. When you experience a success in life—whether financial, creative, or emotional—it triggers your false negative belief(s). This causes you to unconsciously sabotage your success in some way. That's how your hidden barriers stop you from sustaining and expanding success in your life.

YOUR LEAP FOR TODAY

The good news is that when you become aware of your hidden barriers, you can systematically dismantle them.

Use these sentences to commit yourself to that process:

I commit to becoming aware of who I truly am.

I commit to freeing myself to experience more and more success at all levels of my life.

Repeat them out loud a few times, then silently in your mind. Finish by writing each sentence twice—once with your dominant hand and once with your nondominant hand. Using your nondominant hand lights up a different part of your brain.

DAY 35
Hidden Barrier #1: Feeling Fundamentally Flawed

The first hidden barrier is the most prevalent one. If you have this barrier, somewhere deep inside you have the feeling:

I'm fundamentally flawed in some way.
OR
Something is wrong with me.
OR
I'm not okay.

As a result, whenever you feel good, a little voice inside pipes up to tell you, "You shouldn't be this happy or creative or successful, because you're not okay."

This creates a problem because the mind can't hold two opposing thoughts—I'm happy, and I shouldn't be happy—at one time. To resolve this uncomfortable mind rattle, your mind chooses one of the thoughts to act on. Either you scuttle your happiness in some way—or you release the limiting belief about yourself and allow yourself to feel happy.

YOUR LEAP FOR TODAY

Sitting quietly, take a couple of deep, easy breaths. Then read through the three feelings listed below. Closing your eyes, scan yourself to see if any of these resonate with you.

I'm fundamentally flawed in some way.
Something is wrong with me.
I'm not okay.

If none resonate at the moment, check again later in the day. If any of them feel familiar to you, make a mental note of it. In the coming days, you'll learn more about this barrier, including how to let it go.

DAY 36
Deepening Your Self-Appreciation

If you've ever intentionally let your awareness linger on a loved one's face, a beautiful sunset, or the delicious coolness of a drink on a warm day, you've practiced appreciation.

If you've ever taken a moment to stop what you're doing to take a deep, conscious breath and simply relish being alive, you've practiced appreciation.

If you've ever sent an email, text, or snail-mail thank-you note to someone who has helped you or inspired you, you've practiced appreciation.

But how are you at beaming appreciation at yourself? How are you at celebrating the ways you are a gift and a blessing in the world? Like most of us, you're probably not quite as skilled at self-appreciation. Today's leap gives you practice in this essential art.

- -
YOUR LEAP FOR TODAY
- -

Take a few minutes right now to appreciate and celebrate *you*. Imagine you're your own best friend and do an inventory of your good qualities and strengths—physical, mental, emotional, and spiritual. Include your contributions to others, your talents and skills, all your accomplishments, and especially your willingness to grow. Write them all down on a piece of paper and keep it handy. You'll use it for tomorrow's leap.

DAY 37
Self-Appreciation: A Key to Genius

Yesterday, you appreciated yourself the way a good friend would appreciate you, listing all the wonderful qualities and strengths you possess. Today, you're invited to reflect on how it felt to do that and what that means for your journey to genius.

YOUR LEAP FOR TODAY

Take out your piece of paper from yesterday and read through it, noticing your reaction. How does it feel to appreciate yourself?

Is it easy or difficult?

Do you squirm inside or feel the warmth of being loved?

Do you feel conceited or as though you're tooting your own horn?

Or does it create an inner smile?

When appreciating yourself becomes easy and enjoyable, you have a renewable resource of immense value. A healthy amount of self-love means you've broken through the barrier of feeling fundamentally flawed. Loving and appreciating yourself liberates your genius better and faster than anything I know.

Pause right now to savor ten seconds of pure, unconditional love and appreciation for yourself. Repeat often throughout the day.

DAY 38
Hidden Barrier #2: Believing Success Is Disloyal

The second hidden barrier is feeling disloyal to your family of origin.

When you have this hidden barrier, success of any kind brings up the false belief that your wins make you disloyal to your roots. You think your success will cause you to abandon all the people from your past, ending up all alone. This belief hinders any happiness or growth you may experience.

YOUR LEAP FOR TODAY

To determine if you have this hidden barrier, ask yourself these two questions:

Did I break any of my family's spoken or unspoken rules to get to my present level of success?

Although I'm successful, did I fail to meet my parents' expectations in some way?

If you answered "yes" to either of these questions, it's likely your successes will trigger your upper limits in the form of guilt. To ease your feelings of guilt, you unconsciously sabotage your success, or create some drama that destroys your enjoyment of that success, or both. Understanding what activates your upper limits and causes you to put the brakes on your joy is an important key to dissolving them.

DAY 39
Hidden Barrier #3: Believing That Success Brings Burden

VARIATION #1

This hidden barrier has two variations. The first variation is based on the false belief that you're a burden to other people. If that's a belief of yours, then you're afraid being successful will somehow increase that burden.

That means the more successful you get, the bigger a burden you are on others. This naturally leads you to do whatever you can to shrink your success.

- -
YOUR LEAP FOR TODAY
- -

To determine if this variation of hidden barrier #3 is one of your upper-limit triggers, ask yourself these questions:

Have I ever felt that I was a burden to my family?

Do I currently feel that I'm a burden to anyone in my life?

You may be surprised to find that one or both of these feelings rings true for you.

If so, acknowledging this barrier is the key first step in letting go of it. You'll have many opportunities to clear this limiting belief out of your life as the year proceeds.

DAY 40
Vanquishing Variation #1

To free yourself of this variation of hidden barrier #3, you need to become aware of two false beliefs: the core false belief that you're a burden to others, and the secondary belief that being successful somehow compounds your burdensomeness.

If you dismantle the first one, the second will automatically vanish. Luckily, you already have some experience dismantling a similar belief.

The belief that you're a burden is a close cousin to the feeling of being fundamentally flawed. Both are based on an inaccurate childhood idea of what other people think of you.

- -
YOUR LEAP FOR TODAY
- -

Explore the possibility that you aren't really a burden to others. Start by asking yourself where you got that idea in the first place. Use these wonder questions to illuminate this area:

Hmmm, when was the first time I remember feeling like a burden to others?

Hmmm, when did I start believing that more success would make me more of a burden?

It's likely to be sometime in your early childhood, but everyone is different. Yours may have come along later in life. Whenever you started believing you were a burden, now it's time to free yourself.

What you'll find, as I did, is that my old false beliefs were not really about me anyway. They were about long-ago situations and the feelings of the people around me. Now you're free to make up the kinds of beliefs you want to live by.

DAY 41
Believing That Success Brings Burden

VARIATION #2

This variation is not about you being a burden on someone else. This one is based on the fear that more success will be a burden on you. The belief is that the more successful you are, the more burdens you'll feel.

For example, if your success includes having more money, you might be afraid that having to manage your wealth will be a burden. You'll have to pay more taxes. Your friends and relatives might start asking you to give or lend them money. And how will you know which investments are good ones?

While these situations might occur and could be burdensome, this fear is just an excuse for your upper limits to step in and stop you from feeling too good or living the life of your dreams. Today's leap gives you a way to get free of this limiting belief.

YOUR LEAP FOR TODAY

There's a difference between ordinary success and dissolving your upper limits so you live in your Genius Zone. Many people who look successful are still at the mercy of their upper limits. I've worked with lots of people at the top of life's game who feel utterly burdened by their success.

If this variation of hidden barrier #3 resonates with you, take a minute now to practice expanding your capacity for feeling good.

Think of a present success in any area of your life and welcome the joy that comes along with it. Then spend a full minute or more breathing and celebrating the joy you experience while thinking of it. Stay with the positive feeling as long as you can. The longer you can let yourself feel good, the more lightly you'll wear success.

DAY 42
Hidden Barrier #4: Letting Yourself Shine

This hidden barrier is based on the false belief that if you're successful, you'll make someone else look or feel bad. This barrier comes up often for adults who were gifted and talented children. As kids, they got a lot of positive attention from their parents and teachers, but also the subtle warning "Don't look too good, or you'll outshine others!"—like other students or siblings. The fear of outshining others stays with the person, often unconsciously, as they grow into adulthood. Even if you weren't an especially gifted child, this barrier can be an obstacle for anyone who is growing or excelling in the present.

YOUR LEAP FOR TODAY

To determine if you're being stopped by the fear of outshining others, ask yourself these questions:

Am I afraid that my success will make others in my life look bad?

Am I afraid that my success will make others in my life feel bad?

Am I afraid that my success will steal attention from someone I've been led to believe needs it more?

If you get a "yes" to any of these questions, reflect for a few moments on who it is you're afraid to outshine. If there's more than one, make a list of their names.

The more you know about your fear of outshining, the better you're equipped to see through that limiting belief and shine your light.

DAY 43
ULPs Can Strike at Surprising Times

I once got a call from a famous entertainer who lived up the road from us. His voice was hoarse and breathless. He said he didn't know what the problem was, but he felt terrified inside. I asked him to come over and we talked out on my back deck.

It was a classic Upper Limit Problem, with the panic triggered by a surprising event. The next day he was supposed to go to Hollywood and have his handprints immortalized in the Walk of Fame. He knew he was supposed to be happy about it but instead he woke up gripped by fear and an old belief that he didn't deserve love.

We spent an hour shining the searchlight of awareness on the old fear. After he understood it and greeted it with loving acceptance, it disappeared, replaced by a feeling of joy at the tribute he was about to receive.

YOUR LEAP FOR TODAY

Take a moment now to discover limiting beliefs you might be carrying. Explore this limiting belief by an opening commitment, followed by a question. Say this commitment several times in your mind and then out loud:

I commit to liberating myself from the limiting beliefs that hold me back.

Next, put your commitment into practice by exploring the most common one, the old belief that troubled my neighbor. Ask yourself this question:

Deep down inside, do I believe I deserve love and the good things of life?

Use your most generous intentions with yourself when you ask these deep questions. Nobody ever criticized their way to the Genius Zone; loving acceptance of yourself is always the path.

DAY 44
The Power of Choosing

In my view, the goal of life is not to attain some imaginary ideal. It's to discover and use fully your natural gifts, the full expression of which I call "genius." The longer I work with people on bringing forth their genius, the more I see it as a calling that we all need to heed.

To ignore the calling is to court boredom and burnout. When you choose to follow the calling, you step off into an adventure the likes of which you may never have imagined.

Wherever you go on your journey, it's always made one choice at a time to favor and cultivate your genius.

YOUR LEAP FOR TODAY

Use this affirmation to strengthen your commitment to your genius:

I make choices every day that allow me to do more and more of what I most love to do.

Say the affirmation a few times in your mind and aloud. Carry it into your day and be sensitive to the choices you make all day. Do they favor your genius?

DAY 45
The Commitment Paradox

You must do the thing you think you cannot do.

—**Eleanor Roosevelt, former First Lady of the United States, author, and activist**

The most important commitments you'll ever make are to things you don't know whether you can do or not. That's where the power of commitment comes in. The sincerity of your commitment and the passion you bring to it draw forth capabilities you didn't know you had. Your commitment also sensitizes you to people and connections who can assist you in your journey.

The commitment to bringing forth my genius was one of the most important choices I've ever made. At the time, I had little idea of how to do it or what it would take. I kept homing in on the commitment, though, and slowly the path began to emerge.

YOUR LEAP FOR TODAY

Today you have the opportunity to deepen your commitment to your genius. None of us have a full idea of how to do it. All we can do is make a passionate commitment to it and watch the results come forth.

Use this commitment to guide you:

I commit with all the powers of my heart and mind to expressing my full genius in the world.

Take a few moments right now to engage, body and mind, with this commitment. Say it mentally and out loud. Feel the passion of it in your body and pause to feel it throughout your day.

DAY 46
Peace of Mind

Many people have a misconception about how to attain the exalted state traditionally called "peace of mind." They think that peace of mind can be attained by shutting out the world.

In my experience, peace of mind is really "peace of heart" and "peace of body." In other words, we feel genuine peace of mind only when we accept all our emotions and sensations in our bodies. When we do that, we get to feel a whole-person peace of mind, not just peace between our ears.

YOUR LEAP FOR TODAY

Further your journey to whole-person peace of mind with this commitment:

I commit to learning about and enjoying the wholeness of myself.

Circulate this commitment through your mind several times. Feel the truth of it in your body. Throughout the day, bring this commitment into your awareness and feel its power in your body.

DAY 47
Benign Vigilance

By now, you understand the roots of the Upper Limit Problem and the mechanics of how it functions. It's time to start spotting how it shows up in everyday life. You do this through what I call "benign vigilance," or paying keen but relaxed attention to every interaction you have with yourself and the people around you.

To make the fastest progress on your Big Leap journey, make this heightened awareness a habit, like brushing your teeth, putting on your seat belt, and washing your hands before meals. The more automatic it is to recognize when you're "upper-limiting" yourself, the easier it will be to course correct.

YOUR LEAP FOR TODAY

Today, continue cultivating heightened sensitivity to your ULPs. As you go about your daily activities, notice any negative thoughts or feelings that come up inside of you.

As soon as you're aware of the negative thought or feeling, switch your focus and try to remember what you were doing, thinking, or experiencing just before you had the negative thought or feeling. Was there a positive thought or feeling? Or had something positive happened to you?

If not, keep tracing your thought/feeling/experience sequence back to see if you find a positive one that may have been a trigger.

If you don't find one, that's fine. It's good practice.

If you do, there's no need to do anything about it. It's enough just to notice.

DAY 48
The "Benign" in Benign Vigilance

Being benignly vigilant means observing yourself and your behavior in a friendly fashion—generously and with an open heart, rather than critically and looking for fault.

Though this may be a new way of dealing with yourself, it's worth cultivating. There's loads of research showing that you're more likely to succeed at establishing new habits when you treat yourself kindly.

YOUR LEAP FOR TODAY

Imagine you've been given the task to monitor someone you love for upper-limiting behaviors. While observing them, you notice one of their barriers come up and see them immediately react by doing something to bring their energy down and block their success. How would you bring this to their attention?

If it's someone you truly love, would you yell at them or call them names? Unlikely.

My guess is you would gently point out the situation and then encourage them to take the necessary steps to dissolve their barriers.

Take a moment now to really register the compassionate approach you'd use with someone you love so you can access it for yourself.

DAY 49
Upper-Limit Symptom #1: Worry

If you've ever washed a car or worked in a garden, I know you've crimped a hose to pause the water. That sharp bend in the hose stops the flow of the water in the same way that your upper limits stop the flow of positive energy in your life.

There are several ways people upper-limit themselves, so it's useful to recognize the signs. The most common one is worrying—usually about something you have no control over.

- -
YOUR LEAP FOR TODAY
- -

Take out a piece of paper and write down at least three things you're worried about now or you've worried about in the last twenty-four hours. No one else is going to see it, so you can be completely honest with yourself.

For each item on your list, ask yourself the following questions:

Is my worry a real possibility?

Is there any action I can take right now to make a positive difference?

If both answers are "no," it's likely you're upper-limiting yourself.

If both answers are "yes," then that's a reality-based concern and you can take action to address it. (People can use valid worries to bring themselves down, but that's a topic for another day.)

If your answer to the first question is "yes," but to the second question is "no," you're probably upper-limiting yourself.

Worrying is useful only if it concerns something we can do something about, and it leads to taking positive action. Otherwise, it's upper-limit static, there to keep us from experiencing too much joy or success.

DAY 50
Letting Go of Worry: Part 1

Like any bad habit, if you worry long enough it starts to feel normal and natural. As if it's the correct response to life. But worrying is like pressing your own misery button. That's why it's such an effective way to bring down your energy, keeping you stuck in the lower three zones.

The longer you worry, the more your worry spirals into new and scarier worries until you're imagining the worst possible scenarios and bracing for impending doom. That's why it's important to catch worry as it starts and learn to let it go.

YOUR LEAP FOR TODAY

Today, practice spotting your worry thoughts and then letting them go.

When you notice you're worrying about something, start by assuming it's an upper-limit symptom. This breaks the ingrained pattern we have of thinking that worry is the normal reaction to life.

Then, you can check to see if your worry is about something real that you can take immediate action to affect. With practice, you can determine in a nanosecond which worry thoughts to pay attention to and which to dismiss.

If your worry isn't something you have any control over, drop it mid-thought without giving it any more energy. You do this the same way you'd drop a ball you were holding in your hand. One second you're gripping the ball in your hand, the next second you open your fingers and the ball drops to the ground.

At first, you may just pick it up again, but if you keep releasing it and letting it fall out of your hand, it will eventually disappear. The more you do this, the better you get at it. Especially when you give your mind something else to do—which we'll cover in tomorrow's leap.

DAY 51
Letting Go of Worry: Part 2

In yesterday's leap, you learned the first three steps of a tool I developed to help you let go of worry: notice that you're worrying, do a quick reality check, then let go of your worry thoughts the way you'd drop a ball in your hand. This process is made much easier when you immediately switch your focus to something new, which brings us to the next part of the tool.

This next step is based on the nature of ULPs: they always occur when you're expanding in joy, creativity, or abundance. The purpose of ULPs is to distract you and lead you away from your genius. If you can look beyond your ULP symptom(s)—in this case, worry thoughts—you'll often find a positive new direction trying to emerge.

YOUR LEAP FOR TODAY

Today's process gives you more practice spotting your worry thoughts and letting them go.

Then, to better understand what your genius is trying to tell you, use these wonder questions:

Hmmm, what is my genius trying to tell me?

Hmmm, what positive new direction or experience is trying to emerge?

As you reflect on these questions, new ideas or thoughts may arise. Or you may notice a body feeling in the place where the positive new thing is trying to be born.

If you have a body feeling, keep your attention on that area and keep breathing into it, letting yourself feel the sensations deeply, for as long as you can. When you feel complete, take one or two deep, slow breaths. An idea of what's trying to come through may float into your awareness then or it may arise sometime later. Whenever it comes, be open to what you discover.

If you find the same worry thoughts recycling, know that your genius is continuing to wave a flag to get your attention. Just keep on letting go and using the wonder questions above. The more you do it, the easier it gets.

DAY 52
Let It Be

I've always liked the Beatles song "Let It Be." Giving yourself permission to relax the tight hold you have on your fears and worries and simply trust and breathe for a while seems like good advice. "Let it be" is also a great formula for letting something go.

YOUR LEAP FOR TODAY

In a recent leap, I shared that you can let go of worry mid-thought in the way you'd drop a ball you were holding in your hand: by simply opening your fingers and letting the ball fall to the ground.

You can also let go of worry by letting it be. To practice, imagine holding a ball in your hand, but imagine gripping it with your palm facing upward. Now imagine releasing your grip on the ball and letting it rest in the palm of your hand. It's still in your hand but there's no tension. You're no longer gripping it—you're letting it be.

Try this technique now with a worry thought you have often. See how it feels to stop clutching it and just let it be. It's still there, but you have a completely different relationship with it.

DAY 53
Worry Often Leads to Conflict with Others

Another way that worry thoughts cause us to upper-limit ourselves is through conflict with others. When you're feeling good, your upper limits cause your mind to start streaming worry thoughts. Once the worries have dive-bombed your good feeling, it's common to want to share your worries with others, so they can join you in your negativity.

If the person you share your worries with doesn't immediately start worrying with you, you'll start criticizing them until you start an argument, and voilà, now you're both flailing around in a pool of negativity. This is an upper-limit doubleheader: you've brought your own energy down and you've created an additional source of pain for yourself in the area of relationship.

YOUR LEAP FOR TODAY

Now that you know that arguments can be an upper-limit symptom, take a deeper look at what's really going on. One conviction I've developed from decades of counseling is this: most arguments don't have anything to do with what's being argued about. They stem from something deeper and are a highly effective way to send your energy plummeting.

If you're doing this leap in the morning, bring this awareness with you as you go through your day. If at any point you feel like criticizing someone or catch yourself mid-criticism, or notice you've just lobbed a critical remark at someone, give yourself a time-out. Then take a deep breath and ask yourself:

Could this be an ULP symptom?

Am I worrying about something related to my intended or delivered criticism?

Or am I feeling ambushed by worry thoughts and just lashing out with criticism?

If you're doing this leap at the end of the day, review your day, noticing if you had any fights or bickered with someone. The conflict might have been about something real, but look more deeply. See if you can identify what was really going on for you by using the above questions in the past tense.

DAY 54
The Rule of Three

A friend asked me why worry and criticism often recycled through her mind. How could she stop those unproductive thoughts from taking up her mind space? I told her that sometimes mental irritants such as worry are a response to a specific event, such as a recent conversation with a friend. Much of the time, though, the patterns of worry and self-criticism come from ancient programming before we could think for ourselves. In other words, you may have inherited a pattern that your parents or grandparents also struggled with.

I developed a simple way for people to know when their worrisome thoughts are in response to a recent event or an old personality pattern of their own. I call it the Rule of Three. If something has recycled three or more times, it's being run by an old pattern, not by recent events. I found that recent triggers faded after a couple of repetitions unless they were part of a long-held pattern.

- -
YOUR LEAP FOR TODAY
- -

Think of a conflict in your outer world or worry thoughts in your mind.

Use this wonder question to illuminate this area:

Hmmm, what conflicts with people or worry thoughts in my mind have recycled three or more times?

When you discover chronic patterns of behavior or thought, invite yourself to explore where those recycling patterns have their origin.

DAY 55
Worry Thoughts versus Creative Thoughts

When we worry, we get caught up in the drama of a problem and fail to generate a solution. Creative thoughts are different from worry thoughts because creative thoughts focus on solutions. Today, you'll have an opportunity to notice that difference.

It's important work, because worry-thinking can be addictive; it requires us to create more and more problems to worry about. Ending the addiction to worry starts with noticing your worry thoughts and distinguishing them from creative thoughts.

YOUR LEAP FOR TODAY

When you notice a worry thought or chain of worry thoughts passing through your mind, a simple and efficient thing to do is interrupt the pattern. A reliable way I've found to do this is by taking three easy breaths and changing your body position.

Practice that right now a few times: take three easy breaths, then change your body position. Any shift in your posture will work just fine. As you move through your day, use this tool to interrupt any pattern of worry thoughts that runs through your mind.

DAY 56
Upper-Limit Symptom #2: Criticism and Blame

Like worry, most criticism and blame have little to do with whatever we're criticizing or blaming. Criticism and blame are usually just ways to upper-limit ourselves.

The problem is that when we're in the grips of criticizing and blaming, we're usually 100 percent convinced that the person we're criticizing or blaming deserves it.

The idea that we could be motivated by an unconscious desire to sabotage our own happiness and success seems completely ridiculous. Yet, whatever our motivation, look at the result: criticizing and blaming not only successfully bring down our energy, but they also disrupt the connection and intimacy in our relationships.

YOUR LEAP FOR TODAY

In rare instances, criticism or blame are justified, such as when they're directed at a specific behavior that someone is engaging in. This is a slippery slope, though, because sometimes the person can be resistant to what you're saying. In general, people seldom appreciate or benefit from being criticized or blamed.

If you want to explore whether your criticism and blame are upper-limit reactions or reasonable responses based in reality, think of someone you're itching to criticize or blame, and ask yourself this question:

Will my criticism or blame of _____ produce a useful result?

If you get a clear "yes," it may be that a conversation is warranted.

Many times, though, you get a clear "no." Then it's time to consider that your blame and criticism is another ULP.

DAY 57
Self-Criticism and Self-Blame

Many people are careful not to blame or criticize others but have no problem blaming and criticizing themselves. The truth is that it doesn't matter whether your criticism and blame are directed outward or inward, they're all great ways to upper-limit yourself.

A unique feature of self-criticism or self-blame—also known as guilt or regret—is that it can be tied to real events but is often a floating dark cloud of general bad feeling. If you're experiencing the dark-cloud variety, it's highly likely you've hit your upper limits and are endeavoring to turn down your level of good feeling.

YOUR LEAP FOR TODAY

To understand if your guilt or regret is a useful response or just a way to bring your energy down, ask yourself the following question:

Is my guilt or regret about a specific action (or inaction) of mine, or is it a generalized sense of guilt or regret?

If your guilt or regret is about something specific, ask yourself this question:

Will my guilt and regret about _____ produce a useful result?

If your guilt and regret are generalized malaise or won't produce a useful result, do a short Big Leap stretching exercise: bring something positive to your awareness and then take a few minutes to savor the good feeling it produces in your mind, heart, and body.

DAY 58
Going Cold Turkey

Every once in a great while, criticism and blame (about something specific with the aim of achieving a positive result) can be useful, but chronic criticism and blame are never about producing a useful result. They're just habits that stop you from making Big Leaps.

There's a simple process I've used to determine if your criticism and blame, directed at yourself or others, are chronic: commit to going without criticizing or blaming for the next twenty-four hours. Today's leap shows you how.

YOUR LEAP FOR TODAY

Anytime you criticize and blame someone or even feel the urge to, make a check mark in your journal or on a piece of paper. If you want to keep track digitally, start a text to yourself and type an "X" into the message space anytime you observe yourself criticizing or blaming, or wanting to.

At the end of the twenty-four hours, count the check marks or X's. Whatever the number, remember, this exercise is about increasing awareness, not judgment, so be friendly with yourself.

DAY 59
Making Friends with Getting Stuck

Everybody gets stuck from time to time. Things stop working well or you stop feeling a flow of positive energy inside. Each of us has our own ways of getting stuck, but some of the most popular ways are to break an important agreement or forget to tell the truth about something significant. The consequences multiply and soon we're feeling stuck. Usually, the impasse can be resolved through clear communication, but it often takes some time before we figure out how to get unstuck.

The important thing I've learned is not to try to cover it up when you feel stuck. That seems to make it worse. People who try to avoid getting stuck stay stuck a lot longer than those who admit it right away.

I like to think of getting stuck as being like a speed bump, designed to slow you down so you can take a close look at something. It's an invitation to focus your awareness on the essentials.

YOUR LEAP FOR TODAY

What is your experience of getting stuck? What triggers it and how do you get unstuck? Use today's wonder question to open up greater awareness of this area:

Hmmm, what are the feelings and sensations that let me know I'm stuck?

Hmmm, what are the most effective, rapid ways for me to get unstuck?

Wonder about these questions right now and carry them through your day. Journaling is also a boon when you're asking big questions like these.

DAY 60
Transforming Emotions into Energy for Genius

Like most people, I did a fair share of struggling with my emotions in my teens and twenties. I was angry but didn't know it, and sad but didn't show it. As far as fear goes, I would never have admitted to being scared of anything. If you've ever been a teenager or a twentysomething, you're probably very familiar with these kinds of struggles. A lot of my most important learnings in my thirties and forties had to do with befriending my emotions and learning to express them in positive ways.

In books such as *The Genius Zone* and *Conscious Luck,* I introduced an idea that transformed my own life profoundly: use your emotions as fuel for your journey to genius. Instead of resisting your feelings, welcome them, and dedicate their energy to serving your genius. How do you do that? Today's leap shows you how.

YOUR LEAP FOR TODAY

Take a moment now to reflect back over your life in regard to your emotions. Of the main ones people struggle with—anger, sadness, fear, shame—which ones have been prominent in your life? For today's process, pick the biggest one to focus on.

Use this wonder question to open up a new conversation with yourself about your emotions:

Hmmm, **how can I use the energy of my emotions to fuel the full expression of my genius?**

Circulate this question through your mind a few times and feel the genuine sense of wonder in your body. It's a big question that affects every day of your life; keep it in the background of your awareness going forward.

DAY 61
Emotional Literacy: A Lifelong Mission

Learning about your emotions and how to express them effectively is a lifelong journey. I've been thinking about the subject nonstop since I first woke up to my feelings in 1968. Even so, I'm just as excited about what I can learn about my feelings today as I was when I first became aware of them.

Emotional literacy is a challenge at any age. Thousands of times in my career I've asked clients, "What are you feeling right now?" Whether I'm working with a troubled teenager or a grumpy CEO, they give me the same blank stare. They don't know because they've never learned how to find out. For many years I've taught a simple way to discover your feelings. It's the subject of today's leap.

YOUR LEAP FOR TODAY

The simplest way to discover your feelings is to do a body-awareness scan of three main areas: upper back and neck; chest and throat; solar plexus and belly. These are the areas that light up when we're feeling anger, sadness, and fear, respectively. Difficulty in dealing with those three emotions causes the majority of problems.

Take a moment right now to experience the body scan directly:

Become aware of the area between your shoulder blades up into the back of your neck. Rest your nonjudgmental attention on the area. You might feel relaxed or tense in this area, but whatever you feel, simply notice it with your natural awareness.

Become aware of the sensations and feelings in your throat and chest. Give your nonjudgmental attention to anything you feel in that area.

Become aware of the sensations and feelings in your solar plexus and belly area.

Pause occasionally throughout the day to give yourself a quick scan of the three key areas. The lifelong process of becoming more emotionally literate proceeds scan by scan.

DAY 62
Upper-Limit Symptom #3: Deflecting

One strategy for stopping the flow of positive energy in our lives is to sidestep it entirely. I call this strategy "deflecting." When you deflect, you block positive energy from landing in your space, refuse to receive it, or simply don't acknowledge its existence.

For example, if someone gives you a compliment about something you've done, to deflect you say, "Oh, it was nothing." Or "Nah, I actually messed it up," and point out your mistakes. Or you simply ignore it and don't respond at all.

If you find you do some deflecting, break up the pattern by doing the exact opposite. Today's leap shows you how.

YOUR LEAP FOR TODAY

As you go through your day, have a gentle awareness of how you respond to praise, compliments, or positive energy of any kind. Notice if you deflect them and, if so, go to the opposite extreme by pausing to let yourself feel them deeply.

Let the positive energy in as if you deserve every little bit of it. Why? Because you do!

DAY 63
Transforming Deflecting into Receiving

Growing up in the South, I was often warned against getting "too big for my britches" or "getting a big head." To avoid appearing conceited, I learned to meet compliments and praise with a downward gaze and a wiggle of discomfort. I thought I was being humble and modest, but I was actually becoming a master deflector.

I learned much later that although deflecting may seem like a virtue, or at worst, a harmless habit, it's a serious obstacle to making the Big Leap. Deflection prevents us from living in the Genius Zone by keeping us from expanding our capacity for feeling good.

The habit of deflecting can be deeply rooted, so it may take time and patience to be free of it. Today's leap builds on yesterday's leap and gives you a chance to practice transforming deflection into receiving *and* acknowledging.

- -
YOUR LEAP FOR TODAY
- -

Today, if you notice you're about to deflect a compliment, pause and consciously register the positive energy directed at you. Let it sink in for a moment, then simply smile and say, "Thank you."

Learning to receive positive energy graciously is a powerful step on your journey to genius. Going forward, be sensitive to moments when positive energy is being directed to you via a kind word, a compliment, or a smile. Focus on expanding your ability to receive more positive energy and watch your genius emerge.

DAY 64
Being Your Own Biggest Supporter

I took up golf in middle age, after wearing out my knees with two decades of squash and thousands of miles as a cyclist, writing three bicycle tour guides to France, Italy, and the UK. Now, I play a leisurely round a couple of times a week and sometimes play in club tournaments. I mention this because of a generalization I've reached about golfers that applies to just about everybody.

I've played with perhaps a hundred different golfers over the last twenty years, most of them people I'd not gotten to know before playing a round of golf with them. Every single one of them, at some part of the round, complimented other golfers on their shot. Not a single one said a positive word about any of their own shots, even if the shot was a brilliant one. The biggest reaction would be a barely perceptible fist pump, but nobody ever said anything like, "Dang, that was a good one!" Not a peep.

Now, for the big generalization: Isn't that exactly true of the rest of humanity that doesn't play golf? In general, people are quick to compliment others but extremely stingy at celebrating their own accomplishments. I'm not suggesting that golfers or anyone else jump up and down and crow about it every time they do something great. That would be braggadocio, never an attractive feature. Celebration is different, whether it's a fist pump or an audible "Wow, that one went just where I wanted it to go."

- -
YOUR LEAP FOR TODAY
- -

Your affirmation for today gets to the heart of a new attitude about celebrating yourself:

I celebrate myself for my positive accomplishments, as I celebrate others for theirs.

Practice this positive thought several times in your mind and speak the positive affirmation out loud. Carry it with you as you proceed through your activities today.

DAY 65
Upper-Limit Symptom #4: Squabbling

I once knew a couple who were constantly arguing with each other—not about serious things, mostly just petty squabbling. We called them the Bickersons.

Perhaps you know people like that. Or maybe you're a Bickerson yourself. There are quite a few Bickersons out there. That's because bickering, arguing, and squabbling are all incredibly common ways people upper-limit themselves.

When you go beyond your capacity for feeling good, you can quickly bring yourself down by starting an argument. These conflicts often drag on, simmering for hours, days, months, or even longer—robbing you of time and energy you could be spending expressing your genius.

YOUR LEAP FOR TODAY

You'll make enormous strides on your Big Leap journey when you learn to recognize arguments as upper-limit symptoms. If you can keep it in your awareness all the time, it will transform your life. It starts with making this commitment:

I commit to recognizing arguing as an upper-limit symptom.

Repeat this commitment in your mind as often as you can—at least two or three times a day.

At first, you may get sucked into conflicts and only remember the truth after the fact. That's fine; it won't take long until you're waking up mid-argument. With practice, you'll easily stop yourself from squabbling before a single cross word is spoken. The goal is to get this commitment so ingrained that you won't even have the urge to argue.

DAY 66
Displacing Squabbling

Recognizing arguments for what they are makes them far less compelling. When Katie and I understood the origins of our squabbling, we were able to significantly reduce conflicts between us.

This had a wonderfully productive upside because we channeled all the conflict energy into creative energy. By eliminating common issues like blame, criticism, and squabbling, we've been able to write fifty-plus books and earn two million frequent flyer miles teaching seminars all over the world. Would we have been able to do all that if we'd been squabbling with each other? Probably not, but for sure it wouldn't have been as much fun!

YOUR LEAP FOR TODAY

If you channeled all your conflict energy into creative energy, what would you create?

Many of us equate being creative with traditional artistic endeavors like composing or performing music, painting, sculpting, acting, and writing poetry or prose. Those are certainly creative activities, but they're not the *only* ways to be creative. I define being creative as creating *anything*.

You create order when you clean or organize a space.

You create nourishment when you cook a meal.

You create connection when you visit or call or write an email to someone.

You create endorphins when you exercise or dance or take a walk.

You create health when you plant or work in a vegetable garden.

You create beauty when you plant or tend a flower garden.

You create more calm when you meditate.

You create fun when you play a game or go on an outing.

With this understanding, make a list of all the creative things you could do instead of squabbling.

If you feel moved, make a second list of the creative things you and your partner (or a family member or a friend) could do together instead of arguing.

DAY 67
Authentic Speaking

One of the most important things you can learn to make daily life better is to speak in such a way that you promote connection. For example, if you're in an argument and you say, "You're not listening to me," you immediately identify the other person as the one who needs to change. Most people don't like hearing that. Instead, say something authentic and unarguable, such as "I'm afraid I'm not connecting with you."

A key to communication, especially during conflict, is to say things nobody can argue with. That's why often the simplest phrases, such as "I'm sad" or "I'm scared," provide the quickest resolution to conflicts.

Nobody argues with you when you say, "I'm scared," but if you say, "You really don't get it, do you?" you can expect an argumentative comeback. Hone your ability to speak unarguable truths and watch your conflicts dissolve.

YOUR LEAP FOR TODAY

Practice, first in your mind and then out loud, several unarguable phrases:

I'm scared.
I'm confused.
I'm angry.
I'm not sure what to do.
I'm sad.

Notice how your body feels when you say things that nobody can argue with. As you go through your day, look for opportunities to say unarguable things.

DAY 68
The Art of Healthy Responsibility

Taking responsibility for things that come up in life is one of the biggest challenges all of us face. It doesn't help that many of us are saddled with a distorted idea of responsibility. I know I was.

My big misunderstanding was to confuse it with blame. It's easy to see how these two things get mixed up together. In childhood, we're likely to hear angry parents say things like "Who's responsible for this mess?" It took me a lot of practice before I was able to take responsibility for something without blaming myself.

Healthy responsibility never involves blame. Healthy responsibility is when you ask yourself, "*Hmmm*, how did I create this issue in my life?" or "*Hmmm*, why would I be requiring this conflict at this time?" Unhealthy responsibility is when you ask, "What's wrong with me?"

In my experience, healthy responsibility feels liberating and joyful. Once I got myself free of blaming myself, responsibility took on a completely different meaning for me. It became an entirely positive experience, as I hope it will be for you.

YOUR LEAP FOR TODAY

Use the following affirmation to establish an attitude of healthy responsibility in your life:

I take joyful responsibility for all my experiences, completely free of blaming myself.

Circulate this new idea through your mind several times. Feel the truth of it in your body and bring it into your awareness throughout your day.

DAY 69
Feeling Good Is Not Boring

Sometimes I get an odd question when I talk to groups about how Katie and I eliminated blame, criticism, and arguing from our relationship. Someone will stick up a hand and ask, "Isn't that boring?" I always assure the questioner that living in harmony with your partner while expressing your genius is decidedly not boring!

The first time someone asked me that, I was baffled, but it brought up an important point: many people seem to believe that problems make life interesting and are afraid that feeling good will be dull. If you think about it, it's a version of hidden barrier #3, the false belief that being successful—in this case, feeling good—will somehow be a burden.

- -
YOUR LEAP FOR TODAY
- -

Feeling good has many textures and flavors. To verify this yourself, close your eyes and think of someone in your life that you appreciate—your partner, a child or other family member, a beloved friend, a pet. Feel into the connection you have with them and, for a full minute, savor it, the way you would a favorite food or drink, enjoying its distinctive essence.

Pick another someone in your life you appreciate and repeat the savoring process. Notice the difference—it may be subtle—between the first savoring and the second.

Pick one more someone you appreciate and repeat the process, enjoying a third unique savoring experience. These three different experiences are just a small sampling of the infinite number of ways that you can feel good.

Imagine adding the joy of doing the things you most love to do and the satisfaction of contributing your unique gifts to the world, and you'll get a feeling for the magnificence of life in your Genius Zone.

DAY 70
Fear Has Four Faces

When human beings get scared, we do one of four things: flee, fight, freeze, or faint. I call these the "four Fs," and they were wired into our bodies long before our ancestors took up residence in caves.

In modern life, the fight reflex might be a sarcastic remark; the flee reflex might be as subtle as crossing your arms and sitting back in your chair.

In animals, the four Fs are obvious: the cat hisses as a fight response, the mouse quivers (freeze) and then runs in a flight response. The opossum faints and plays dead. In humans the faint reflex might be to space out with an old *Star Trek* episode, and the freeze might be to tighten your neck muscles. Learning about your habitual responses to fear can be very helpful in freeing yourself from its grip.

YOUR LEAP FOR TODAY

Take a few moments right now to think about how you respond to fear and anxiety. Use these wonder questions to illuminate this area of your life:

Hmmm, when I'm scared, do I tend to get angry and lash out?

Hmmm, when I'm scared, do I tend to pull back and avoid conflict?

Hmmm, when I'm scared, do I tend to tighten up and freeze?

Hmmm, when I'm scared, do I tend to space out and lose focus?

As you go through your day, take note of any of the four Fs that you experience. Most of us have one particular pattern that shows up more than the others. Learning whether you're a fighter, fainter, fleer, or freezer can help you navigate fear more easily. Tomorrow's leap shows you how.

DAY 71
Turning Fear into Fuel

The great value of learning about your emotions, particularly fear, is that you can turn them into fuel for your journey to genius. The key principle: when we stop resisting emotions and turn our attention to acknowledging and embracing them, the energy that's been expended in resistance becomes available for higher uses.

Fear deserves special attention, because it's one of the main ways we hold ourselves back from the Genius Zone. Instead of letting your fear hold you back unconsciously, shine the light of your awareness on it so it becomes your friend.

In our cave-dwelling days, our fears were often survival related. When a hungry saber-toothed tiger appeared on the scene, our choice to flee or fight had life-or-death consequences. In modern life, the fears are often social rather than physical. In your boss's office asking for a raise, you're probably not afraid that your boss will punch you. Also, you're probably not worried you're going to flee shrieking from the office if you get turned down.

Whether the fear is social or physical, though, we still have the same wiring left over from our cave-person days. Every moment you spend exploring your emotions is an investment in your genius.

YOUR LEAP FOR TODAY

Use this commitment to turn the energy of fear, anger, and sadness into fuel for your genius:

I commit to befriending all my emotions, so I can use their energy for my genius.

Say your commitment a few times in your mind, then a few more times out loud. Get the feel of it in your body. As you move through your day, circulate the commitment through your mind and body.

DAY 72
Upper-Limit Symptom #5: Getting Sick or Hurt

Another common way people upper-limit themselves is by getting sick or hurt. Things start to go well and boom—you feel ill or fall off your bicycle or twist your ankle. . . . There are a million different body-related ways to bring your energy down.

Of course, not all injuries or illnesses are upper-limit symptoms. Sometimes, an accident is just an accident, and our health takes a nose dive because we ate something wrong or were exposed to a virus.

It's still a good idea to explore whether there's a connection between exceeding your capacity for joy and getting sick or hurt.

YOUR LEAP FOR TODAY

Reflect on your own recent accidents or illnesses. For each one you can remember, ask yourself:

Did it come during, or just after, a big win at work?

Did it come during, or just after, a creative breakthrough?

Did it come during, or just after, a period of happy times in a relationship?

You may see a pattern, you may not; it's worth exploring. Becoming conscious of upper-limit symptoms takes away their stealth, an important reason they're so effective at bringing down your energy.

DAY 73
The Driving Force

There are three possible driving forces behind upper-limit-induced accidents and illnesses. I call them the three Ps: punishment, prevention, and protection.

You unconsciously get sick or have an accident to *punish* yourself or to *prevent* yourself from doing something you don't really want to do or to *protect* yourself from feeling emotions you don't want to feel. (Prevention and protection almost always occur simultaneously.)

Your physical symptoms and injuries can be warning signs, much like the check-engine light flashing in your car, saying:

- Slow down.
- Stop what you're doing and pay attention.
- Something is out of alignment here.

YOUR LEAP FOR TODAY

All upper-limit symptoms are signs you're unconsciously bringing your energy down and that you need to wake up and interrupt your pattern. When those symptoms are an illness or injury, they may also bring an important message that you need to pay attention to.

To prepare yourself to decipher that message, let this wonder question resonate inside you throughout the day:

Hmmm, how can I stay open enough to hear whatever it is my deeper self is trying to tell me?

DAY 74
P Is for Punishment

If you experience a sudden onset of illness or have chronic health issues, it's possible you feel guilty about something and are trying to punish yourself. Same goes for having a serious accident or continually getting hurt in minor ways. It never hurts to ask yourself what's going on inside you at a deeper level.

YOUR LEAP FOR TODAY

Take a few minutes today to reflect on this wonder question:

Hmmm, **is there anything in my life that I feel guilty about?**

I invite you to approach this exercise with curiosity and openness.

Author and Stanford lecturer Shirzad Chamine calls this approach being a "fascinated anthropologist." Your only goal is to discover exactly what's happening, without judgment, and without trying to change or control the situation.

If you find anything, just make a mental note of it. Your awareness is a powerful first step. You'll have the chance to take more steps in tomorrow's leap.

DAY 75
Forgiving Yourself

Unacknowledged guilt leads to unconscious self-punishment. It's something to celebrate when you make progress turning that around.

In yesterday's leap, you became aware that your illnesses and injuries could be ways to punish yourself, and then you did an inner inventory for feelings of guilt. Awareness alone may not always be enough to stop the guilt and subsequent self-punishment, but it's *always* a great foundation. It will allow you to address your feelings of guilt in a far more healthy and effective way.

YOUR LEAP FOR TODAY

Go through this checklist for each thing you feel guilty about:

If your guilt is about something you did that hurt other people, is there a way you can make amends to them? Perhaps a communication to them is in order, either in person or through a call. The intent is simple: fix what you broke. Clean up any messes you made. Help someone you hurt. Donate to a related cause.

You may not be able to undo what you did or directly repair any damage you caused, but you can always take action to improve the lives of others.

Most important, forgive yourself in the way you would forgive a friend or a beloved child. Encouragement, patience, and love are the best ways to create lasting positive change.

DAY 76
P Is for Prevention and Protection

Over the many years I've been studying the Upper Limit Problem, I've seen that illness and injuries sometimes occur to help you avoid doing or feeling things that on a deeper level, you don't want to do or feel. When you recognize what it is you're trying to avoid, it may seem irrational or irresponsible to your conscious mind, which is why you haven't made a conscious move to avoid it.

But on an unconscious level, there's an alarm blaring—"Danger! Danger! Abort mission!" In response, your unconscious comes up with an effective (and usually painful) way to avoid the problematic course of action.

For example, I once had a client who had been offered a new job that paid significantly more but required a longer daily commute, which he wasn't crazy about. On a conscious level, he felt that it was irrational to turn down the job simply because of a time concern. But on an unconscious level, he was afraid of the negative impact having less time with his girlfriend would have on his relationship.

The day he was supposed to accept or decline the offer, he came down with a horrible case of the flu, allowing him to avoid making the decision—and to avoid feeling that his priorities were wrong, or that he was being disloyal to his girlfriend.

YOUR LEAP FOR TODAY

Whether or not you've had a recent illness or injury, take a few minutes today to sit with these wonder questions:

Hmmm, is there anything I have to do that I don't want to do?
Hmmm, is there anything I'm trying not to feel?
Hmmm, is there any emotion I'm afraid to feel?

Again, do your best to approach this exercise like a fascinated anthropologist. If you discover something, jot it down. If you didn't find anything, tomorrow's leap should be helpful.

DAY 77

Looking at Prevention and Protection from a Different Angle

If you're currently dealing with some form of physical setback and didn't get any answers yesterday, today's leap could be helpful.

What the client you met in yesterday's leap was trying to avoid doing and feeling when he came down with the flu was fairly straightforward and obvious, but sometimes what you're trying to avoid with illness and injuries is more subtle and harder to pinpoint. You may need to start with the result and work backward.

YOUR LEAP FOR TODAY

Ask yourself the following questions:

What action (or actions) is my illness or injury preventing me from taking? (Or if the illness or injury is in the past, what action did it prevent me from taking?)

What feelings are my illness or injury protecting me from feeling? (Or if the illness or injury is in the past, what feelings did it protect me from feeling?)

Questions such as these are profound, affecting the way you live your life. Give the questions plenty of time and space to send you creative answers.

DAY 78
What Are the Results Telling You?

When I was first exploring the Upper Limit Problem in myself, I committed a glaring example of one. I was offered a book contract for a book on writing. It was early in my relationship with Katie, and we were struggling to make ends meet every month. Along came a publisher offering a generous chunk of up-front money to write the book and I eagerly signed up. I got to work on the book right away, even before I received the contract or the advance money.

I was fifty pages into it when one day I "accidentally" turned off the hard drive before it had fully backed up the manuscript. When I quickly tried to turn it back on, it crashed, taking my precious fifty pages into the void, never to be seen again. This took place in the early days of computers, and I made a mad dash to our town's only computer store to see if they could recover it. They couldn't.

After much gnashing of teeth, I calmed down and asked myself why I'd done such a seemingly dumb thing. In a brutal flash of honesty, I realized I'd never wanted to write it in the first place. I'd just said yes because I wanted the money. I sat down and wrote a humble letter to the publisher, bowing out of the project. They forgave me graciously and offered the project to another one of their authors.

YOUR LEAP FOR TODAY

When you hit an ULP, do your best not to judge yourself harshly. An ULP often has an important message to it. Ask yourself if there's hidden wisdom to be learned. With me, the message was "Don't do stuff you don't love to do, even if it comes with compelling benefits."

Think of a recent ULP you experienced, perhaps a flurry of worry thoughts or something that looked like an accident. Reflect on it and ask yourself:

Hmmm, what message was my ULP trying to bring me?

Get in the habit of asking this question frequently and watch your ULPs decrease.

DAY 79
Upper-Limit Symptom #6: Integrity Glitches

When you sail past your upper limit of love, abundance, or success, an effective way to bring yourself down is to do something that violates your integrity. The most common integrity glitches are withheld truths, lies, and broken agreements.

In your journey to genius, I encourage you to keep close tabs on yourself for any of these behaviors. Integrity glitches eat up a lot of energy, but the sooner you catch them, the easier they are to fix.

YOUR LEAP FOR TODAY

To avoid adding guilt or shame to this symptom—giving your upper limits more fuel to bring you down—try on the following definition of integrity from the realm of physics:

When a system is whole and complete, it's in integrity.
If anything interrupts that completeness or wholeness, the system is out of integrity.
To restore integrity, you simply need to identify the breaks in the system and reverse them.

Based on this understanding, make the following commitments:
I commit to being vigilant for integrity glitches in myself.
If I find them, I commit to using them as cues to restore myself to wholeness.
Let these circulate in your mind a few times. Say them aloud and feel the power of the commitments in your body. As you move through your day, look for any integrity glitches, large and small. If you encounter any, pause and refresh your commitments.

DAY 80
The Two Steps of Healing Integrity Glitches

Healing your integrity glitches is often a two-step process: first, you explore whether the glitch is an upper-limit symptom, and second, you address the glitch itself.

Recognizing that your integrity glitch was sent by your upper limits to bring down your energy is the first step in dealing with the ULP. It helps you stop adding to the drama your upper limits create.

This frees up more energy and intelligence to focus on mending your integrity, by sharing the entirety of your experience with yourself and others, telling the truth, and repairing and renegotiating broken agreements.

YOUR LEAP FOR TODAY

Use the following questions to take a brave look at yourself in this area:

Am I telling less than the whole truth to anyone in my life—including myself?

Am I lying (actually making false statements) to anyone in my life—including myself?

Do I have any broken agreements (past or present) with anyone in my life?

The more thorough and fearless you are with your answers, the more quickly and easily you'll be able to reclaim your integrity.

DAY 81
Integrity Glitches in
Communication: Withholding Truths

Communication is a flow of energy. When you're out of integrity in your communication, within yourself or with others, you stop that flow of energy—just like crimping a hose stops the flow of water.

One way integrity glitches happen in communication is when you choose not to acknowledge or express everything you're aware of in a situation. For example, your uncle asks you a question about a controversial subject, and you avoid answering by changing the subject, or by giving an answer that only partially expresses your views.

Here's another example: you ask your coworker how she is and accept her answer of "fine," when it's clear to you that she's not fine.

You may have a good reason for not being completely honest with your uncle or for not digging deeper with your coworker, but that glitch still stops the flow of energy between you.

YOUR LEAP FOR TODAY

As you go through your day, be aware of any instances of withholding the truth from others. If you find them, for now, you don't need to do anything about them, just get a sense of how often they happen.

Notice how many of them are with people who are important to you.

DAY 82
Withholding Truths: Part 2

In yesterday's leap, you brought your awareness to the integrity glitch of withholding the truth from others. In today's leap, I invite you to look at what may be going on inside you to cause this glitch—specifically the way you withhold the truth from yourself to conceal feelings you don't want to accept consciously.

There are a lot of reasons you might want to stop the flow of communication within yourself. For example, if you're attracted to someone you don't think you should be. Or you don't like someone or some activity that's important to your partner. Or you feel upset about something, but you think your upset is unreasonable.

Letting yourself be fully aware of your deeper feelings might lead you to express or act on them, and that could be inconvenient (at best) and disastrous (at worst). To avoid all that, you break the flow of energy between your true self and the world around you.

YOUR LEAP FOR TODAY

Today, take some time to look for ways you withhold the truth in your communication with others. When you find one, check in with yourself to discover if your external glitch is based on an internal one.

To see if you're hiding important information from yourself, float this wonder question:

Hmmm, what thoughts and feelings am I avoiding because I don't want to accept them?

If you find any, follow up with these questions:

Hmmm, why don't I want to accept those thoughts and feelings?

Hmmm, what am I afraid will happen if I do?

Give these questions time and space to produce useful answers. They're also good for journaling later, so keep the questions alive in your awareness as you go through your day.

DAY 83
The Value of Microscopic Truths

In fifty years of helping people clear up conflicts, from the bedroom to the boardroom, I've developed a great reverence for the power of simple truths to restore harmony. In fact, one of my key principles in problem-solving is this: problems will tend to recycle until someone tells a fundamental truth. I call these deeper truths "microscopic," because you often need to focus the magnification power of your awareness to notice them. An example will show you what I mean.

I once was called in to help resolve a conflict between business partners that had been raging for three days. According to them, they'd been "yelling at each other with no resolution" the whole time. It took a sweaty hour, but I finally got them out of the anger zone to tell a more fundamental level of the truth: what they were scared and sad about.

Shortly, the conflict was over and good solutions emerged. With simple truths like "I'm scared we're in over our heads" and "I'm sad our friendship has broken down," they moved out of three days of being stuck recycling their anger at each other. Once they got their microscope focused on the feelings under their anger, resolution was quick to follow.

YOUR LEAP FOR TODAY

Think about a recent conflict or one that has recycled a few times in the past. Bring it to mind and ask this wonder question:

Hmmm, what is the simplest microscopic truth I need to communicate in this situation?

Perhaps it's something you're scared or sad about that you haven't communicated. Perhaps it's "I don't really want to do this." If you don't feel resolved in any situation, look for the microscopic truths that might lie just under the surface. Communicate those truths and notice the freedom you feel.

DAY 84
Lies

Another common integrity glitch is lying. You may have the best of intentions for not telling the truth—sparing someone's feelings, avoiding rejection, not losing money or position, but lying always brings down your energy.

Authenticity is a key to integrity. When you are aligned with what you authentically feel and speak honestly about it, your whole being registers it. When you're not being authentic, covering up your inner experience, your whole being registers that, too. Today's leap helps you stay in alignment with your authentic self.

YOUR LEAP FOR TODAY

Look for any places in your life right now where you're not being truthful with others.

If you find any, use these wonder questions to gently explore what's going on:

Hmmm, how does not telling the truth in this situation protect me?

Hmmm, how does not telling the truth in this situation protect others?

The intent in asking big questions like these is to increase your awareness, not to judge, criticize, or shame yourself. Treat yourself as your own best friend as you go about exploring these significant issues.

DAY 85
Looking for Miracles

You're allowed to be a masterpiece and a work in progress, simultaneously.

—Sophia Bush, American actress and activist

As we go through life, it is often the case that we think of ourselves as a work in progress (and sometimes a failed one at that). However, if we shift our attention slightly, we can also see the perfection of ourselves in the same moment. We are all both a work in progress and a living miracle at the same time.

While we're busy feeling bad about ourselves, we are also living in bodies that have been evolving for millions of years.

While we think about our failures, we're walking around on a planet spinning through space at eighteen thousand miles per hour and listening to podcasts on earphones that took engineers years to develop.

In other words, miracles are everywhere, if we choose to look for them.

YOUR LEAP FOR TODAY

As you go about your regular activities, slip the following idea into your thought stream:

I'm a magnificent masterpiece who's also constantly learning and evolving.

If it's hard to think of yourself as a masterpiece, keep trying. Seeing yourself as a living miracle is a great antidote to any negative thoughts that buzz through your mind.

DAY 86
Dismantling the Upper Limit Problem

When I first began studying my own ULPs, I found much to study. Once I started looking for how I interrupted or blunted the flow of good feeling in myself, I was amazed and dismayed to find that some days I had more ULPs than good feeling. I ultimately came to see that I had several unconscious habits that reliably brought my flow of good feeling to a screeching halt.

One of the unconscious habits I had for making myself feel bad was to break an agreement. Usually the situations were minor—showing up five minutes late or forgetting to pick up the eggs on the way home—but as I later learned from famed business consultant Tom Peters, "There's no such thing as a minor lapse of integrity." Our nervous systems register small broken agreements with the same mechanisms as big ones.

YOUR LEAP FOR TODAY

Take a moment now to explore the current state of agreements in your life. Open a friendly conversation with yourself with these wonder questions:

Hmmm, how do I use breaking agreements as a way to limit the flow of good feeling in myself?

Hmmm, how do I use breaking agreements as a way to limit the flow of connection in my relationships?

It took me many months of increasing my awareness in this area before I eliminated my pattern of not keeping my agreements. Be patient and generous with yourself as you go about clearing out your own ULPs.

DAY 87
Know Thy ULPs

When I was young, my diet was terrible—fast food, ice cream, do-nuts, chips. It makes me cringe now even thinking about it. I carried a hundred extra pounds around on my frame and wasn't even re-motely comfortable in my body. A year later I was a hundred pounds lighter. What did I do to achieve this diet miracle? I started eating healthy food!

One of the first things I did was to go through my refrigerator and pantry and throw away or give away all the cookies, candy, and sodas that I might be tempted to eat. This was useful for two rea-sons: not only did it take the undesirables out of easy reach, but it also helped me pinpoint the exact items that I gravitated toward in the universe of less-healthy foods.

After tossing out or donating five different kinds of cookies, three pints of ice cream, and a case of Pepsi, I knew I needed to care-fully monitor the overactive pull of my sweet tooth. I steered clear of bakeries and made sure I had some healthy sweet alternatives on hand. Being prepared made it easier to resist backsliding. It's the same with your go-to upper-limiting behaviors—being aware of them will help you resist their pull.

YOUR LEAP FOR TODAY

Make a list of your top three upper-limit behaviors. Here are the most common ones:

Worrying
Blaming and criticizing—yourself and others
Getting sick or hurt
Squabbling
Withholding truths—hiding important feelings and not commu-nicating significant truths to the relevant people
Breaking promises or agreements
Deflecting—ignoring or minimizing compliments and praise

Knowing which ones you tend toward will help you know the specific red flags to watch for as you make the Big Leap. When you find you're no longer significantly upper-limiting yourself in a way you listed, cross it off and select another behavior to add to the top three. Repeat this until you've dissolved all of your ULPs. It's your upper-limit diet, and it works well, no matter how much your ULPs are weighing you down with excess baggage.

DAY 88
Preventing Life-Whacks

At one point in my life, I thought I'd arrived: bestselling books, packed seminars, coaching top executives at the world's largest corporations, ever more money pouring in. But the truth was, all the activities that fed my success were getting a bit stale. I could do them in my sleep.

The sparks of creativity had been replaced by a dull, sluggish feeling in my body, which I realized had been there without my fully noticing it for months, maybe years.

After getting a full medical checkup that ruled out any physical issues, it finally dawned on me: I had been so hypnotized by success in my Excellence Zone that I had been ignoring the calls of my genius. My gray fog of malaise was both an ULP and a "life-whack" sent to wake me up. Fortunately, I got the message in time and made a deeper commitment to expressing my genius.

YOUR LEAP FOR TODAY

To avoid getting hit over the head with a life-whack, wake yourself up gently by reflecting on the following questions:

How much of my day is spent "going through the motions"?

How often do I feel truly creative?

There are no right or wrong, good or bad answers. Whatever you find is important intel that will help you on your journey to genius.

DAY 89
Adventure

The big question is whether you are going to be able to say a hearty yes to your adventure.

—**Joseph Campbell, American writer and professor**

Thanks to the venerable Miss Emma Williams, Latin teacher to two generations of my family at Leesburg High, I know that our word for adventure comes from *advenire* (to arrive) and *adventurus* (something about to happen).

The idea of leaving point A to arrive at point B has no special magic, whereas the same trip when framed as "going on an adventure" becomes exciting and fun. At the start of an adventure, our whole being vibrates with anticipation and energy, ready to tackle whatever lies ahead. The vision of finally arriving at our destination, triumphant and better for the experience, keeps us going if we're ever tempted to give up.

I suggest you view the Big Leap journey you're on now as an adventure—one of growing awareness and joy. It will transform your feelings about the process and keep your energy high.

YOUR LEAP FOR TODAY

To keep the spirit of adventure alive on your journey, use this wonder question:

Hmmm, how could I turn every moment of my life into an adventure?

Bring this question into your day today, especially if you encounter situations that feel uncomfortable. Discomfort is often part of adventure, but if you know it's in the service of your genius, it turns into excitement.

DAY 90
Embrace a New Story

As a young man, I spent a lot of time chewing on my problems and frustrations, and complaining about all the ways I was being blamed and criticized unfairly. A lot of my energy was tied up in telling and retelling the story of my disappointing life, as I focused on everything I didn't want.

When I discovered the role of my upper limits and began making the Big Leap, I made a conscious decision to switch my focus to the things I *did* want. I began telling and retelling the story of what life would be like in my Genius Zone. *That* story was uplifting and exciting and inspiring—and ultimately helped me live my genius. Today's leap offers you the opportunity to tell your best story.

- -
YOUR LEAP FOR TODAY
- -

Take a few minutes today for honest reflection. Think about the following questions and use them to find your Genius Zone.

If I were living in my genius, what work would I be doing?

If I were living in my genius, what qualities would I want in my relationships?

Embrace the story of expressing your unique genius and being surrounded by people who have an unlimited capacity for feeling good.

You may notice some internal resistance or back talk when you ask big questions like these. If so, thank that part of you for sharing its concerns, and gently put it aside for now. It's just your upper limits trying to maintain their hold on you. You know their game and you've got a better one to play.

DAY 91
The First Genius Question

When you first started thinking about what activities belong in your Genius Zone, you may have thought it would be those you were very good at doing. That makes sense given the common definition of "genius"—being exceptionally skilled at something.

But as you know from earlier leaps, those activities belong in your Excellence Zone. To qualify for your Genius Zone, the activities must also be connected to what you most love to do. In today's leap, we'll revisit that question and take it a step further.

YOUR LEAP FOR TODAY

Deepen your Genius Zone inquiry with this wonder question:

Hmmm, what do I love to do so much that I can do it for long stretches of time without getting tired or bored?

Your mind might light on activities—like binge-watching Netflix or playing solitaire or eating ice cream—that don't represent your deepest needs and desires. If that happens, just keep going. Continue to float the wonder question without fear or judgment.

You don't have to have a clear or specific description yet, just a general sense of it in your body is enough for now.

You are now a quarter of the way through Your Big Leap Year! Congratulations on completing your first quarter of growth. Over the next few days, try to identify the ways that you feel different from and the same as the person who started this journey. If you've been journaling, take some time to read through your answers and notes from the past thirteen weeks. Take time also to celebrate your achievement, in whatever way makes sense for you.

DAY 92
Find What You Love To Do and Do It Every Day

I was in my thirties when I began to home in on what I most loved to do. I've known people who discovered their true passion in their teens and twenties, and I've also known those who didn't find theirs until later in life.

The late Max Weisman, MD, was a friend and role model for me, although I didn't meet him until he was in his seventies. Max didn't find his passion for helping people until midlife when he decided to become a medical doctor. He couldn't find a US medical school who would take a forty-four-year-old student, but he eventually found a school in Holland. School started in six weeks, and he didn't speak a word of Dutch, so he immersed himself in the new language and started school fluent enough to understand medical lectures.

Max was one of the most vibrant elders I'd ever met. When I asked him the source of his radiant aliveness, he immediately said, "Find what you love to do and do it every day."

- -
YOUR LEAP FOR TODAY
- -

Focus in for a few moments on what you most love to do. Even though you've explored this topic before, revisit it from the perspective of courage. In the spirit of Max Weisman's unstoppable pursuit of his genius, use this affirmation to instill the same determination in you:

I feel the confidence and courage to do what I most love to do.

Circulate it through your mind several times. Feel the truth of it in your body and bring it into your awareness throughout your day.

DAY 93
My Big Leap

Inspired by meeting Max Weisman, whom I introduced you to in yesterday's leap, I went home that evening and spent an hour asking myself what I most loved to do. I came up with one big thing at first, although later I would discover other facets.

Of all the things in my workday world, the thing I loved most was being with groups of interested people solving the central problems of living and opening up new dimensions of awareness. I was a university professor at the time, and the set curriculum plus the publish-or-perish pressures did not leave much time for doing what I most loved to do.

After I met Max, though, I decided to offer a class of my own on Thursday nights. At first, it was six people sitting on cushions in the living room of my apartment, but within a year it took a hotel ballroom to accommodate the participants. Once I started doing the thing I most loved to do, I could barely keep up with how quickly the world responded.

Through these meetings, I homed in further on what I most loved to do. I realized I had a gift for explaining complicated things in a simple way that people could use to make their daily lives better. That awareness led me to start writing non-academic books such as *Learning to Love Yourself* and later *The Big Leap*.

YOUR LEAP FOR TODAY

Where will your journey to genius take you? Wherever your path goes, it will likely contain twists, turns, and loops you never expected. All you can do is make the commitment and watch the results emerge.

Strengthen your commitment with this sentence:

I commit to learning more every day about what I most love to do.

Circulate the commitment through your awareness as you go through your day. Look for opportunities to do more of what you most love to do.

DAY 94
The Second Genius Question

In today's leap, you're going to add another dimension to your inquiry about what you most love to do. Whatever your profession, start zeroing in on your favorite part of your work life. When you're doing it, you feel your happiest. You might even have the thought, *This is why I do what I do!* If you're lucky, you get to do that part a lot.

If you dedicate yourself and work diligently on it, you'll wake up one day and realize you're in the Genius Zone.

YOUR LEAP FOR TODAY

To get a better sense of your genius, play with these wonder questions:

Hmmm, what work do I do that doesn't seem like work?

Hmmm, what work can I do all day long without feeling tired or bored?

Sometimes, exploring these questions makes you realize that you spend too much of your workday dealing with necessary trivia and other activities that don't excite you or make your heart sing. Instead of feeling unhappy about it, I invite you to celebrate this new awareness. Becoming aware of a problem is a healthy and necessary step in addressing it.

Be easy with any discomfort you feel—it's a sign that you're headed in the right direction. Your genius won't accept anything less than a life lived in the Genius Zone.

DAY 95
The Third Genius Question

The third part of your genius inquiry involves exploring what activities in your work produce the greatest abundance and satisfaction. In other words, what do you do at work that you love doing and that also creates the best results?

For me, it's what I call free mind play. Time when I can just let ideas tumble through my mind without pressure or structure and without any criticism or constraint. Sometimes it goes nowhere; other times I'm astounded by where it leads.

Some of my most creative and lucrative ideas have come from letting my mind play freely. What will your genius activities do for you?

YOUR LEAP FOR TODAY

Use this wonder question to identify the essential aspect of your work that produces the biggest payoff:

Hmmm, **what activity in my work provides the greatest joy and value for the time spent?**

It might be interacting with the people you work with or vendors or customers. It might be taking time to sit quietly and organize your thoughts as you plan your day. It might be doing research of some kind. When you discover what yours is, make it a priority to do (at least a little) every day.

Here's a Big Leap tip: do your highest priority activity *first* each day. I schedule time each morning for my meditation and free mind play—before I start doing anything that looks like work. I find it makes the rest of the day far more productive and enjoyable.

DAY 96
Resistance and ULPs

I've had ample opportunities to study the subject of resistance, both in my own life and in the people I've worked with. One thing I've noticed still surprises me to this day: even if people understand their genius and have experienced the benefits of focusing on it every day, many still have resistance. They get distracted by ULPs large and small, and stop investing the time every day necessary to keep the flow of genius strong. If you struggle with resistance from time to time, as most of us do, today's leap gives you a friendly way to triumph over it.

YOUR LEAP FOR TODAY

To uncover any resistance you may have, make a commitment to doing one of your genius activities first each day, before you do any of your other work. Even if you only budget ten minutes for your genius, put it as your highest priority work. Use the following commitment:

I commit to doing a Genius Zone activity *first* each day for the next week.

Then immediately scan your body, mind, and emotions for any pushback. If you feel any inner objections to doing your Genius Zone activity first—or at all—list your reasons on a piece of paper. They'll often reveal your specific upper-limit symptoms.

For example, you might feel worried that changing your schedule that way will upset people in your life. Or that doing your Genius Zone activity first will make you feel irresponsible. Or that it will be a waste of time—maybe you're not as good as you think at the activity you chose. Whatever story your inner voice pipes up with, thank it for sharing and make the commitment anyway.

As you go through the week, be prepared to keep thanking the voice of your upper limits for sharing and then continue your journey to genius. Your life in the Genius Zone is waiting for you.

DAY 97
The Fourth Genius Question

When I was in preschool, I set up a cardboard box as a desk in my grandmother's living room. My job? "Helping people solve problems." I was clear that I didn't solve medical problems. People could go to the doctor's office for those. I helped with problems "around the house."

No one knew what had inspired my idea. There were no psychiatrists or psychologists in the tiny Florida town where I grew up. (And this was a decade before the *Peanuts* character Lucy sat in her cardboard booth offering "Psychiatric Help" for five cents.)

I like to think that even then, I knew that solving people's problems was connected to my unique genius. In today's leap, you can take some time to think about yours.

YOUR LEAP FOR TODAY

To reflect on your own strengths and talents, let this wonder question settle into your mind and heart:

Hmmm, what is my unique ability?

You have a special and priceless gift that you carry within yourself. This unique skill or ability when fully realized and used brings enormous benefits to those around you. This skill can often be traced to your childhood.

Your quest for genius doesn't have to be all serious. Have some fun brainstorming on this topic. You'll know you're on the right track when you feel an inner glow of wonder and exhilaration.

DAY 98
Russian Dolls

My favorite aunt, Lyndelle Hoover, was an avid collector of just about everything, but I particularly remember her collection of Russian dolls. She delighted in showing me different ones, each with its own version of the doll-within-a-doll concept. Later, when I began to seek my own genius and work with others on theirs, I found the Russian doll analogy to be useful in understanding genius.

When you first start your journey to genius, you probably don't have a full appreciation for exactly what it is. You may have a general sense—"I love teaching" or "I love writing"—but that's only the biggest Russian doll.

Inside it there are deeper treasures. At a deeper level you realize that it's not just teaching or writing, it's something more essential such as the look on students' faces when they really grasp something you're teaching. Use today's leap to delve deeper into your appreciation of your genius.

YOUR LEAP FOR TODAY

Use your journal to journey down through the Russian dolls of your genius. The following fill-in-the-blank sentences will open up this area for you.

I describe my genius in one word as _____.

When I'm doing my genius, what exactly am I doing? _____.

What I love most about doing my genius is _____.

If I were to describe one moment when my genius was fully engaged, it would be when _____.

Keep going deeper into what is most essential about your genius. The deeper your understanding, the easier it is to focus on it and grow its presence in your life.

DAY 99
Primal Longing

Your primal longing is the deepest yearning you have; the essential desire that brought you here to earth; the reason why you're alive; the goal that's most important for you to strive for this lifetime; your core driving force.

—**Rob Breszny, American astrologer, author, and musician**

The phase "primal longing" is another way of saying "what you most deeply want." When you live in your Genius Zone, your primal longing is fulfilled because you're doing what's most deeply meaningful for you and making your biggest contribution to the world around you. As you proceed along the path to the Genius Zone, it's important to stay in touch with your primal longing. It will help you choose the activities that most express your genius.

YOUR LEAP FOR TODAY

Focus your exploration today on a wonder question:

Hmmm, what do I most want to accomplish in my time here on earth?

Initiate this wondering by circulating it through your mind a few times. Then, say it out loud to get the feel of it in your body.

DAY 100
Pronoia

The universe is conspiring in your favor, bringing you all of the perfect people and situations to answer life's only question: Who am I?

—**Neale Donald Walsch, American author**

One of my favorite books, *Pronoia* by Rob Brezsny, is about a state that's the opposite of paranoia. Pronoia is the growing awareness that the universe is constantly conspiring in your favor. In my lifetime, I've made the transition (mostly) from paranoia to pronoia, but I never had a name for it until I met Rob and read his book.

As you move toward your Genius Zone, you'll find that you're riding an upward spiral: you get more and more support from the people around you for moving toward your Genius Zone. This positive feedback loop accelerates your journey.

YOUR LEAP FOR TODAY

Making the Big Leap requires being open to being supported.

Contemplate this wonder question:

Hmmm, how am I letting myself be supported by people in the world around me?

Savor the question as you go through your day. Look for opportunities to be more open to receiving support.

DAY 101
Falling in Love with Your Genius

A successful [marriage] requires falling in love many times, always with the same person.

—**Mignon McLaughlin, American journalist and author**

My grandmother, married sixty years to my granddad, said that marriage is a noun, but it ought to be a verb. It's the way you express your love for your mate that makes the difference. She said, "Treat each other with honesty, love, and respect and you can weather any storm."

Katie and I are now in our fifth decade together, and I believe my grandmother's wisdom more than ever. What I also discovered is that the same principle holds true for your genius. If you treat it with love and respect every day, you may be surprised by the priceless nature of the rewards you receive.

YOUR LEAP FOR TODAY

Wonder for a moment about how you treat your genius. Do you regard it with doubt or suspicion? Do you think of it as difficult to discover and maintain? These are all natural and common attitudes toward an unfamiliar part of yourself. Going forward, make a new commitment:

I commit to loving and respecting my genius.

Say your commitment in your mind several times, then say it aloud several more times. Bring it to mind and say it aloud throughout the day.

Bring to life—in your body and mind—a deep commitment to your genius and be willing to be astonished by the results.

DAY 102
The Centering Breath

In the early 1970s, while I was still in my doctoral training, I spent time volunteering in my daughter's kindergarten and first-grade classrooms. One thing I noticed was how much time it took to get kids settled again after recess or to get them focused on the task at hand. I got inspired to write a little book of centering activities teachers could use to get kids relaxed and focused more efficiently. Eventually, it turned into *The Centering Book*, which appeared in 1975 and is still in wide use today.

One of the breathing practices worked so well I've used it over the past fifty years in hundreds of sessions and seminars with grown-ups. I call it the "centering breath," and it's the quickest way I know of to get centered again after some stressor has impinged upon your well-being. Today's leap shows you how to put the simple power of breathing to work for you.

YOUR LEAP FOR TODAY

When we get stressed our belly muscles tighten, which prevents the full range of a relaxed breath. With tense belly muscles, the breathing gets pushed up into the chest. Usually, this happens unconsciously and so fast that we don't realize why we're suddenly not feeling good. Today's process will help you bring consciousness and insight to an often overlooked part of well-being.

First, tune in to the muscles around your navel area. Slowly and mindfully tense and release those muscles three to five times. Feel how tensing your belly muscles pushes your chest up and forward. Feel how relaxing your belly muscles lets your chest relax, too.

Next, relax your belly muscles as much as you can and take three easy breaths, letting your belly expand with each in-breath. Feel how natural and easy it is to breathe when your belly is relaxed.

As you go through your day, tune in to your belly muscles, noticing if they are tight or at ease. Notice how your body, particularly the muscles around the center of you, tense and relax in response to events.

DAY 103
Ordinary Creativity or True Creativity?

Creativity is one of the great gifts we have as human beings. Yet, all too often we end up expressing our creativity to benefit other people but not ourselves. I call it "ordinary creativity" when you're using your creativity for the sake of others. I call it "true creativity" when your creative work benefits both you and the people around you.

For example, I had the pleasure of getting to know the late mystery author Elmore Leonard in the 1980s when he was at the height of his fame. Before striking out on his writing career, he used his ordinary creativity to write advertising copy for local car dealers, banks, and supermarkets. Finally, one day he made the Big Leap to his true creativity and lived to see Paul Newman and John Travolta play his characters onscreen.

- -
YOUR LEAP FOR TODAY
- -

Take a few minutes right now and think about your creativity. Consider how you're expressing your creativity in your daily life. Make a distinction between ordinary and true creativity, as I defined them above.

Two wonder questions illuminate this area:

Hmmm, to what extent am I using my creativity in my daily life?

Hmmm, am I using my creativity to benefit myself as well as others?

I've found that the happiest people are those who bring their creativity to the world in ways that are also fulfilling to themselves.

DAY 104
We Have No Control Over the Past or Future

The past and the future have one big thing in common: we don't have any control over either one. The past has already happened, despite the maddening tendency of the mind to replay previous situations over and over, hoping for a different outcome.

As to the future, we can certainly influence it by good planning, but in actual fact we don't have any control over what eventually happens. The power to change our lives occurs only in the present.

YOUR LEAP FOR TODAY

Focus on some event from the past that still comes into your mind from time to time. Then, shift your focus to some event in the future that's been coming into your mind.

With this fresh experience of the past and future, use these affirmations to focus your power on the present:

I relax and let go of trying to control the past or the future.

I focus my attention on my commitments in the present.

Say these a few times in your mind and aloud. Feel the truth of them in your body. Tune in from time to time during your day to reaffirm them in your awareness.

DAY 105
The Feeling of Genius

After I'd been working on my genius for six months or so, I noticed a new feeling in my body. When I was fully engaged in an activity that contributed to my genius, I felt a combination of ease and excitement that was unfamiliar to me. It was a blend of deep peace and quiet exhilaration. I began to use that feeling as a reliable sign that I was serving my high intention to liberate my full genius.

We all have our own version of the "genius feeling." Yours may be very different from mine, but whatever it is, there is great value in learning about it. It's very handy to have an instant recognition system for letting you know you're in your genius. Today's leap gives you an opportunity to get clearer on how genius feels to you.

YOUR LEAP FOR TODAY

Take a few moments now to think about your genius and how it feels in your body. Imagine that you are doing something you really love to do, an activity during which you lose track of time.

As you imagine that in your mind, tune in to what you're feeling in your body. Notice any feelings, even subtle ones, that are different from how you usually feel.

As you go through your day today, stay tuned to your "genius feeling" and choose activities that bring it forth.

DAY 106
Getting Clear About Why You're Not Clear

One common stumbling block for people on their Big Leap journey is not knowing what their genius is. Unfortunately, there are many reasons you might not have even let yourself explore this deeply fundamental part of your being. Here are a few:

You feel you're too busy to even think about your genius, much less pursue it.

You're afraid of rocking the boat—there are people counting on you, and you don't want to disappoint them.

You feel that doing what you most love to do is selfish or simply a fairy tale.

You're afraid you might not have any real talents or strengths.

You're afraid that you'll discover your genius is impractical. You won't be able to make a living doing it, so why torture yourself?

To clear this obstacle, I invite you to make the unconscious conscious. Then you'll find it easier to address it.

- -
YOUR LEAP FOR TODAY
- -

If you're one of those people who doesn't know what your genius is and has even a tiny bit of resistance to exploring it, review the reasons above and see if any resonate with you.

To own your situation, whatever it is, fill in the blanks below:

I don't want to try to figure out what my genius is because

_____.

If I figure out what my genius is, I'm afraid _____.

Whatever you find, I encourage you to place it in your mental file labeled "Noted," and keep going. All explorers face a multitude of fears about their expeditions, but the successful ones don't let those fears stop them from pursuing a new and larger world.

DAY 107
Why Can't You Do What You Most Love to Do?

Maybe you're one of those people who is clear about what you most love to do but is convinced that you can't because of certain circumstances in your life. If I asked you to complete the following sentence, "If it weren't for _____, I could be doing what I really want to do," you'd know exactly what to write. My guess is you've probably spent a lot of time complaining about whatever you'd put in that blank.

Although the circumstance you'd list is valid and truly feels restricting, the truth is your "circumstance story" is a distraction from what is really holding you back, which are your fears. You've explored some of your fears earlier. Now, go a little deeper into what holds you back.

YOUR LEAP FOR TODAY

Start by filling in the blank in this sentence:

If it weren't for _____, I could be doing what I really want to do.

Give yourself a minute or two to write down everything that comes to your mind. But don't spend more than that focusing on what's stopping you. Instead, get in touch with what lies beneath the obstacles by asking yourself this wonder question:

Hmmm, what am I afraid would happen if I were free to do what I really wanted?

Whatever surfaces, give yourself time and space to feel it. Imagine that your fears are shy friends of yours. They're there because of a misunderstanding at an earlier time in your life and are trying to protect you. Notice them, acknowledge their existence, even give them a friendly wave. Then switch gears and turn your attention to the important matter at hand—making the Big Leap into your Genius Zone.

DAY 108
When You Commit to the What,
the How Will Follow

A good time to commit (or recommit) to a goal is immediately after you've examined your fears about it. Based on yesterday's leap, which took you to a deeper level of your being, you'll be able to make a more profound commitment to living in your Genius Zone.

If that prospect makes you nervous, you're not alone. Over the course of my long counseling and seminar career, I've noticed many people resist making what they felt was a binding commitment—especially if the person was successful. I quickly figured out that those in positions of responsibility are often hesitant to promise something before they know how they can deliver it.

YOUR LEAP FOR TODAY

In an earlier leap, you learned that when you truly make a commitment to a goal before you know how to make it happen, something powerful happens—the universe conspires to aid you in ways you couldn't foresee.

But did you know there's a scientific basis for this phenomenon? When you set your mind on something, your brain recalibrates its filters to help you notice anything and everything around you that will help you achieve your desired goal.

Knowing that your firm commitment will physically enhance your ability to succeed, mentally repeat this sentence at least five times:

I commit to living in my Genius Zone, now and forever.

Let go of any worry about how you'll do it; simply make the commitment with your whole heart and mind. Let the "how" come out of the power of your commitment.

DAY 109
Out of the Box and onto the Spiral

When astronauts break free of the earth's gravitational field they have to learn to function in a new way. Getting around is easier—as evidenced by those comically large bounds that serve as steps—but it does take some getting used to.

When you're no longer being held down by your upper limits and are free to soar into your Genius Zone, you also need to become accustomed to a different way of being.

At first, you may feel off-balance, but with time, the large amounts of joy, love, and abundance you experience on a daily basis will seem completely natural. Today's leap will help you start acclimating.

YOUR LEAP FOR TODAY

The first order of business is to switch up your thinking about how life works. I tell people when you're in the Genius Zone, "You need to get out of the box and onto the spiral."

In the Genius Zone, you move in a continuous upward spiral. There's no limit to the amount of love, abundance, and creativity you can experience.

In your Incompetence, Competence, and Excellence Zones, you live inside a box. Your joy, love, abundance, and creativity are kept in check by your upper limits.

Use your imagination to feel the difference between the two experiences in your body.

Sit comfortably and close your eyes. Feel the space all around you. Let your awareness move outward in all directions until you bump up against the walls, floor, and ceiling. Take a breath or two, aware of the container you're in, and then let that feeling of limits go.

Now imagine walking on a path that curves around in ever higher circles. If you've ever visited the Guggenheim Museum in New York City or seen photos, you can start with that image and then, in your mind's eye, stay on that ascending path, spiraling up as high as you can. Feel the giddy pleasure of unlimited upward movement.

DAY 110
The First Shortcut: Your Ultimate Success Mantra

Living in your Genius Zone is a whole new way of being. Gone is the back and forth of expansion and contraction—a growing swell of good feeling that triggers your upper limits and then causes you to contract, repeating over and over in an endless loop.

In the Genius Zone, your experience is one of almost continual expansion. You may have some upper-limit symptoms here and there, especially when it's all new, but they're fewer and you learn to see them approaching so you can deal with them earlier.

To reinforce your experience of expansion, I've found a few shortcuts that help. The first is impressing a central guiding intention on your conscious and unconscious mind. As we go along through your Big Leap Year, you'll have abundant opportunities to develop your own version of a central intention. Until that crystallizes, I invite you to use my tried-and-true mantra. I call it the "ultimate success mantra," and I use it every day.

YOUR LEAP FOR TODAY

Say the following intention several times in your mind and out loud:

I expand every day in love, creativity, and abundance, as I inspire others to do the same.

After you've said it several times, notice how your body is receiving the information. Does the intention feel harmonious to you? The more you can embody the intention, the faster it manifests.

DAY 111
Using the Ultimate Success Mantra

You can use the ultimate success mantra (USM) in two ways: formally, as a regular meditation practice, or informally, by bringing it to your awareness throughout the day. In today's leap, we'll explore how to use it as a meditation practice.

YOUR LEAP FOR TODAY

Practicing meditation is really very simple. It doesn't require any special equipment or skill. To start, find a place you can sit undisturbed for five or ten minutes, and close your eyes.

In your mind, say the USM once:

I expand in abundance, success, and love every day, as I inspire those around me to do the same.

Sit quietly, letting the words resonate for ten or fifteen seconds. This open space is vital to allow your conscious and unconscious mind to digest this new idea.

Then repeat the USM again. You don't have to pronounce the words clearly in your mind, it's okay if it's just a feeling.

Let yourself rest easily for another ten to fifteen seconds.

Repeat this process for the next five to ten minutes, alternating in your mind between the USM and a mental rest. Be prepared for some mental chatter—*This is stupid. This won't work,* and so on. It's just your old conditioning resisting your new direction. If thoughts arise, simply let go of them and come back to the USM.

It's important not to give yourself a hard time when your thoughts stray. It's a normal part of meditating. Be openhearted and generous with yourself.

When you're done, sit for a minute or two, letting yourself come back to regular thinking. Wiggle your fingers and toes if that feels good, then open your eyes.

DAY 112
Going Public

The second way to use the USM is informally—by thinking it or reading it or saying it occasionally throughout the day. When I started using my ultimate success mantra, I worked with it mostly in my mind. After my morning meditation, I would spend a few minutes circulating it through my mind: "I expand in love, abundance, and success as I inspire others to do the same."

One day I was sitting in a traffic jam when an idea came to me. Instead of stewing in the traffic jam I could be working on my genius. I made a batch of sticky notes with key ideas written on them such as "*Hmmm,* what do I most love to do?" Each day when I drove off to the university, I stuck a new note on my dashboard. Getting stuck at a traffic light became a different experience. Spending the time either letting wonder questions work their magic or saying my ultimate success mantra out loud made the time whiz by.

YOUR LEAP FOR TODAY

Make a few notes to post in your car, on your refrigerator, and on your bathroom mirror. Use the ultimate success mantra and other key ideas you want to make your own.

Going public with your affirmations has another benefit, too. People who ride in your car or see your "genius notes" elsewhere will often ask you about them, opening the door to conversations with them.

DAY 113
Embracing Opposites

You cannot have a positive life and a negative mind.

—Joyce Meyer, American author

Positive energies like love, kindness, and creative expression exist alongside their opposites. Depending on what you focus on, you can see examples of both wherever you look. Learning how to embrace both positive and negative energies gives you a sense of wholeness in yourself. Embracing all your energies gives you more fuel for the journey to genius.

When you live in the Genius Zone, you're aware of both energies but lean into the positive. Learn to savor positive feelings in your body and your mind. It not only feels good, it's a direct way to dissolve your Upper Limit Problems. Letting yourself savor good feeling for longer and longer periods of time means fewer and fewer ULPs.

- -
YOUR LEAP FOR TODAY
- -

Pause occasionally throughout the day to notice what you're focusing on. Is your focus on the positive or the negative or a bit of both? Whatever you notice, let yourself embrace the wholeness of what you're feeling.

Use this affirmation to deepen the sense of wholeness in yourself:

I embrace all my energies and focus them on the full expression of my genius.

Express this affirmation in your mind and out loud several times. As you go through your day, take a moment now and then to refresh the idea in your mind.

DAY 114
Taking on Your ULPs Is an Act of Bravery

I've seen magnificent things happen to people who make Big Leaps in their lives. In every case, including my own, we had to go outside our comfort zone. That allowed us to keep adjusting the setting upward that controls how much abundance, love, and success we enjoy.

In my view, taking on your ULPs and seeking your genius is a rare form of bravery. You may think bravery is for big, physical things like jumping out of airplanes, but doesn't a deep inner journey require equivalent courage? Today's leap will help you find the flavor of bravery that best fits you.

YOUR LEAP FOR TODAY

Read through the following list of synonyms slowly, letting them resonate in your mind and heart:

Courage
Fearlessness
Fortitude
Grit
Boldness
Daring
Valor
Pluck
Nerve
Guts
Heroism

Which one feels right for you? Which will best help you take on your ULPs? Write it on a sticky note and reread it before you do tomorrow's leap.

DAY 115
Action, Action, Action

Do one thing every day that scares you.

—Eleanor Roosevelt

Veteran movie producer Avi Lerner made Hollywood history by giving a three-word prescription for movie success: "Action, action, action." It's also a good philosophy for making Big Leaps in your life.

As you've seen, it requires conscious commitment, recommitment, action, and more action. It's a constant process of getting out of your comfort zone—either your Incompetence, Competence, or Excellence Zones—and putting yourself where your genius can shine.

What can you do today to nudge the edge of your envelope and express more of your genius? Today's leap gives you exciting options to explore.

YOUR LEAP FOR TODAY

Think of one small (or not so small) step you want to take but have been putting off because you're scared. Summon up your "bravery" word from yesterday and take it into action:

Make the call.
Send the email.
Book the appointment.
Sign up for the class.
Ask for support.
Offer your help.

Notice how you feel before and after you take the action. I've taken many such actions in my own life and witnessed countless others with my clients. No matter how scared I was about making the call or booking the appointment, the relief I felt afterward made it worthwhile.

DAY 116
The Second Shortcut: The Enlightened "No"

When I first made the Big Leap and began soaring free in my Genius Zone, I found that I had to watch out not to get sucked back into my Excellence Zone activities. After all, those activities had been supporting me in grand style for many years. Plus, I was good at them—even if they didn't fulfill me or use my unique genius.

Since there was a constant stream of invitations and opportunities for Excellence Zone work, I had to learn to turn down anything that didn't fit into my Genius Zone. Declining them with what I call the "enlightened 'no'" was another shortcut that helped stabilize my new state.

When you say an enlightened "no," you're really saying "yes." You're saying "no" to living in a box but saying "yes" to living in your Genius Zone. What surprised me was that by choosing to say "no" in service to my own genius, I inspired others to do the same.

YOUR LEAP FOR TODAY

Commitment is always a good first step for any undertaking. Use the following affirmation to commit to the enlightened "no":

I commit to saying no to any activity that takes me out of my Genius Zone.

Say it out loud a few times, then repeat it mentally. If you'd like, write it on a sticky note and post it alongside your USM.

You may find, as I did, that it can be challenging to turn down the income you'd make from non–Genius Zone work. Even so, know that every time you do, you're strengthening the foundation you're building for yourself in your Genius Zone, which, I guarantee, in the long run will be far more profitable.

DAY 117
Saying an Enlightened "No" to Yourself

A vital part of making the Big Leap is transitioning from your "box" activities to your Genius Zone spiral. In yesterday's leap you committed to saying no to invitations and opportunities for work outside your Genius Zone, but what about the activities you choose to do in your leisure hours? It's every bit as important to say an enlightened "no" to yourself.

YOUR LEAP FOR TODAY

Take a moment to reflect on your routines *outside of your work.* Make a list of the things you do on a daily, weekly, monthly, and yearly basis. How much of your free time is spent doing what you most love to do—that also taps into your unique gifts and strengths?

Start saying an enlightened "no" to as many non–Genius Zone activities as you can. Remember, they take up energy and time you could be using to express your genius.

DAY 118
Don't Eat the Marshmallow

Another variation of the "enlightened no" is the "healthy no." Self-discipline consists of saying no to gratification in the short-term so you can experience greater happiness later on. Based on copious research done on the subject, it's clear that learning to say a healthy no pays off.

The most famous delayed-gratification study was done at Stanford in the 1960s. The researcher left children, ages three to five, alone in a room with a marshmallow on a plate. The child was told that if he or she didn't eat the marshmallow right away, but waited till the researcher came back in a few minutes, the child would get two marshmallows instead of just the one. It turned out that only 30 percent of the children delayed gratification and resisted eating the marshmallow till he got back.

In the years that followed, the researcher tracked the lives of every child who had been in the study and found that the kids who hadn't immediately eaten the marshmallow did better academically, had higher self-esteem, better emotional coping skills, and were less likely to use drugs. Those who ate the marshmallow were more likely to be overweight and to be less healthy overall.

YOUR LEAP FOR TODAY

Today, don't eat the marshmallow—hold out for two later. Practice saying healthy noes. Here's a way to start that practice:

Whenever you face a choice, like taking the elevator or the stairs, eating the fries or the salad, staying up to watch another show or going to bed on time, focus on the thing you're saying "yes" to—being more fit, enjoying better health, feeling fresh the next day.

Focus on what you truly want in the future; you'll find it's easier to say "no" to something that will only feel good right now.

DAY 119
Technology and Genius

Recently, I was thinking about how much technology has changed since my mother's time. Norma Hendricks wrote for the *Leesburg Daily Commercial* and the *Orlando Sentinel* from 1957 to 1990, first as a reporter, and later as a daily columnist. The soundtrack of my childhood was the clatter of her ancient Underwood typewriter in the early morning and evening as she filed her stories and columns. She had to drive to the bus station every evening to put her typed stories aboard a bus to Orlando. On occasions when the family car wouldn't start, she would mount my brother's old bike and pedal off in the night to get to the bus on time.

By contrast, I'm writing these words on the quiet keyboard of a laptop. When I finish editing them, I'll click a button and send them off into thin air to my publisher, who will collect them out of the air, and put them into print. That's much easier than riding an old Schwinn bike to the bus station. But is it better?

In my emphatic view, *yes*! I love my phone. In ten seconds, I can get the weather in Kuala Lumpur before calling a client there. I love my computer, too. As a writer, it makes my life so much easier than it was back in the typewriter days. What's your experience of technology? Today's leap gives you a useful look at this issue in your life.

YOUR LEAP FOR TODAY

In my view, the important thing is to let technology serve your genius. Whether or not you feel comfortable around computers and other tools of the electronic era, we can all agree that technology is here to stay.

Use the following affirmation to establish a friendly relationship with your electronic companions:

All the technology I use makes the journey to my genius easier and more fun.

Every year is likely to bring us new technologies, so let your intention be to have technological innovations serve you and your highest aspirations.

DAY 120
The Past

Knot by knot, I untie myself from the past
And let it rise away from me like a balloon.
What a small thing it becomes.
What a bright tweak at the vanishing point, blue on blue.

—**Charles Wright, American poet, "Arkansas Traveler,"**
from *The Other Side of the River*

What *is* the past, actually? Most people have some vague sense of the past and its significance, but very few really realize how the past keeps us tied to our upper limits. Until you've made the Big Leap, the past is where and when you were governed by your limiting beliefs.

Those beliefs are like the knots in the poem. When you dissolve your upper limits, as the poem describes, you untie yourself from the past and let it float away behind you.

YOUR LEAP FOR TODAY

Devote a few minutes of your full attention to the following wonder question:

Hmmm, what else can I do to untie the knots of the past to experience more of my Genius Zone in the present?

Gently ask the question, tune in to your body/mind, then repeat the question, then tune in again. In your day, be aware of moments in which your mind slips into the past. Gently untie the knot and let it float free.

DAY 121
The Third Shortcut: Renewing and Refining Your Commitment

After you make your transition to the Genius Zone, you may still have moments of wobbliness as your old programming tries to hijack you. The first two shortcuts, the USM and "enlightened no," are great tools for keeping yourself focused on your genius.

The third shortcut—renewing and refining your commitment—is a safety net and the most advanced form of course correction available, all rolled into one.

- -
YOUR LEAP FOR TODAY
- -

This leap will help you nip wobbles or even backsliding in the bud.

Take a moment now to practice the third shortcut by first bringing your attention to any ways you're upper-limiting yourself at present or in recent days. Then when you find one—no matter how small or large the symptom is—take a deep breath and give yourself permission to let it go. Remember, be gentle with yourself.

Then find something good in your life to savor and spend a minute enjoying the experience of feeling good.

Finally, renew your commitment by thinking or saying the following sentence:

I commit to expressing my genius in the world in ways that help me, and others, thrive.

Say it a few times to get comfortable with the idea, and keep it in the background of your awareness as you move through your day.

DAY 122
Future Thinking

If you think in terms of a year, plant a seed.
If in terms of ten years, plant trees.
If in terms of one hundred years, teach the people.

—Confucius, ancient Chinese philosopher

I had the pleasure of getting to know the English anthropologist Gregory Bateson toward the end of his life. A story he told made a big impression on me. When he was at Oxford as a student, some of the beams in one of the dining halls needed replacing. They were huge beams that had been there for several hundred years since the university was founded. The administrators had numerous discussions about what to do, but finally they asked the university forester for his ideas on how to replace the beams.

"No problem," the forester said. He revealed that the founders had foreseen that the beams wouldn't last forever and had planted the kind of trees they would need to replace them. The trees had been growing for several hundred years, just waiting to be used for the replacement.

I was very touched and impressed that the founders had the kind of foresight to think hundreds of years down the line.

YOUR LEAP FOR TODAY

When you live in the Genius Zone, you do what you most love to do while at the same time contributing to others.

Your contributions may not impact the world for hundreds of years, but there are lots of things you can do to have a lasting effect. For example, planting a tree, arranging for a bench to be put up in a park, establishing a scholarship and fundraising for it, and so on. Take time today to reflect on this question:

What can I do to positively impact the world beyond my lifespan?

This question calls on a deep part of you, the urge of human beings to affect the future beyond their individual lifetimes. Keep this question alive in your awareness today and going forward on your journey to genius.

DAY 123
Being in the Genius Zone Keeps You in the Genius Zone

Energy is more attractive than beauty. . . .

—**Louisa May Alcott, American author**

Based on my own experience, as well as the thousands of successful people I've worked with over the years, I believe there's truth to the old saying "Success breeds success."

Once you're in the Genius Zone, you just keep spiraling up to higher levels of abundance, success, and love. The main reason is that once you stop upper-limiting yourself, you can tolerate more positive energy.

But another reason is your "posture." When you live in the Genius Zone, you smile more, are friendlier and more relaxed, and even have a better sense of humor! Simply put, you're more attractive energetically. People are drawn to you and want to work with you, invest with you, buy from you, and generally support you.

YOUR LEAP FOR TODAY

Today, consciously appreciate the people around you and from your past. When you've found that warm feeling inside, imagine sending that positive energy to them in an "energetic hug." The person you're sending a hug to could be a thousand miles away or no longer among the living. The important part is that you are feeling and sending positive energy.

Once you've beamed your appreciation to them silently in the form of the energetic hug, feel free to express your appreciation in words.

DAY 124
Building Your Toolkit

By now you're familiar with tools we use for your Daily Leaps such as affirmations, commitment statements, and wonder questions. Visualization is another powerful tool in your genius toolkit, but I tend to use it less often because not everybody is a good visualizer. In doing transformational processes with live audiences for five decades, I've found that only about a third of people in audiences tend to be good at picturing images in their minds. In fact, I've had people tell me outright that they aren't good visualizers.

If you're one of those folks who considers themselves unskilled at mental movies, rest easy: I've found a workaround in the form of body visualization. I'll show you how to do it in today's leap.

YOUR LEAP FOR TODAY

Practice this new tool with something you're familiar with: the ultimate success mantra. First, refresh the concept in your mind by saying it to yourself. Here's the version of it I'm using now:

I expand in love, abundance, and creativity every day as I inspire others to do the same.

Then, take a moment to do a body visualization with love, abundance, and success:

Feel yourself giving and receiving all the love you possibly can. As you feel it in your body, let your mind spontaneously produce any images it wants to. Do the same with abundance: feel in your body a sense of being wealthy to your satisfaction. Do the same for creativity: feel yourself being creative by every standard you measure by. Let any images emerge from your mind as you feel the creativity in your body.

Body visualization works because you let the images come spontaneously and naturally. You don't force yourself to create a picture; your inner creative self makes it for you. Take note of any images you receive; they make good subjects for reflection and journaling.

DAY 125
Time in the Genius Zone

As you spend more of your time doing what you most love to do, your relationship with time gets friendlier and friendlier. Hurry disappears, as does boredom. You're no longer serving time. Time is serving you.

What that means, practically speaking, is that you're no longer wasting your precious time doing things you don't want to do. You're no longer complaining about time or blaming the lack of it for your shortfalls. In the Genius Zone, time is easy. There's always plenty of it because you take responsibility for creating the amount you need.

YOUR LEAP FOR TODAY

In the Genius Zone, time feels free and easy. Use the following affirmations to invite more freedom and ease into your day:

I feel completely at ease with time in my life.

I make all the time I need to do the things I love to do.

Take a moment now to run those through your mind, say them out loud, and feel them in your body. Pause occasionally through your day and renew these affirmations.

DAY 126
It's About Time

In *The Big Leap*, I devoted a chapter to a truly radical concept I call "Einstein Time." The word "radical" comes from a Latin word that means "root," and that's the way I mean it. Once you understand how Einstein Time works, it changes your thinking at the very root.

The life-changing idea of Einstein Time is this: take ownership of time and quit thinking of it as something outside yourself.

When you take responsibility for being the source of time, you open up a new superpower you can use to turn your dreams into reality. We'll revisit Einstein Time many times during *Your Big Leap Year*. Today's leap gets you started.

YOUR LEAP FOR TODAY

Tune in for a moment to your relationship to time. Start with this wonder question:

Hmmm, do I have any recurring patterns in my relationship to time?

For example, many people have a pattern of showing up late. Others have the opposite issue, being excessively concerned or anxious about showing up on time. Use your wonder question to open up a friendly conversation with yourself about time.

DAY 127
Einstein and the Elastic Nature of Time

In 1915, when Einstein introduced his general theory of relativity, it sent shock waves around the world. The idea that gravity warps space, and that time isn't the constant we all believe it is, was revolutionary.

Yet over a hundred years later, most of us still embrace the Newtonian concept of time as something "out there" that we have no control over, but which affects us internally producing a variety of responses—including anxiety, stress, boredom, and delight.

Humans in general haven't grasped the concept of Einstein Time, which works the other way: when you're functioning in Einstein Time, *you* are the source of your experience of time.

To help you better understand how this works, I offer this unscientific yet relatable explanation of Einstein's theory: sitting with someone you love for an hour feels like a minute, while touching a hot stove for a minute feels like an hour.

In other words, how you feel about what you're doing affects your perception of time.

- -
YOUR LEAP FOR TODAY
- -

Today, as you go about your normal routine, notice when time flies by and when it drags along. Observe what you're doing and how you feel in your body. It's enough just to pay attention today.

Later, you'll use this information to stay in your Genius Zone and to switch over to Einstein Time when necessary.

DAY 128
Contraction, Expansion, Time, and You

When I first heard the hot stove example of Einstein's theory, I remember thinking, "Why does touching a hot stove make time slow down?" Perhaps you have the same question.

I found the answer by imagining that I was doing something unpleasant and noticing what happened in my body: I contracted—trying to get away from where I was and what I was experiencing. When I imagined I was doing something I love to do, like being with Katie, I noticed my body relaxing and expanding, opening every cell wide to experience everything I could.

Try it for yourself. You'll find, as I did, that when you're contracted, time slows down, getting sticky and sludgy. When that happens, you feel stressed, which makes it hard to get things done.

When you're open, you forget about time. Hours fly by like minutes as time simply disappears. Your energy and creativity are free to flow, and you get more done in less time—effectively generating more time.

YOUR LEAP FOR TODAY

In yesterday's leap, you paid attention to which activities dragged and which flew by and how that felt in your body.

In today's leap, you're going to repeat yesterday's assignment, but when you feel your body contracting, reverse the feeling by closing your eyes and taking at least three deep, slow breaths—the more the better. When you feel complete, open your eyes.

Observe what happens after you relax and allow more energy to flow in your body. You'll find that you're able to get more done and feel happier while you're doing it.

When you take responsibility for the amount of time you have at your disposal, you'll see that time is not a big external pressure always about to overwhelm you. The truth is you are the source of both the time *and* the pressure you feel about it.

DAY 129
You and Time

When I was coming up on my sixth birthday, my grandparents and my mom teamed up with an offer I couldn't refuse. I was already a good reader, but for some reason I was having trouble figuring out how to read a clock. Then came the deal: if I learned to tell time by January 20, my birthday, I'd get something I really wanted, a wristwatch. The one I wanted cost about two dollars, an astronomical sum to my eyes in 1951 Florida.

I got extra tutelage from Granddad and hit my mark with a few days to spare. I'm sure everybody was relieved, because I heard later they'd already bought the watch!

I still have it, although it's beat-up to the extreme from a rowdy childhood. (I recently did a search for a 1951 Benrus watch and found that my two-buck timepiece was now worth several hundred dollars!)

Why am I telling you all this? Because for the next three days I want you to take a deep excursion into how you think about time.

YOUR LEAP FOR TODAY

Get out your journal or a good friend and tell your time story.

When did you first become aware of time?

Have your thoughts and feelings about time changed over your life?

See if you can remember any anecdotes like mine about your early relationship with time. Turn the searchlight of awareness on you and time.

DAY 130
Family Time

Today, we go on a deeper exploration into your early experience of time. As you know, we're all born into a situation that was going on long before we got there. It has its own rules, values, and communication styles. It's like coming to a party that's been going on for a while. Some of the new rules are taught explicitly, but most are imbibed in a kind of osmosis. The question becomes: What family values and attitudes about time did you osmose before you knew how to choose for yourself?

In my family, time was often the subject of frantic communication. One of my mother's favorite phrases, uttered at high volume, was "There simply aren't enough hours in the day!" In addition to the usual frantic pace of keeping two boys clothed and fed as a single parent, she also had to write her column for the daily newspaper and had a deadline to hit every day.

Overall, the lessons I osmosed were that time was a constant, relentless force and there was never enough of it. What lessons did you learn about time?

YOUR LEAP FOR TODAY

Reflect on your family's attitude toward time.

Was it frantic like mine, or serene, or something other?

Was hurry a common feature or did things move slowly?

Take these questions to your journal or to a good listener in your network. Learning as much as you can about your early time story comes in very handy at unwinding any issues you have with time now.

DAY 131
Connecting the Dots

How does your early experience of time, in your family and elsewhere, affect your relationship with it now? Are there any connections between time issues that give you trouble in your daily life now and the early lessons you picked up about time before you could think for yourself?

These are powerful questions, ones I've asked myself many times. Part of my personal growth has been to get my early learnings about time scarcity out of my head and body. Until I started focusing on my time issues in my late twenties, I had a chronic "hurry-up" feeling in the background of my awareness. Then, like a few million other people, I read the watershed book by Meyer Friedman, MD, *Type A Behavior and Your Heart*. I'll give you two of the punchlines: Type A behavior is feeling like you're in a hurry all the time. Type A people have more heart attacks than their more easygoing counterparts.

Your experience may be completely different. Each of us has our own time signature, the composite of learnings about time that affect our life now. Zoom in on that signature today.

YOUR LEAP FOR TODAY

Take a moment to imagine asking a friend, "What do you notice about my relationship with time?" Or, even better, ask a friend for real.

In your imagination, what did your friend say? If you're doing it in real life, listen carefully to what your friend says. As you listen to the descriptions from outside, tune in to how you feel about your own relationship with time. Do the two mesh?

In these deeper questions, there are no wrong answers. Be friendly to yourself and welcome any sort of answers.

DAY 132
What's Your Time Persona?

A persona is a role you occupy, either consciously or unconsciously. I remember kids with various personas in my school years: class clown, shy kid, teacher's pet, brainiac, rebel. When I went to my fiftieth high school reunion, I was amazed to see how many of us were still occupying the same roles as sixtysomethings.

My students gave playful nicknames to the two extremes of time personas: time slacker and time cop.

Time slackers are largely oblivious to time, chronically showing up late or not at all.

Time cops are hypervigilant about time; they show up early or on time, and don't think very highly of those who don't.

YOUR LEAP FOR TODAY

Using the two time personas we discussed above, ask yourself this fundamental wonder question:

Hmmm, if I had to pick one, do I tend to be more of a time slacker or a time cop?

Neither of these personas are good or bad, right or wrong, so do your best to avoid judgment. Be friendly to yourself as you do all your explorations.

DAY 133
Nurturing Creativity

If you have a burning, restless urge to write or paint, simply eat something sweet and the feeling will pass.

—Fran Lebowitz, American author

Not everybody should write or paint or sculpt as an outlet for their creativity. However, to live in your Genius Zone, creativity itself needs to be nurtured in some way every day. Sometimes in our daily life, creativity gets set aside in favor of the 1,001 details that need handling.

In my view, making soup can be just as much a genius activity as composing a symphony. At their best, both soup and symphony are expressions of love. Both also contribute to the lives of others as well as the maker. Love and contribution are the best practical definitions of genius I've found. Today's leap brings these qualities into your awareness in a very practical way.

YOUR LEAP FOR TODAY

Pick a ten-minute block of time today and put it on your calendar. When the time comes, go in a room by yourself and reflect on this wonder question for the ten minutes:

Hmmm, what are the ideal expressions of my creativity at this point in my life?

Circulate the question through your mind, feel it in your body, and say it out loud. When you finish your ten minutes, sort through the ideas and discover if there are things you can take action on right away.

DAY 134
The Spiritual Value of Boredom

A team of British mega-nerds invented an algorithm that analyzed three hundred million data points and concluded that a particular day in 1954 was the most boring day in history. Nothing of significance happened that day, anywhere; no famous people were born that day, no weather catastrophes, etc. I was around in 1954 and I'm inclined to agree. Although I was only nine, I was already highly accomplished at being bored.

It reminded me, though, of what I've always thought of as the silver lining of boredom: it acquaints you with the feeling of nothingness, a state that people practice meditation to experience.

I now think of boredom as resistance to nothingness. As a longtime meditator, the open space of nothingness is one of meditation's great rewards. I savor those moments of pure consciousness, free of thoughts of any kind, simply being in the best kind of nothing.

YOUR LEAP FOR TODAY

Take a moment to reflect on things you find boring. Make a list if there are more than a few. Pick one, perhaps the thing you find most boring, and bring it clearly to mind.

Instead of resisting the boredom, go ahead and let yourself feel deeply bored. Sit with the feeling of boredom until it turns into pure nothingness. It may take a few seconds or a few minutes, but if you keep focusing your awareness on it you'll feel the shift from boredom to the open space of nothingness.

As you move through the day, be sensitive to moments when you're bored and instead, use your new insight to enjoy the pure open space of nothingness.

DAY 135
Peace of Mind with Time

When I go on podcasts and talk shows, time is the subject I talk about that causes the most controversy. It gets people especially stirred up when I say, "I'm where time comes from," and "You're where time comes from." It sounds like a radical idea but is actually quite simple: either you take responsibility for creating the time you need to do the things that are important to you, or you don't.

If you don't, you treat yourself as a victim of time. I know, because that's the way I thought of time for the first half of my life. Either there wasn't enough of it and I was harried, or there was too much of it and I was bored. I didn't find any real peace of mind until I stepped out of the victim position with time and took charge of it in my life. I wish the same for you.

YOUR LEAP FOR TODAY

Take a bold step out of any victim relationship you may have with time. Use this commitment to step fully into ownership of time:

I commit to creating all the time I need to bring forth my full genius.

Circulate the commitment through your mind and feel it in your body. As you go through your day, pause occasionally to renew your commitment to taking charge of time.

DAY 136
Time Isn't a Good Excuse

Earlier in my life, if I were invited to a social engagement, I'd usually beg off explaining that I didn't have time to attend. I'd usually use work as an excuse. But if, on that same evening, my daughter wanted to talk to me about something that was bothering her, I'd put away my work and give her my full attention.

Clearly, time wasn't the issue. Doing what I wanted to do was the important thing: I wanted to talk to my daughter. I didn't want to go to the social engagement. I used time as an excuse—which only reinforced my victim relationship with time.

If that sounds familiar, do whatever it takes to accept the reality that you're the source of time. Begin with a complete abstinence of complaining about time—especially your lack of it.

YOUR LEAP FOR TODAY

Start by monitoring every time you speak from the victim position regarding time. For example, "I don't have time for that." Or "I wish I had time for that." Or "I'd love to stop and chat but I'm late for an appointment."

If you notice that you're about to say one of those (or are even in the middle of saying one), stop yourself and switch it to: "I'm not willing to make the time for that right now." Or "I want to _____ (finish my work, exercise, whatever you're going to do instead) before I do that."

This takes you out of the time-victim position and puts you in the ownership position, which is a place of power and a step along the way to genius.

DAY 137
Using Your Relationship to Upper-Limit Yourself

When good things happen to you—causing more positive energy to run through your body than you're used to—relationship problems are a surefire way to bring your energy down to a more manageable level.

What I've witnessed is the more successful someone is, the rockier that person's relationships tend to be. (And if both people in the relationship are successful, that rockiness is doubled.)

As soon as you understand how your upper limits work, you can defuse relationship problems much more quickly—eventually stopping them before they even start.

Relationships involve deep emotions, and it's easy to get so caught up in the drama that you overlook the possibility that one or both of you are upper-limiting yourself. Today's leap helps you develop a new response for when relationship trouble strikes.

YOUR LEAP FOR TODAY

Remember fire drills when you were in school? Whenever the fire alarm went off, you jumped up from your desk, got in line, and exited the building as quickly and calmly as you could. You didn't know if there was a real fire—probably not—yet you still took the appropriate action.

Today, any time you feel tension brewing in your relationship, imagine it's a benign fire alarm. But instead of exiting the building, exit the interaction just long enough to scan yourself for any possible successes that could be triggering your upper limits.

Instead of upper-limiting, take a moment to savor the good feeling inside yourself. Use the interaction to increase your tolerance for positivity.

DAY 138
Big Leaps in Your Relationships

During your Big Leap Year, we'll visit the subject of relationships many times. Yesterday, you practiced recognizing relationship problems as possible ULPs. Today, we focus specifically on how those ULPs show up in your relationships.

When I began studying my own ULPs, one of the first places I noticed them was in my relationships. I was in a new relationship with Katie, now my wife of forty-plus years, but I had not yet made a commitment to her. Spotting and dealing with my ULPs with her led to being able to make a full-hearted commitment to her in 1981.

Arguments are probably the most common ULP in relationships. However, as I explained in an earlier leap, "It's never what you think it is." Sex problems are never about sex, and money problems are never about money.

Of the four main things couples argue about—sex, money, kids, and chores—all of them are surface manifestations of unconscious struggles for control and approval.

YOUR LEAP FOR TODAY

Even though you've probably thought about your relationships many times, start a brand-new conversation in yourself with this wonder question:

Hmmm, how do my Upper Limit Problems show up in my relationships?

It's a big subject, so be generous and friendly with yourself as you pay closer attention to your relationships. In future days you'll have the opportunity to explore relationship in fine-grain detail. For now, though, simply circulate today's wonder question through your consciousness often throughout the day.

DAY 139
A Deeper Look into Relationship

When Katie and I began to focus our awareness on our ULPs, we caught a surprising pattern right away. We would get along fine for about three days, then something would spark an argument. Someone would make a critical or sarcastic remark, and then we'd be off on a cycle of conflict that would go on sometimes for weeks.

Spotting the patterns helped us clear it up so that we could spend longer and longer time in harmony.

YOUR LEAP FOR TODAY

What kind of patterns are at work in your relationships?

How much time do you spend in an easeful flow of connection and how much time do you spend out of sorts in your key relationships?

These questions are important for the health of any relationship.

Open up this new dimension of your awareness with this commitment:

I commit to spotting and clearing up any pattern that keeps me from enjoying an easeful flow of connection in my relationships.

Say it a few times in your mind and aloud. Feel your commitment in your body. Refresh it in yourself often as you go through your day.

DAY 140
A Powerful Relationship Question

Katie and I have asked each other a special question throughout the five decades of our marriage. It's a question we found so useful that we've taught it to thousands of couples in our office and seminars. Every week or so, one of us will lean over and whisper, "Is there anything I could be doing or saying differently that would help you feel more loved and treasured?"

Early in our life together, the question would sometimes get a practical answer such as "Remember to pick up your socks." Other times the answer might communicate specific desires, perhaps "I loved snuggling in front of the fireplace the other night. Let's do that more." For the last twenty years or so, the answer is usually "Just keep doing what you're doing!"

The question is good in any relationship, not just with mates and lovers. I've consulted in business situations where a version of the question has helped executives get through boardroom impasses.

YOUR LEAP FOR TODAY

Asking a bold question can stir up anxiety in the asker. That's why it's a good idea to do some mental rehearsal before you try the question out in one of your close relationships.

Take a moment right now to think of one of your closest relationships. Imagine sitting across from the person and asking, "Is there anything I could be doing or saying that would help you feel more loved and treasured?" (If it's a friend or business relationship, say ". . . help you feel like I was a better friend or colleague?")

Do this process for several different loved ones and key people in your life. Then, if you feel it would be a useful addition to your relationship life, try out the question in real life.

DAY 141
About Projection

Projection is one of most important habits to overcome in close relationships. Practically speaking, projection is when you see something in another person that's actually going on in you. For example, watch the political news for a day. You'll see known liars accusing the opposition of lying. That's projection.

At home, projection is when one partner who's feeling angry about something but hasn't realized it says to the other, "What's going on with you? You look angry about something."

Learning to notice when I was projecting was essential in the early days of my relationship with Katie. I was one of those people I mentioned above. I'd be angry about something but unaware of it. Instead of saying, "Katie, I'm angry and would like to talk about it with you," I'd say, "You look upset, Katie. What's wrong?" It took me years to clear that habit out of my consciousness, but every moment of it was worthwhile.

YOUR LEAP FOR TODAY

Clearing the projection habit out of your relationships is not a simple process for one big reason: most of the time we don't know when we're doing it. By its very nature, projection is an unconscious process that needs to be made conscious.

Use this wonder question to open up the conversation in yourself:

Hmmm, how do I project onto others things I'm feeling in myself?

Circulate the question through your mind and feel the wondering of it in your body. Genuine curiosity helps unlock the secret of these troublesome relationship habits.

DAY 142
A Deeper Look at Projection

Once I started spotting projections in my relationships, I saw them in places other than home. I was a university professor at the time, and while I loved teaching and research, the faculty politics drove me nuts. Particularly, I got into a long-running contentious relationship with the dean of my department. At first it never occurred to me I was projecting onto him, because almost all my colleagues had contentious relationships with him, too. He was notoriously hot-tempered, authoritarian, and stingy.

One day, though, after an unsatisfying conversation with him about budgets, I had a revelation that changed my relationship with him entirely. I realized I was projecting onto him some of my unresolved issues with my father. Regardless of what he was bringing to the table, I was bringing a lot of undealt-with issues with my father, whom I never knew in real life. Once I owned the projection, I had a much more congenial relationship with the dean.

YOUR LEAP FOR TODAY

There's a simple way to bring your projections to light: listen carefully to what you complain about repeatedly. I found that recurring complaints on my part always involved some kind of projection I was importing into the situation.

Use these wonder questions to explore this area in yourself:

Hmmm, **what have I complained about repeatedly in my relationships?**

Hmmm, **what is it in me that causes these issues to recycle?**

Reflect on these questions now and use them as seeds for further exploration as you move forward in your life. Spotting your projections will allow you to be more in the present with people you're close to.

DAY 143
Being Present for Others

In our seminars we teach a process called "conscious listening." The key to it is to give the other person space to communicate without being interrupted by the listener. The purpose of conscious listening is to draw forth the essential communication of both people.

What gets in the way of conscious listening? There are many varieties of unconscious listening, such as interrupting, mocking what the other person says, arguing, and minimizing.

When we teach conscious listening in seminars, we hear from many people that they've never been listened to nonjudgmentally and had their emotions welcomed into the conversation. Today's leap gives you an opening into the world of conscious listening.

YOUR LEAP FOR TODAY

Use the following affirmation to open a new dimension when you listen to people:

I enjoy being present to other people's experience and expression of their emotions.

Think it, feel it, and say it several times until you feel it take root in you. Circulate it through your awareness often as you go through your day.

DAY 144
Becoming a Source of Appreciation

Earlier in your Big Leap Year, we discussed appreciation from the perspective of the receiver. We focused on increasing your willingness to receive more and more appreciation, rather than deflecting it. That's an important thing to do, an action that extends beyond appreciation into every part of life. For example, so many things go easier when you become willing to let yourself receive more support from people and the world around you.

While it's important to open your receiver more and more each day, it's equally important to keep strengthening your giver. Giving appreciation is an art form that's worth a lifetime's study and practice.

Today's leap focuses on enhancing your ability to appreciate the people and situations in your life. Tomorrow we'll focus on how to sharpen and refine your giver so it's more effective.

YOUR LEAP FOR TODAY

Take a moment right now to work with several fill-in-the-blank statements about you and appreciation:

One very important person in my life is _____.

One thing I could do to appreciate _____ is to

_____.

Another thing I could do to appreciate _____ is to

_____.

A second very important person in my life is _____.

One thing I could do to appreciate _____ is to

_____.

Another thing I could do to appreciate _____ is to

_____.

I suggest you continue to reflect on and journal about how you can appreciate more people in your life until you've covered all the people closest to you.

DAY 145
Customizing Appreciation

For appreciation to be effective, it needs to be as specific as possible. People have many different ways they like to be appreciated, and to make matters more complex, most of us haven't given much thought to the types of appreciation we like best. To improve your skills as a giver of appreciation, you need to tune in to what really lights people up.

Here's an example: my wife, Katie, loves flowers and goes to the farmer's market every Sunday to get fresh ones for our house. After the hour or two it takes to go get them, she spends another couple of hours arranging them in vases and putting them around the house. I mention the hours she puts in because up until I met her, I don't think I'd spent two minutes in my whole life thinking about flowers.

Early in our relationship, I learned that one way to make Katie's face light up was to compliment her on the flower arrangements. At first, my appreciations were general: "Hey, great flowers this week." Then, I learned that the more specific I made my appreciation, the more she lit up. Now, I say things like, "What are those red flowers with the black center called? They're really vibrant!"

YOUR LEAP FOR TODAY

Take a moment to customize an appreciation for an important person in your life. Bring the person to mind and ask yourself several wonder questions:

Hmmm, what does _____ deeply value?

Hmmm, what could I appreciate about _____ that would be most likely to bring a big smile to their face?

When the time is right, deliver your customized appreciation to the person and see if it brings light to their face. It's an art form you can develop your whole life, so be willing to receive feedback on your skills.

DAY 146
Expand Your Capacity for Intimacy and Connection

Often, when we reach a new level of intimacy and connection—romantically or otherwise—our upper limits get triggered and find a way to bring us down.

To avoid coming down to earth with a thud after moments of deep connection and shared joy with others, find a positive way to ground yourself. I suggest doing something that literally connects you to the ground.

Here are a few ideas:

Dancing, especially barefoot on the earth.

Taking a walk in a natural setting, preferably with your feet touching the earth.

Working in a garden.

Picking up trash on a local trail.

Stargazing while lying on the ground.

YOUR LEAP FOR TODAY

Make a list of grounding activities that appeal to you. Choose from the list above and see if you can think of more. The next time you experience a relationship high, do one of the activities on your list.

To make your grounding even more powerful, do some savoring at the same time. Think of something positive in your life and, taking long, slow, easy breaths, savor the good feeling for as long as you can.

DAY 147
Stopping Relationship ULPs Before They Begin

There are several ways we limit positive energy in relationships:

Starting arguments (thereby avoiding intimacy)
Withholding significant communication
Needing to control and dominate your partner (or be controlled or dominated by your partner)

One way to counter these in a relationship is to take time by and for yourself. If you do this consciously, you won't have to do it unconsciously by starting arguments, and so on.

There are many ways to recharge your batteries. You could go on a solo walk, putter in the garden, window-shop around town, take in a movie, or soak in the tub. Whatever works for you, make it a priority within your relationship. It will allow you to spend more and more time enjoying intimacy and connection with your partner.

YOUR LEAP FOR TODAY

What are your battery-charging activities?

Make a list of those you know you enjoy and add a few that you're curious to try. Then, get out your calendar and schedule at least one solo date a week for the next month.

Remember, time apart enriches your time together. You're not doing this to get away from your partner, you're doing it to come back closer.

DAY 148
Emotions Are for Expressing

When I was a child, I remember very clearly being told "Don't cry." Partly because boys of my generation were not supposed to cry, but also because airing *any* negative emotion was strongly discouraged, as you can see from other admonitions from my childhood: "There's nothing to be angry about." "Shut up and sit down." "Stop making such a fuss." "You're being a scaredy-cat."

When I had my own child, I personally tried to take a more enlightened approach, but I noticed that most of the parents around me were still strongly dissuading their offspring from expressing any upset.

If a parent was taught to suppress their emotions as a child, their children's emotions will trigger their own. To restore their equilibrium, the parent will try to discourage their kids' emotional expressions, and the cycle continues.

If you were a discouraged from voicing your emotions as a child, it's no mystery why you might still be trying to stifle and conceal your emotions—and those of your partner. You learned at an early age that it wasn't okay to express them. Unfortunately, this tendency causes a lot of problems in relationships.

YOUR LEAP FOR TODAY

Undo this generational maladaptation by starting with yourself.

Today, when you notice any emotions coming up, if it's appropriate for the situation, let yourself feel whatever it is you're feeling until the feeling naturally subsides.

If you're sad, let yourself feel sad till you don't feel that way anymore. Same goes for anger, fear, and hurt, as well as positive emotions. (If it's not an appropriate situation, as soon as possible find a private space to let your feelings run their course.)

If your partner (or a family member or friend) is feeling something, don't try to tamp down their emotion; encourage them to feel it completely. Feelings are meant to be felt.

DAY 149
A Key Principle in Relationships

Since the nineties, Katie and I've taught a seminar for single people who want to attract genuine love. When graduates write us afterward to report on their successes, they often cite one of the key principles from the seminar as the reason for their success: you can only love another person to the extent you love yourself.

Another way to say this is that as we come to treat ourselves with loving acceptance—our anger, our grief, our fears—we get the ability to love others when their deep emotions come forth. Today's leap turns this principle into something you can see and feel in your daily life.

YOUR LEAP FOR TODAY

Use the following affirmation to give yourself the gift of unconditional loving acceptance:

I accept and love myself more each day as I accept and love those close to me.

Savor the affirmation several times in your mind. Feel it in your body and speak it aloud. When you have time, do some journaling to add more dimensions to how this powerful idea affects your life.

DAY 150
Find Your Big Leap Circle

We can't choose our family, and we often can't control who our neighbors or coworkers are. Some of the people we're around on a regular basis are wonderful—positive, supportive, encouraging. Others, not so much.

Today we focus on understanding the power of our associations. The people around you either help you expand your genius or keep you tethered to your upper limits. Today's leap helps you apply the same "benign vigilance" you use to recognize your ULPs to the people you spend time with.

YOUR LEAP FOR TODAY

Take out your phone and spend some time going through your contacts. As your eyes fall on each name, notice what you feel in your body.

Do you expand or contract? Do you instantly smile and feel a spark of happiness in your heart? Or do you cringe a little and feel your chest or stomach tighten?

Write down the names of those who light up your world. Make a commitment to spend more time with them and look for ways to contribute to their lives.

DAY 151
Dealing with People Outside Your Circle: Part 1

The people you didn't include in your Big Leap Circle are still there, populating your world, many requiring interaction. As you reflect on them, always remember that sometimes your visceral response to people can be about *you*, not *them*.

If you feel guilty or resentful about something that's passed between the two of you, that will definitely color your reaction to them. Today's leap sharpens your ability to distinguish between what's yours and what's theirs.

YOUR LEAP FOR TODAY

Go through your contacts again and this time, if someone doesn't light you up, pause to consider your reaction. Ask yourself these wonder questions to open up this essential conversation with yourself:

Hmmm, do I have uncommunicated issues with them that might be affecting how I feel?

Hmmm, if I didn't have feelings I was harboring, would I still dislike this person?

There are no right or wrong answers to these questions. They're designed to fill you with wonder, not self-criticism. Keep these questions in the background of your awareness as you go through your day.

DAY 152
Dealing with People Outside Your Circle: Part 2

Sometimes it's possible to eliminate people from your life in a way that's friendly to all parties. Usually, though it's neither feasible nor friendly to yourself or others to avoid further interactions with them entirely. The best you can do is be aware of their influence and take effective actions.

YOUR LEAP FOR TODAY

Reflect on the people in your life who don't light you up and consider taking these actions I've used and recommended to my clients:

- Limit the time you're around them.
- When you're together, find ways to stay centered so you don't get sucked into their negative energy. For example, all the breathing processes and references in this book will guide you in how to use your breathing to stay centered.
- Don't share your enthusiasms and your genius-related activities with them. Save these to share with people who support your genius.

Be patient with yourself. It took me years to learn to resist the pull of some people's negativity.

Also believe in people's ability to change, evolve, and grow, including yourself. Always be open to re-testing your response in the future.

THE
SECOND
CYCLE

- - - - - - - - - - -

Don't be afraid to start over again.
This time, you're not starting from
scratch, you're starting from experience.

—Unknown

DAY 153
The Genius Spiral

In my early work to liberate my own genius in the eighties, I noticed something that puzzled me at first. If I handled some challenge, say, an ULP about fear of outshining, the issue would recycle a month or two later, but in a subtler form.

One day, an image popped into my mind of an eagle soaring up into the sky in a widening spiral. I realized that the spiral explained why the same issue might recycle several times in subtler forms before it cleared out.

Each of us has recurring challenges. Whether they involve the seductions of addiction, power struggles for control, seeking approval, or some other pattern, the challenges tend to recycle until we finally do something that makes them disappear. If you think of your journey as a spiral upward toward your full genius, it suddenly makes those challenges appear very different.

Instead of shrinking from them, you learn to welcome them as you go around the spiral. You see what you missed last time you encountered the challenge, and you get another opportunity to self-correct and soar higher to the full expression of your genius.

- -
YOUR LEAP FOR TODAY
- -

Think of two or three challenges that have recycled several times since you started focusing on liberating your genius.

Use these wonder questions to open up the dialogue with yourself:

Hmmm, what are the main challenges that keep recurring for me?

Hmmm, how often do my challenges tend to occur?

Hmmm, what actions can I take to move through my challenges with greater ease?

Entertain these questions in your mind for a few moments now, and pause occasionally today to treat yourself to a few moments of reflecting on them.

DAY 154
Fine-Tuning the Power of Commitment

Commitment is one of the major themes of your Big Leap Year. If you really understand how commitment works, you're powerfully equipped to turn your dreams into reality. I tell my students, "Commitment costs nothing, but requires everything." Any moment you spend learning about commitment is well spent.

The secret to unlocking the deep power of commitment is embedded in the word "heartfelt." It's important to have a clear commitment in your mind, but if you want it to produce results you must feel it in your body.

YOUR LEAP FOR TODAY

Revisit the first powerful commitment you made when you began your Big Leap Year:

I commit to expanding my genius every day of my life.

Say it in your mind a few times to refresh your awareness of it. After you establish it in your mind, feel the commitment in your body. Using "heartfelt" as a measure, notice how heartfelt your commitment feels.

Add this conscious intention or affirmation to your day:

I deepen my commitment to expanding my genius every day of my life.

DAY 155
Well Begun Is Half Done

Have you ever seen a dog that's had a blanket thrown over them? They twist and turn beneath the blanket, lunging in all directions as they try to escape what they perceive as the many enemies surrounding them.

We humans often react the same way to our challenges. We feel we're battling numerous separate adversaries on multiple fronts, when in truth, we're like that dog, struggling under the one confounding blanket. In our case, the blanket is our upper limits.

Not knowing about the Upper Limit Problem keeps us stuck under the blanket. Now that you're aware of it and committed to leaving it behind, you're more than halfway there.

YOUR LEAP FOR TODAY

Take a moment now to celebrate this major victory: you've broken through the fog of un-knowing, seen the problem clearly, and are committed to doing what it takes to leave your upper limits behind.

Take a deep breath and enjoy the clarity and calm that come when you can see the path ahead.

DAY 156
Return to Wonder

I encourage you to bring a spirit of wonder and enjoyment to all the wisdom and tools you learn in your Big Leap Year. Based on my experience of leading hundreds of seminars since 1975, I can testify that people learn better and faster when they're having a good time and open to wonder.

Wonder and enjoyment are also tools you can use to keep yourself on track in daily life. In any moment, you're either enjoying a spirit of wonder as you go about your life, or you're not.

When you notice you're stuck in some other state of consciousness, such as working too hard or feeling stressed, pause on the spot and recover the spirit of wonder in yourself. Today's leap shows you an easy way to do it.

YOUR LEAP FOR TODAY

Refresh the feeling of wonder in yourself by using this wonder statement:

Hmmm, I wonder how much good feeling I can enjoy today.

Repeat it several times in your mind and out loud until you feel a genuine sense of wonder in yourself. As you move through your day, tune in now and then to notice if you're enjoying that sense of wonder. If not, pause on the spot and recover it.

DAY 157
The Antidote to ULPs

The sure cure for the Upper Limit Problem is to cultivate and nurture longer and longer periods of positive energy. Positive energy includes both the flow of good feeling inside you and the flow of loving connection with the people close to you.

Focus on extending both your inner and outer flow, and your ULPs will recede. Today we focus on the flow of inner good feeling; later in the year, we'll explore the flow in relationships.

In my own early work, I measured my periods of good feeling in hours and days. Now I measure it in years. It took a lot of focused awareness over a decade or so to grow my ability to tolerate more positive energy. It was all done the same way, though, with commitment and one choice at a time, just as today's leap demonstrates.

YOUR LEAP FOR TODAY

Even though you've made similar commitments earlier in your Big Leap Year, take a moment now to refresh this crucial idea in your consciousness:

I commit to feeling good for longer and longer periods of time every day.

Say the commitment a few times mentally and speak it out loud. Get the feeling of it in your body. Pause occasionally during the day to refresh it in your awareness.

DAY 158
Undefended Openness

Like any worthwhile goal, your journey to genius requires a number of important ingredients—a compelling vision of your destination, a willingness to change, firm commitment (and recommitment) to your goal, kindness with yourself, and dedicated practice.

Making the Big Leap also requires what I call "undefended openness." What makes openness undefended? The courage to be open, no matter what.

Many times, people start out open, until something happens that makes them contract and fall into old patterns of blame and criticism (of themselves or others), and they become guarded going forward.

Being able to remain open—even after setbacks or lapses—and trust that all that happens to you is ultimately for your good is the attitude you're aiming for as you go through your Big Leap Year.

YOUR LEAP FOR TODAY

To create undefended openness in yourself, use these affirmations:

I embrace every opportunity to grow.

I live in a benevolent universe.

Repeat them silently a few times throughout the day and feel the inner lightness and expansion they bring.

I also suggest you write them on a sticky note and put the note somewhere you'll see it often.

DAY 159
How Do You Feel When Things Go Well?

The Upper Limit Problem has been around for a long, long time. Evidence of humans feeling afraid and uneasy when they feel good can be found across many different time periods and cultures.

How many of these expressions have you heard?

"It's too good to be true."
"I'm just waiting for the other shoe to drop."
"I'm afraid I'll have to pay for this later."
"All good things must end."

Today's leap allows you to gauge your growth in this area over the last few months.

YOUR LEAP FOR TODAY

On a scale of one to ten, rate how you feel your life is going now. If your score is a nine or above, go to the next paragraph. If your score is eight or lower, remember a time when you felt your life was going well enough to rate it a nine or ten, then continue.

Take a moment to lean into that positive energy—close your eyes and really feel the joy, love, or success you're experiencing. As you continue to savor that wonderful feeling, do a quick scan for any little flickers of fear or discomfort.

If you feel any, you don't need to dwell on them. Just notice they're there.

If you don't feel any, simply continue to enjoy the experience. The more comfortable you are with feeling good, the easier your path to genius will be.

DAY 160
Does Your Inner Discomfort
Lead to Outer Self-Sabotage?

Even though you're well into your Big Leap Year, it's important to keep returning to the essential concepts that make the journey easier and more effective. For example, you may still have a limited tolerance for things going well in your life. It's totally natural to experience this internally as fear and discomfort, which you may have noticed in yesterday's leap. The inner fear and discomfort can go a step further, showing up on a physical level.

Even seasoned travelers on the path to genius do things, usually unconsciously, when they've exceeded their tolerance for feeling good and doing well in the world. Then, up come ULPs such as getting into arguments, making bad money decisions, or even suffering physical injuries. The effect is always the same: the act of self-sabotage brings your positive energy down to a more familiar level.

YOUR LEAP FOR TODAY

I invite you to revisit this foundational concept. Think of the most recent time you had some drama in your life—you got into a fight with a partner, friend, or family member. Or possibly your ULP took a physical direction. You cut yourself chopping vegetables or sprained your wrist or bit your tongue.

Now, reflect on the period that directly preceded the drama. Was there a positive event that happened around that time? A success at work, an increased feeling of connection with a friend or partner, a win in any area of your life?

If you can identify a positive catalyst, great. It reinforces your awareness of how ULPs work. If not, it's okay. With continued practice, you'll notice it more clearly in yourself, as well as in the people around you.

DAY 161
Turning Fear into Excitement

I got acquainted with Gestalt therapy through one of my mentors, the late Jack Downing, MD, who had trained with Fritz Perls, MD, the founder of the approach. One of Perls's quotations that made an impact on me was "Fear is excitement without the breath."

Jack explained that the same mechanisms in the body that run fear also run excitement. Though when we get scared, we often hold our breath, making the fear intensify. If you remember to breathe fully when you get scared, you discover that you can transform your fear into excitement.

It's one of the most useful principles I've ever learned. I've done it myself hundreds of times and shown three generations of students how to do it. Today's leap shows you how.

YOUR LEAP FOR TODAY

Take a few moments now to think of something you tend to get scared about. Perhaps it's public speaking or heights or a particular person. Whatever it is, gently bring it to mind.

First, greet it as many people do, by holding their breath. Clutch a breath and hold it as you think about the feared object or person. Just hold it for a few seconds, then let it go, and take some big, easy breaths. Breathe until you can feel a wholesome flow of good feeling inside you.

As you go through your day, notice any situations when you find yourself holding your breath. Note what the trigger was and introduce big, easy breaths into your body again.

DAY 162
Stillness as Radiance

Learning how to be still, to really be still and let life happen—that stillness can become a radiance.

—**Morgan Freeman, American actor**

I didn't read that quotation from Morgan Freeman until many years after I met him, in a Red Carpet Club at the airport in Chicago. Although I only talked with him briefly, I was impressed with his stillness and ease. It wasn't the kind of "nobody's home" emptiness that a lot of actors have. He was right there, fully present, in as heartfelt a conversation with a stranger as anything I'd seen him do on the screen.

YOUR LEAP FOR TODAY

Pause for a moment to contact your inner feeling of stillness. How do you experience it? Is it an open space like the sky or an unblemished surface such as a pond without ripples?

As you go through your day today, be aware of the stillness within. Everybody has it, but it's often covered up by stronger sensations such as fear and anger. Morgan Freeman says it's a radiance. Can you feel what he's referring to?

DAY 163
Your "Going Home" Outfit

In yesterday's leap, I told you about my conversation with Morgan Freeman. At the time, he was wearing jeans and cowboy boots, with a cowboy hat resting on his lap. When I mentioned how comfortable he looked, he said it was his "going home to Memphis" outfit.

At its best, clothing is an outer expression of your inner spirit. For Morgan, it was jeans, boots, and a cowboy hat. For me, it's workout pants, a rainbow selection of sweatshirts and T-shirts, along with a similarly technicolored selection of socks.

If you think of your Genius Zone as your true home, what is your "going home" outfit?

YOUR LEAP FOR TODAY

Take a moment to think about your clothes. Do you dress to fly beneath your upper limits? Or does your clothing reflect your genius?

Use this wonder question to "think outside your closet":

Hmmm, if I could wear what truly felt like me, what would it be?

I created a life in which I can always wear exactly what suits me. Not everyone has that luxury. If you need to wear a uniform or suit at work or for some other reason can't wear what you like all the time, do it part-time.

Make sure you're spending some of your time dressing for your genius, wearing your ideal "going home" outfit.

DAY 164
The Art of Letting Go

In *The Big Leap* and its sequel, *The Genius Zone,* I explore the powerful concept of *letting go.* Particularly, I emphasize the value of letting go of trying to control things you don't have any control over anyway. For example, many people expend energy worrying about whether other people like them. Our intellectual mind may know we have no control over how other people feel, but that doesn't keep us from fretting over it.

What is your experience of letting go? I found it challenging at first to let go of things I had no control over, such as how much the scale said I weighed. Eventually I learned to put all my attention on things I could actually control, such as what I put in my mouth and how much exercise I got. Today's leap gives you a gentle way to explore this area of your life.

- -
YOUR LEAP FOR TODAY
- -

Here is a commitment I found useful in illuminating my letting-go process. Try it on for yourself and find out if it serves you:

I commit to controlling the things I can control and letting go of the things I can't.

Such a powerful commitment usually takes time to come to full fruition in your life. Until you've mastered it, be friendly with yourself in the process. Criticism only slows you down.

DAY 165
Maintain Your Focus on Time

As you've now seen, how you spend your time is a crucial factor in your journey to genius. Even though I've been working with Big Leap ideas for more than half my life, I still go back and review the essentials every once in a while. Today continues our focus on time, all intended to help you create a productive relationship with this crucial force in life.

The Incompetence Zone and the Competence Zone are two of the biggest time consumers. I was appalled when I began to see how much time I was spending doing things I wasn't good at or things others could do just as well. I put a big priority on getting out of those two zones and urge you to maintain a focus on doing so.

YOUR LEAP FOR TODAY

Do a present-moment review of time you spend in the Incompetence and Competence Zones.

Use these wonder questions to illuminate this area:

Hmmm, how much time am I spending each day doing things I'm not good at and don't enjoy?

Hmmm, how much time am I spending each day doing things I can do but others could do just as well?

Remember to be loving toward yourself as you focus your awareness on questions such as these. The process is never about finding fault with yourself; it's about freeing up more time for your genius. Whatever you find, the following two leaps will help you decrease the time you spend in these two zones.

DAY 166
A Deeper Look at the Incompetence Zone

Today, we're going to take another, deeper look at the Incompetence Zone. Spending a lot of time in that zone wastes time and energy you could be using toward more enjoyable and effective pursuits.

However, if you're in the Incompetence Zone as the first step of learning a skill or talent, that's a different story. Then it's a necessary stage that you'll want to embrace, pushing through it with patience and persistence on your way to mastery.

- -
YOUR LEAP FOR TODAY
- -

Review a typical week in your life. Write down all the things you do that are in your Incompetence Zone (and are not part of any skill-acquisition process).

Study each item on your list to see if there's a way to avoid doing it.

Put a D by the items you can delegate to someone else.

Put a P by the items that you can pay someone else to do.

If you can't afford to pay someone else to do it, is there some item or skill you can barter in exchange? If so, put a B next to that item.

If you don't see a way to avoid doing an item, use this wonder question to inspire some out-of-the-box creativity:

Hmmm, how could I avoid doing _____ in a way that has only positive consequences?

Let the question swirl around inside you every so often throughout the day and see what arises.

DAY 167
Revisiting Your Time in the Competence Zone

A lot of people spend far too much time and energy in the Competence Zone because it feels easier to do things yourself than delegate tasks to others.

This ends up being penny-wise, but pound-foolish. You may save a little time in the short run, but you waste hours, weeks, probably years of your life that you could be spending using your genius. This is unfortunate not just for you, but for everyone, because you also deprive the world of your special gifts.

- -
YOUR LEAP FOR TODAY
- -

Make another list, this time of the tasks you do in an average week that fall into the Competence Zone. You can do these activities well, but no better than many others.

In the same way you did for the Incompetence Zone, review the list to see which activities you can delegate, and which you can pay or trade with others to do. Mark them accordingly.

Use the same wonder question you used before for the activities that you don't see a way to transfer to others:

Hmmm, how could I avoid doing _____ in a way that has only positive consequences?

This may feel more challenging because you'll have to keep reminding yourself that even though you *can* do it, it doesn't mean you *should* do it. Clearing your schedule of non–Genius Zone tasks is a vital step toward living your genius.

DAY 168
Competence Zone Exceptions

If you discover you're doing something in your Competence Zone, it doesn't automatically mean you should discard it. Even though I've had the great joy of living in my Genius Zone for many years—doing what I truly love to do and inspiring others to do the same—I also load the dishwasher and take the trash out. I'm not especially talented at either of those tasks, but I happily do them both. Why? Because I enjoy them, and they contribute to a smoothly running household.

I'm also in charge of making sure our cats, Greta and Ali, have tidy litter boxes. I have no great skill in that area, either, but I enjoy doing it because I like to be a good cat parent.

These are examples of the healthy reasons why you might choose to continue doing things that are squarely in your Competence Zone.

YOUR LEAP FOR TODAY

Review your list from yesterday and again look at the items you designated as ones you could delegate, pay, or trade with others to do, as well as the ones you couldn't see a way to avoid doing.

Ask yourself:

Are any of these activities I enjoy and would like to keep doing?

Are any of these activities in service of something I value?

If so, feel free to take them off the "avoid" list. And from now on, when you do them, do them consciously, at your own pace, savoring the experience.

DAY 169
Possible ULPs and the Competence Zone: Part 1

One of my clients found the process of shifting some of her Competence Zone activities to someone else especially challenging. Even though she knew those activities weren't the best use of her time and didn't engage her unique strengths and talents, she felt strongly that she would do them better and faster than anyone else. Was her issue an ULP—keeping her stuck in her Competence Zone?

It might be, since the need to control can be driven by fear—and we know that fear is often a component of ULPs.

But maybe not. There are times when other forces are at work.

If you have resistance of any kind to shifting your Competence Zone activities, it's helpful to learn to recognize if it's an ULP or something else.

- -
YOUR LEAP FOR TODAY
- -

Go back to your updated list and look at the items you designated as ones you could delegate, pay, or trade with others to do, as well as the ones you couldn't see a way to avoid doing.

Go through each item and notice if you feel any resistance in yourself to letting go of that activity. If you do, then ask yourself this wonder question:

Hmmm, why am I resisting letting this activity go?

Simply sit with the question and see what comes up. If you don't get an answer right away, stay with it. Often, it will take a little while before the deeper reason emerges.

Repeat this process for each activity that you have resistance to relinquishing. In tomorrow's leap, we'll look at what to do with this information.

DAY 170
Possible ULPs and the Competence Zone: Part 2

In yesterday's leap, you identified your feelings of resistance to taking certain Competence Zone activities off your plate and you also explored why you felt that way.

As you probably noticed, sitting with a "why" question about your feelings is often like peeling the layers of an onion. As you delve beyond your initial answer, you usually uncover deeper reasons that might seem silly, illogical, or even unreasonable.

Know that whatever answer you arrived at is okay. It's valuable information that you'll use now to take the next step on your journey to genius.

YOUR LEAP FOR TODAY

Today you'll explore how each Competence Zone activity that you resist letting go of is either helping or hindering you. Depending on what you find, you'll know what to do next.

For each activity, ask yourself:

What is the payoff for continuing to do this activity?
What is the cost of continuing to do this activity?
Is the payoff worth the cost?

If the cost is greater than the payoff, reflect on these two questions:

What's one step I can take to begin letting this activity go?
What support would I need?

If the payoff for doing that activity is greater than the cost, just add the activity to the list of Competence Zone activities that you enjoy doing.

When you do that activity, do it consciously, appreciating the benefits it brings to your life.

DAY 171
Acknowledge Your Awesome Power

Whether we realize it or not, we all have the power to make massive positive changes in our lives. Many people may not realize or use that power, but it's there in potential form, ready to be turned on and directed toward your chosen goals.

How do I know you have this awesome power? Because you've already created your life the way it is now. If you can do that, you have the power to create it some other way.

You may not think you created the life you have. I certainly didn't when I first started working on my genius. I didn't realize I'd created the life I had based on a lot of unconscious choices. It was a joyful day when I realized I could make *conscious* choices that turned my life in a positive direction.

- -
YOUR LEAP FOR TODAY
- -

What are some conscious choices you can make today that will move you closer to your genius? Do you need to make new choices in the areas of health, happiness, relationship, or another area of your life?

Treat yourself to a wonder question that will illuminate this area for you:

Hmmm, what conscious choices can I make today to move more into my Genius Zone?

Turn this question over in your mind a few times and wonder about it. As you go through your day, look for moments of choice that serve your genius.

DAY 172
In Our Own Way

The legendary spiritual teacher Alan Watts spent his long career writing about and teaching the wisdom of Zen and other Asian spiritual traditions. At the same time, according to his autobiographical writings, he had five marriages, countless affairs, and fought a lifelong battle with the alcoholism that eventually killed him.

I found out about this amazing man by reading his autobiography, *In My Own Way*. The title has a double meaning: it was about how he lived his life his own singular way, but it was also about how he got in his own way.

As I read how his human habits often sabotaged his spiritual intentions, I realized he was describing the Upper Limit Problem. Upper Limit Problems are the way we get in our own way.

YOUR LEAP FOR TODAY

Take a moment to reflect on times you have formed new goals—losing weight, reading more, keeping a journal—only to "get in your own way" by sabotaging those good intentions.

Sometimes sabotage looks like a forbidden pint of ice cream or an extra hour of *Desperate Housewives of Omaha*, but whatever the distraction, it takes us off-track.

Use this wonder question to open up the conversation in yourself:

Hmmm, how do I get in my own way?

As answers to this question come to light, either now or later, always remember to be friendly with yourself as you're being honest with yourself. I mention this instruction often because a feeling of loving acceptance of all your foibles is the fastest way to move beyond them.

DAY 173
The Relationship Between Genius and Success

Today, we focus again on one of the essentials of your journey to genius. Whether you're someone who's already attained a good degree of success or someone struggling financially or creatively, you're being held back by your Upper Limit Problem. I started out working with juvenile delinquents and ended up working with rock stars and White House aspirants. They all had their ULPs.

You and I and everyone else have the equivalent of a thermostat that regulates how much love, success, and abundance you'll allow yourself to experience. When you exceed your setting, you sabotage yourself so you can re-enter the familiar zone where you feel secure.

Wherever and whenever your thermostat got set, this year you're in the process of shifting it upward. As you establish yourself in your Genius Zone, your thermostat will fade into the background. You'll live in waves of greater and greater love, success, and abundance. Along the way, it really helps to have a vivid picture of your Genius Zone life. Today's leap is about exploring where you're headed.

YOUR LEAP FOR TODAY

What does your most beautiful fantasy for your best life look like? Your automatic response might be generic—riches, romance, beauty, fame, and power—the stuff of movies. Is that *really* what you want?

Take some time today to go deeper and find the details of your unique vision. Ask yourself:

What's my personal version of the ultimate in love, success, and abundance?

Make a list and continue to add to it as more and more clarity dawns. Your vision may come fully formed or may evolve over the course of your journey to genius. The important thing is to know that it's entirely possible—no matter where you start.

DAY 174
Key Skill: Increasing Your
Tolerance for Good Feeling

The perfect is the enemy of the good.

—Voltaire, French writer and philosopher

Perfection is a construct of the mind, but good feeling is something you experience in your body. When you find yourself focusing on any form of perfection, focus instead on increasing the amount of time you enjoy good feeling.

When you cultivate and extend the amount of time you spend feeling good, you make a direct investment in your genius. The more you enjoy feeling organically good, the less likely you are to get stopped by ULPs.

YOUR LEAP FOR TODAY

Make the expansion of good feeling in your body a high priority today and every day.

Use a wonder question to facilitate:

Hmmm, how can I enjoy the maximum amount of good feeling as I go through my life today?

Circulate this question in your awareness as you go through your day. Treat yourself to as much good feeling as you possibly can.

DAY 175
Small Steps, Big Results

An acquaintance from the gym where I work out retired from his corporate job after forty years, carrying an extra pound for each year in the executive chair. He wanted to weigh 170 instead of 210, but he also never enjoyed exercising. Finally, he talked himself into joining the gym and working out in the weight room for ten minutes before going for a swim or a walk around the indoor track. Pretty soon, though, he was spending fifteen and even twenty minutes with resistance training.

By the end of his first year, he was doing a full hour-long workout in the weight room in addition to his aerobic exercise. And he'd shed thirty of the forty pounds he wanted to lose. I only crossed paths with him every week or two, so watching his body change was like watching a slow-motion slide show.

YOUR LEAP FOR TODAY

What is something you could do in ten minutes today that would increase the flow of good feeling in your body?

You might try on something brand-new, like I did when I was first invited to a dance therapy group. I immediately declined, saying, "I don't dance." Fortunately, I worked up the courage to give it a try and ended up happily married to a dance therapist for forty-plus years. The guy who didn't dance has spent thousands of hours dancing.

Give yourself the gift of ten flow-increasing minutes today and see where it takes you.

DAY 176
Feeling Flawed Starts Early

Feeling fundamentally flawed often comes from internalizing negative messages from caregivers and siblings. It also happens in your encounters with bullies and other conflicted relationships.

These messages get into your head before you're old enough to effectively evaluate their truth. To make matters more complicated, these old negative messages usually live beneath the conscious level. Today's leap gives you an opportunity to make the unconscious more conscious.

- -
YOUR LEAP FOR TODAY
- -

To uncover unconscious feelings of being flawed, sit quietly for a few minutes and float the following wonder question through your mind:

Hmmm, **what do I most deeply believe about myself?**

Make a list of your answers—both the positive and the negative. For example, I'm not a team player, I'm unattractive, I'm good with animals, I have a talent for math, I can't cook. . . .

Reviewing your list, item by item, ask yourself two questions: "Whose voice is that?" and "Where and when did I start believing that?"

To make the Big Leap to the full expression of your genius, take every opportunity to examine your beliefs and make sure they fit the life you're creating now.

DAY 177
A Surprising Discovery

I remember the surprise of discovering a specific ULP in a successful person I saw for a first session. On the surface, she looked like she had it all: wealth, fame, accolades in her profession, and a solid partnership with her beloved.

As we delved into why she felt so miserable in spite of all these blessings, one of the major fears that cause ULPs came to light. She was convinced she didn't deserve good things happening to her, because of things she'd done in her past that she hadn't forgiven herself for. When good things did happen, she had to feel bad about them to match the old inner feeling of being terminally flawed. She had everything but didn't think she deserved anything.

Later, as I worked with other prominent people, I realized that it was almost an epidemic among the highly successful. Almost none of them thought they'd actually earned being where they were, even ones who had worked their way up from tiny clubs to stadiums, or from the mail room to the CEO chair.

YOUR LEAP FOR TODAY

You don't have to be a rock star or a corporate executive to suffer from what has been called "impostor syndrome." Almost all of us have at least a bit of it, a part of ourselves that doesn't quite believe it or celebrate when good things happen to us.

Use today's affirmation to open a bigger openness to positive energy, no matter what you've done in the past:

Whether I think I deserve it or not, I celebrate more and more success and positive energy in my life every day.

Whether you "deserve" something is a thought you make up in your mind. Celebrating positive energy and success is something you do all over. Put your attention on celebrating your good fortune as you go through your day today.

DAY 178
Learning to Love Yourself

We must fall in love with ourselves. I don't like myself, I'm crazy about myself.

—Mae West, American actress

Think of learning to love yourself as a lifelong process of deepening your acceptance and valuing of yourself.

Like a spiral, every time you go higher, you pass by aspects of yourself or the world you've seen before. Now, you have an expanded ability to love them. Each time you encounter the issue you get the opportunity to extend loving acceptance to any aspect of it that remains unloved.

YOUR LEAP FOR TODAY

Pause occasionally in your daily round and float these wonder questions through your mind:

Hmmm, **what in me most needs love?**

Hmmm, **what in the people I love most needs love?**

These are big questions, worthy of your sustained attention. As you go through the events of the day, look at the people you meet through a new lens: What most needs my loving acceptance?

DAY 179
Ramifications of Feeling Fundamentally Flawed

The belief that you're fundamentally flawed often creates two more related limiting beliefs.

The first: if you fully commit to expressing your genius and really try to do it, you'll fail.

The second: your genius must also be flawed, so if you succeed at truly expressing it, that expression wouldn't be good enough.

As a result, you decide it's better to not even try. Or if you do, you opt to play small, so you'll fail small. Fortunately, there's an antidote, and today's leap gives you a direct way to apply it.

- -
YOUR LEAP FOR TODAY
- -

The thing about hidden barriers is that they're hidden. It's hard to identify an obstacle that's invisible—except by the presence of its effects. The only reliable way I've found to do this is to look at the results it's producing.

Explore whether you might be running up against this barrier by asking yourself these questions:

Am I afraid I'll fail at discovering and expressing my genius?

Am I afraid my genius won't be good enough?

A few times today, just let these questions run through your mind and feel what comes up.

DAY 180
More Awareness About
Feeling Fundamentally Flawed: Part 1

In yesterday's leap, you spent time exploring how feeling fundamentally flawed might show up on your journey to genius.

If asking yesterday's question about being afraid to fail brought up any feeling of "yes," it will be helpful to shine more awareness on the subject.

YOUR LEAP FOR TODAY

Playing it safe means never putting yourself in a position to fail. If you don't try, you can't fail.

To get more clarity about whether this dynamic is at play in your life, consider these wonder questions:

Hmmm, how do I play it safe in my life?

Hmmm, what excuses do I use to avoid even trying things?

Be gentle with yourself as you bring awareness to behaviors that have served you in the past. Once you know better, you can do better.

DAY 181
More Awareness About
Feeling Fundamentally Flawed: Part 2

In yesterday's leap, you explored how feeling fundamentally flawed can zap your willingness to even try to make the Big Leap.

Today, you'll have the chance to address the question from two days ago about whether you were afraid your genius might not be good enough.

If you found any "yes" inside to that question, today's leap invites you to bring more awareness to bear.

YOUR LEAP FOR TODAY

Playing it small is about protecting yourself from humiliation and ridicule.

When you're in the habit of comparing yourself to other people and coming up short, you'll hesitate to do your very best, because then you and the rest of the world will be able to see your best is not as good as everyone else's best.

If that sounds familiar, use these wonder questions to go deeper:

Hmmm, how do I play small in my life?

Hmmm, what reasons do I use to justify not taking on more difficult or more meaningful projects, adventures, or relationships?

Again, be gentle with yourself. The goal is to shine a light on the beliefs holding your hidden barriers in place. A lot of their power comes from their invisibility.

DAY 182
Transforming Emotion

I had a profound experience of transforming emotion not long after my mother passed away in 1990. You can read the details in my book *Conscious Luck*, but in brief, I discovered a letter when my brother and I were cleaning out our mother's house. It was stuck behind a picture in a frame, dated my birth year of 1945, and it was about how much shame my mother felt during and after her pregnancy with me.

As I read the letter, I became aware of where I could still feel the shame in my own body. At first, the awareness of all that shame made me squirm, but as I stood there a new idea came into my mind: instead of resisting the shame or feeling bad about it, I could embrace it and use its energy for my genius.

Emotion is energy in motion. For example, the butterflies you feel in your stomach when you're anxious or scared are the energy of blood leaving your stomach and heading out toward your muscles. Because emotion is energy, that energy can be dedicated to whatever purpose you choose. I chose using the energy of my emotions for genius. That decision gave me a new relationship with all my feelings. Today, you have the opportunity to do just that for yourself.

YOUR LEAP FOR TODAY

Use the following affirmation to anchor this new idea into your awareness:

I appreciate all my emotions and use their energy to bring forth my genius.

Make this new idea your own by circulating the affirmation through your mind several times and saying it out loud. Open your heart to the idea and feel the sincerity of it in your body. Pause a few times throughout your day to refresh the affirmation in your mind.

DAY 183
Handling ULPs with Ease

One useful metric to keep your eye on is how quickly you move through ULPs. The metric *not* to use is whether you have any ULPs at all. Just accept, as I still do even after decades of benign vigilance, that occasionally you're going to hit an Upper Limit Problem.

Focus always on things you can do to move through them quickly and efficiently. That will also help you spot them on the horizon and make early moves that lessen or ward off the ULP.

Resistance makes ULPs persist. Resistance to admitting you're in an ULP, resistance to looking at the fears underneath it—these unconscious moves put the brakes on the process. By contrast, shining the light of awareness on the ULP and underlying fears speeds things up.

YOUR LEAP FOR TODAY

Use the following affirmation to increase your ability to move through your Upper Limit Problems with efficiency and ease:

I greet my Upper Limit Problems with awareness and move through them with wonder and ease.

Say this positive idea in your mind and feel it in your body. Pause occasionally today to refresh it in your awareness.

You are now halfway through your Big Leap Year! Congratulations on completing your second quarter of growth. Over the next few days, try to identify the ways that you feel different from and the same as the person who started this journey. If you've been journaling, take some time to read through your answers and notes from the past twenty-six weeks. Take time also to celebrate your achievement, in whatever way makes sense for you.

DAY 184
Building Habits

How do you make something a habit? It requires willingness and commitment (and lots of recommitment), but a habit can also be reinforced by pairing it with an action you already do naturally.

A good example of that is a custom observed in some Jewish households I've visited. Every time a person enters or exits their house, they touch their lips and then touch the mezuzah, a small box containing Jewish scripture nailed to the doorframe.

Connecting something extraordinary, like this act of devotion, to something ordinary, like going through a door, makes an extraordinary feeling such as love for God a habit.

YOUR LEAP FOR TODAY

Take a moment right now to review your daily activities. Look for some mundane, everyday action of yours—like putting on your shoes or brushing your teeth—to connect to one or more of your Big Leap commitments and affirmations.

Every time you do your chosen action, say or think one of your commitments or affirmations. As you do, make a point to consciously savor positive feelings in your mind and heart.

DAY 185
Turning on a Light

When it comes to your upper limits, ignorance is not bliss—it keeps you stuck. It was unsettling for me to realize how much I had unconsciously sabotaged myself in the past. I had to remind myself I'd been on automatic pilot, set to keep me in a limited comfort zone.

The same goes for you. All the work you're doing now is to turn on the light, or become conscious of how you've been limiting yourself. Once the light is on, you can see the situation—*and* more easily do what's necessary to dissolve your upper limits and start living your genius.

YOUR LEAP FOR TODAY

Ram Dass once wrote that everything in life—positive and negative—is "grist for the mill." When it comes to your Big Leap Year, that means any limiting beliefs and negative patterns you're uncovering are just material to process on your journey.

To cement your commitment to this process, run this statement through your mind a few times right now:

I commit to doing what it takes—for as long as it takes—to be free of my upper limits.

Take this bold, positive commitment into your day today by pausing occasionally to refresh it in your mind.

DAY 186
Celebration

Maitake mushrooms are known in Japan as "the dancing mushroom." According to a Japanese legend, a group of Buddhist nuns and woodcutters met on a mountain trail, where they discovered a fruiting of maitake mushrooms emerging from the forest floor. Rejoicing at their discovery of this delicious mushroom, they danced to celebrate.

—Paul Stamets, American mycologist and author

The word "celebrate" comes from the Latin verb *celebrare*, which has a number of ancient meanings. To celebrate something is to honor it and to sing the praises of it.

Whatever the meaning of the words, the actual experience of celebration is what really juices up our experience of living.

YOUR LEAP FOR TODAY

Pause several times today to consciously celebrate what you've created in your life.

Each time, dedicate a full ten to fifteen seconds to full celebration (which, inspired by the dancing nuns who found the mushrooms, may include dancing).

DAY 187
The Power of One Thought

When I was in elementary school, a man named Roger Bannister ran a mile in less than four minutes. Nobody had ever done it before, but long before Roger broke the record, he had a breakthrough in his thinking. He changed a single thought in his mind from "Nobody has ever done it" to "I commit to doing it."

Not only did his own life change with an empowering new thought, Roger changed the lives of many others through his example. In the sixty years since his record, more than fifteen hundred runners have broken the four-minute barrier.

YOUR LEAP FOR TODAY

Use Roger Bannister's story to change a single thought in your own life. Take a moment to think of a limiting thought, such as "I can't find time to exercise" or "I can't get enough sleep."

Change the "I can't" to "I can" and say it a few times, as in "I can find time to exercise."

You may not know how yet but changing to "I can" opens up possibility where before there was none.

DAY 188
Creativity

Curiosity about life in all of its aspects, I think, is still the secret of great creative people.

—Leo Burnett, American advertising executive

One of my heroes, developmental psychologist Erik Erikson, first inspired me to think about the relationship between creative expression and psychological growth.

He says that we have to keep the creativity taps turned on full flow in order to keep growing. Not to do so is to stagnate. (This is especially true after fifty years of age.)

In kindling creativity at any age, curiosity is our best friend.

- -

YOUR LEAP FOR TODAY

- -

Invoke several wonder questions:

Hmmm, what am I most curious about right now in my life?

Hmmm, what am I most interested in finding out how it works?

Let them circulate in your awareness, giving yourself space and time for creative answers to emerge. Carry the questions in your awareness throughout your day.

DAY 189
Three Major Emotion Zones

In the quest to embrace your emotions, it's helpful to know where specific emotions reside in your body. It's information we could have learned in the first grade, but I can testify that many grown-ups, even super successful ones, don't have a clue about where their emotions are located.

Here's a review from an earlier leap: three zones of our bodies give us clear signals when we are angry, scared, or sad.

The anger zone is from your mid-back up through your neck and jaw muscles. If you learn to pay attention to this zone, it will send you signals by tightening up when you're angry.

The sadness zone is in the chest and throat; it signals us with a constricted sensation when we're feeling sad.

The fear zone is in the solar plexus and belly region. This area signals us through butterflies and tensing of the belly muscles when we're scared.

YOUR LEAP FOR TODAY

Use this simple process to explore the emotion zones of fear, anger, and sadness. Sit comfortably and tune in to your body's sensations and feelings. Rest your attention on your anger zone, first on the area between your shoulder blades. Move your attention up into the neck muscles and out into your jaws. Notice whether it feels tight or at ease.

Shift your attention to your sadness zone, your chest up into your throat. Notice if you feel constricted in your chest or have the well-known lump-in-the-throat sensation.

Shift your attention to the fear zone. Notice if you feel the racy, queasy, tight-belly sensations of fear.

As you go through your day, tune in to these zones often. Noticing your specific emotions can help you communicate about them in effective ways.

DAY 190
A New Way to Look at Addiction: Part 1

I've treated a variety of addictions in my work, and handled a couple of my own along the way. Addictions are one of the main ways we upper-limit ourselves. One of my university colleagues took twelve years to get his PhD, compared to three years on average. Every time he'd get close to finishing, his alcoholism would escalate and he'd drop out.

It was in handling my own food addictions in my twenties that I first conceptualized the Upper Limit Problem. I would lose weight, sabotage myself, lose more weight, and sabotage myself again. After a few iterations of this pattern the light began to dawn on me. I gradually stopped upper-limiting myself and attained a healthy weight.

You may never have been addicted to any of the usual substances such as alcohol, opioids, or nicotine, but even if you haven't, many other things in life can be addictive ULPs. For example, many people find that bingeing television, social media, or food are ways they bring their energy down or distract themselves from working on their genius. Others find that they upper-limit themselves through repetitive relationship dramas.

YOUR LEAP FOR TODAY

Take a few moments to do a review of the role of addiction in your life right now. Do you consider yourself addicted to any chemical substances such as alcohol, drugs, or nicotine? How about social addictions such as social media, video games, or relationship conflict?

Whether or not you find any addictions in your current life, use this affirmation to set a helpful intention:

I easefully spot and clear up any habits that hinder my path to genius.

Let this positive idea resonate in your mind and body for a few moments now, then take it into your day to guide your actions.

DAY 191
A New Way to Look at Addiction: Part 2

When I started my career, I mainly treated alcoholism, pot, and cigarette addictions. I was working with delinquents and repeat offenders at the time; those were the main addictions my clients had. Later, when I ran a halfway house, I also worked with cocaine and heroin addiction.

After working with a few hundred addicts, as well as kicking my own addictions to cigarettes and unhealthy food, I came to see that all addictions have one thing in common: addicts always lie about their addictions. Eventually, I came to agree with the blunt conclusion of the late addictions expert Anne Wilson Schaef. In her view, an addiction is anything you lie about.

One of my writer friends struggled with alcohol and drugs for thirty years but now has twenty years of sobriety. She told me once that one of the greatest days in her life was when she stopped lying to friends and family about her addictions. Instead, she went to her first 12-step meeting and told the truth: "My name is Sally and I'm a drug addict."

- -
YOUR LEAP FOR TODAY
- -

Be friendly and nonjudgmental with yourself as you take a clear-eyed look at this new aspect of addiction. Take a broad view that includes food, drugs, media, relationship drama, sugar, and anything else you can think of. Use this wonder question to initiate your inquiry:

Hmmm, what, if anything, do I lie about regarding addictions?

Take a few moments now to reflect on this question. It's a big one, though, so take it into your day to wonder about "in the heat of action."

DAY 192
Ending Worry

Worry is a thin stream of fear trickling through the mind. If encouraged, it cuts a channel into which all other thoughts are drained.

—**Arthur Roche, American Catholic Bishop**

Worry is the most common Upper Limit Problem. The quickest way to stop feeling good is to manufacture a stream of worry thoughts.

As I began to study this in myself early in my career, I realized that my worry thoughts were all fueled by fear. As you go through your Big Leap Year, you'll learn a lot about your emotions. Fear is a primary one, along with sadness and anger, that cause repetitive problems in daily life. Much of our happiness depends on our ability to embrace these natural feelings and get the wisdom they offer.

YOUR LEAP FOR TODAY

Deepen your understanding of the relationship between worry and fear by engaging with this wonder question:

Hmmm, **when I have worry thoughts, what am I afraid of?**

Ask the question several times in your mind, aiming for that "*Hmmm*" of authentic wonder. Then, say it aloud several times, doing your best to feel the question in your body. As you go through your day, pause occasionally to focus on the question.

DAY 193
Getting Rid of Getting Rid

One problematic way of thinking I encountered in my clients early in my career was the notion of "getting rid" of something. One client would talk about getting rid of her tension headaches; another would talk of getting rid of his fear of public speaking.

It's certainly understandable to want to get rid of the pain of a headache or the fear of public speaking, but ironically, trying to get rid of pains and angst in ourselves doesn't work very well. In fact, the act of trying to get rid of something often locks it into your body. When you "get rid" of something, you drop it like a rock or banish it from your house, but try doing that with a headache or fear and it often gets worse.

The solution is inclusion, not banishment. I ask my clients to explore their symptoms, to feel the fears, grief, and anger that come along with them, and ultimately to own them with loving acceptance.

It often seems like magic to the client when the headaches stop occurring or the fear of public speaking is replaced by excitement. It's not magic; it's the application of an ancient principle—what you resist runs you. Once you stop resisting the feelings underneath the symptoms, once you extend your loving acceptance to them, they often disappear . . . as if by magic.

- -
YOUR LEAP FOR TODAY
- -

Tune in and ask if there are old, unproductive parts of yourself you want to get rid of. If yes, give yourself a few moments of loving acceptance toward those parts of you.

Use this affirmation to replace your "get rid of" thinking:

I welcome and lovingly accept any part of me I want to get rid of.

Repeat the affirmation a few times in your mind. Try it on out loud and feel yourself welcoming those parts of you into yourself. Take the affirmation into your day, being on the lookout for things you might still want to get rid of.

DAY 194
Your Relationship with Time

When I started looking into my own ULPs, I was surprised to see how many of my worry thoughts involved time. If you study your thoughts closely, you will likely see that even when you're not working and you're enjoying downtime, a substantial number of these thoughts still pass through your mind.

One of the best ways to turn off worry thoughts about time is to shift your focus. Take your attention off of time and put it on doing more things you love to do. When you're doing what you love to do, you transcend time. It's been my experience that busy humans need some time-transcendence every day. Today's leap offers you another experience of my tried-and-true method.

YOUR LEAP FOR TODAY

Scan your schedule for the last few days and today with the following question in mind:

What did I do that I absolutely love to do and what did I do that I don't love to do?

Come up with a percentage that reflects how much of the day you spent on things you love to do and don't love to do.

Next, reaffirm your commitment to spending more time doing what you love to do. Use the following statement:

I commit to spending time every day doing things I most love to do.

Even if you've made similar commitments before, home in again on this crucial issue. Circulate the commitment through your mind. Feel the resonance of it in your body and keep it in your awareness throughout your day.

DAY 195
Generosity

The Choctaw people have a history of helping others. Only 16 years after they began their long, sad march along the Trail of Tears, the Choctaws learned of people starving to death in Ireland. With great empathy, in 1847 Choctaw individuals made donations totaling $170, the equivalent of several thousand dollars today, to assist the Irish people during the famine.

—Judy Allen, Choctaw historian

Gratitude, appreciation, and generosity are all part of the deep impulse to fully express your energy. As I expanded my ability to receive in my life, I found that a great way to do that was to give generously.

It's all about energy—your ability to receive a maximum flow of inbound energy in the form of abundance, love, and good times, and your ability to express a maximum flow of outbound energy in the form of contributions of various kinds.

YOUR LEAP FOR TODAY

Float two wonder questions through your consciousness a few times right now and take them into your day:

Hmmm, how would my life be if I were fully willing to receive generosity?

Hmmm, how could I fully express my generosity?

Generosity is an expression of gratitude, which is a feeling I've found to be very facilitative of genius. The formula is simple: the more grateful and generous you are, the more you live in the Genius Zone.

DAY 196
Guilt and Regret

Have you ever been feeling good, perhaps celebrating a win in your life, when out of the blue you remember some past screwup? I've had that happen more than once, and I bet you have, too. It's one of the classic ULPs, stopping the flow of positive energy and causing you to beat yourself up for it. The timing is not a coincidence. Guilt and regret are highly effective ways to bring down your energy.

YOUR LEAP FOR TODAY

All of us have a "greatest hits" list of actions and inactions we regret or feel guilty about. Today, with a clear understanding of how our upper limits can use these hits, introduce these affirmations:

I expand my capacity for feeling good.

I spot guilt and shame when they occur and continue to expand my good feeling.

Float these affirmations through your mind a few times and then write them down. As you go through your day, keep these positive ideas fresh in your awareness by pausing to think or say them.

DAY 197
Finding the Source of
Recycling Criticism and Blame

In an earlier leap, you used the Rule of Three to identify recycling thoughts of worry. You then explored which events or experiences in your past might have triggered the worry thought initially.

Today you're going to do the same exploration, this time to determine the origin of any recurring thoughts of criticism or blame—either directed inward or outward.

YOUR LEAP FOR TODAY

Take a minute to bring up the recycling experience of either criticizing or blaming others, or the repeated cudgel of guilt or regret you use on yourself.

See if you can remember the first time it happened. It may have been a long time ago—in childhood—or more recently. It's fine if you can't pinpoint the exact moment it started; my guess is that the experience feels familiar in some way.

That's because whether it's the third or fourth time you've noticed it or it's a long-term pattern, you're running an old script. Try to come up with a sentence that describes this experience. For example, "I feel like I'm too much." Or "I've done something wrong and need to pay for it." Or "I need to make sure others don't make mistakes." "If I'm wrong, I'll suffer."

Whether or not you find the original source or come up with a descriptive sentence, give yourself a moment of sincere self-appreciation. Expanding your awareness is always a step forward.

DAY 198
Gratitude or Entitlement: Pick One

Gratitude starts where entitlement ends.

—Anonymous

What's the difference between feeling you deserve love, success, and abundance, and feeling that you're entitled to them? Though it may seem like semantics, the difference is profound.

Deserving means feeling worthy. After you've dissolved the ULP of feeling fundamentally flawed, you get to feel an ongoing, organic sense of worthiness. Feeling worthy leads to gratitude and appreciation, furthering the cycle of positivity.

Entitlement has a demanding quality to it. Relationship expert Alison Armstrong explains it this way: When you get something you think is owed to you, it's like getting a paycheck. There's very little gratitude or wonder generated in your heart at receiving it.

Along the path to your genius, become aware of any feelings of entitlement and transform them into gratitude. Feel your genuine worthiness in every cell of your body.

YOUR LEAP FOR TODAY

Notice how you feel today when something goes your way or someone is kind, loving, or pleasant toward you. Are you grateful? Or do you feel it was just your due?

If you notice yourself feeling entitled in any way, pause to turn it into gratitude. Take a few deep breaths and savor the joy of being alive.

DAY 199
Celebrating Wonder

The fully integrated person is capable of being both an adult and a child simultaneously. Recapture the childlike feelings of wide-eyed excitement, spontaneous appreciation, cutting loose, and being full of awe and wonder at this magnificent universe.

—**Wayne Dyer, American author and motivational speaker**

The experience of wonder is its own reward. It feels good to slip out of the field of the known into genuine curiosity about the unknown. It's a pleasure I've enjoyed thousands of times. Wonder also has another reward, a highly practical one, that I've also used thousands of times to help people transform issues large and small.

Wonder is a powerful tool for insight and change. As I've told three generations of people in our seminars, "If you can wonder about it, you can change it." The reason is that a moment of true wonder pops you free of your previous conceptions about the subject. Today's leap gives you the opportunity to feel the power of wonder for yourself.

YOUR LEAP FOR TODAY

Reflect for a moment on a recurring challenge in your life, something that's been resistant to change. Call it to mind, picture it, feel how it shows up in your body. Next, bring this wonder question to bear on the issue:

Hmmm, what do I need to know, do, and be to free myself from this pattern?

Focus on launching the question, not on getting answers. Think of your question as a searchlight you're sending into the unknown, illuminating things previously unseen.

DAY 200
The Power of Stillness

You do not need to leave your room. Remain sitting at your table and listen. Do not even listen, simply wait, be quiet, still, and solitary. The world will freely offer itself to you to be unmasked, it has no choice, it will roll in ecstasy at your feet.

—Franz Kafka, writer

In much of our lives, we're focused on doing—getting things done, handling our responsibilities, taking actions that further our goals. But a focus on doing needs to be balanced out by a focus on being.

I was once much more of a doer than I am now. I still get plenty done, but as I matured, I learned to balance my doing with equal attention to being. Today's leap gives you an opportunity to explore your relationship with being.

YOUR LEAP FOR TODAY

Here's an experiment that gives you an up-close look at what I call "pure being." Designate ten minutes in your calendar every day for the next seven days. Pick a different time each day.

When your ten-minute block comes up on your calendar, go into a room by yourself and don't do anything for the full ten minutes. Don't meditate or focus on your breathing or do anything with your mind or body. Just be. Notice urges to do something that come up during the ten minutes; each time you get an urge, go back to pure being.

Notice how you feel afterward and on throughout the day. Many people are surprised to discover that a brief period of pure being can have a beneficial effect on their whole day.

DAY 201
The Truth About Manifestation

You've no doubt heard a lot about manifestation over the past twenty years. It's been the subject of dozens of books and movies. With all that input coming from different directions, you have every right to have some confusion about what's genuinely useful and what's just blather.

Here's the basic idea of manifestation I've used and taught in my life: it's simply the practice of bringing your goals into visible reality. The essentials of manifestation are straightforward and easy to learn. Today's leap delves into this important subject.

YOUR LEAP FOR TODAY

If we think of manifestation as simply the art of turning your goals into reality, the obvious starting place is your goals. Open up the conversation with yourself about your aims and objectives by asking this wonder question:

Hmmm, **what do I most want and need right now in my life?**

Ask the question several times in your mind, genuinely wondering about it. Then, ask it aloud several times. Make a hum of authentic wonder that you can feel in your body. Focus on the wonder and be open to the spontaneous emergence of answers as you go through your day.

DAY 202
Celebrating the Natural Way

One of the weird inconsistencies of my pre–Big Leap life was the tolerance I had for artificial ways of feeling good through alcohol, sugar, and other temporary fixes. As I woke up and began my journey to the Genius Zone, I created more space inside to feel and appreciate *natural* good feelings.

Today, we focus on a direct way to expand your capacity for things going well in your life. Start exactly where you are, by noticing the many good things that happen to you every day. Savor your good feelings about them. The more you celebrate them, the more good things happen.

YOUR LEAP FOR TODAY

Celebrate your life today with natural intoxicants:

Chug a tall glass of connection with others.
Toast to the ways you were brave.
Eat a pint of creative expression.
Light up . . . the world with your unique contribution.

Once you start looking for ways to celebrate your life in natural ways, you may notice, as I did, that your craving for unnatural intoxicants disappears into the past.

DAY 203
Making the Connection

When you are grateful—when you can see what you have—you unlock blessings to flow in your life.

—Suze Orman, American author and financial advisor

I go with the flow. Whatever music you play for me, I'll dance.

—Gael García Bernal, Mexican actor

When you make the connection between gratitude and flow—the sustained experience of feeling good—you acquire a skill of immense practical significance.

The tool is simple: whenever you notice you're hitting up against your upper limits, which interrupts you feeling flow, figure out something you're grateful for and express gratitude for it. Then notice how quickly the feeling of flow returns.

YOUR LEAP FOR TODAY

This process comes from my wife, Katie, who began her career as a dance/movement therapist. Try a ten-minute experiment she does with her clients. Put on some dancing music you like and spend ten minutes doing a gratitude dance.

As you move, let your eyes fall on different things in your awareness: furniture, clothing, art, food. Each time your eye falls on something, feel gratitude for it. Notice how you feel afterward.

Remember as you go through your day to keep the dance of gratitude going, even if you're sitting at your desk.

DAY 204
Trying to Out-Victim Others

Even if you increase your awareness about arguments and ULPs, fights may still happen. To handle them effectively, it helps to understand the dynamic underlying conflicts.

In our relationship seminars we say, "All arguments between couples are a race to occupy the victim position."

One person says, "You're making me miserable."

The other counters, "No, *you're* the one making *me* miserable."

Back and forth you go, slinging blame at each other.

The truth is it doesn't matter who started the conflict. You can debate that point forever. If one of you succeeds in capturing the coveted "biggest victim" award, then what? That person may have won a single skirmish, but you're both no closer to ending the larger conflict.

YOUR LEAP FOR TODAY

Resolving conflict starts with stepping out of the victim position. You do this by taking 100 percent responsibility for resolving the conflict. To try on this process, allow these wonder questions to settle into your mind and heart:

Hmmm, how would it feel to free myself from being a victim?

Hmmm, what can I do to resolve conflicts without claiming victimhood?

This approach works best when both parties take 100 percent responsibility, but even if it's just you, I predict the energy between you will change.

DAY 205
Practice Recognizing Projection in Conflicts

When two people are stuck in conflicts with each other, very often they're both feeling the same deeper emotions. But since they've hidden those emotions from themselves, they do a lot of projecting onto each other, which only escalates the tensions.

Rather than deal with their own unresolved pain, it's easier to fight. As a result, people can get locked into their struggles—trying to prove each other wrong—for a very long time. As you can imagine, this is a very effective and very troublesome upper-limiting tool.

When the two people finally start sharing their deeper feelings, allowing authentic energy to flow between them, they begin to heal the glitches in their communication.

YOUR LEAP FOR TODAY

Think of the last argument you had with a significant person in your life. Take a moment to check if there were any recent positive events in your life, or your life together, that might have triggered your upper limits.

If you think it might be an ULP, ask yourself about the emotions that may have triggered it. Use these wonder questions for your exploration:

Hmmm, was I angry?

Hmmm, was I sad?

Hmmm, was I scared?

These are the three most common emotions that trigger ULPs. When people in conflict quit projecting blame onto each other and start communicating their fears, angers, and griefs with each other, problems get resolved.

As you move through your day, look for instances when you think you might be projecting. Tune in and do a body scan, looking for signs of anger, sadness, and fear inside you. Acknowledge the emotions and consider if it feels appropriate to communicate them clearly to the relevant people.

DAY 206
Recommitting to Benign Vigilance and Openness

The settings on your success/feeling good thermostat can cause you to create accidents and illnesses for yourself, whether you're aware of the connection or not.

To accelerate your journey to genius, look carefully at *anything* in your life that causes you pain. Check to see if it might be a way you're upper-limiting yourself. Use the same benign vigilance and attitude of openness you adopted earlier in the year.

Today's leap takes you through committing to do this at a deeper level.

- -
YOUR LEAP FOR TODAY
- -

It's one thing to commit to being vigilant and open when you don't know what you're agreeing to be vigilant *of* and open *to*.

It's another to understand what's being asked of you—and perhaps feel some resistance to it—and still make that commitment. Your recommitment requires more of you and will produce a more powerful result.

Knowing what you do now, use these affirmations to recommit yourself to your Big Leap journey:

I commit to examining anything in my life that causes me pain to determine if it's an upper-limit symptom.

I commit to being gentle and patient with myself during the process.

I commit to staying open to what I find—even if I feel resistance to it.

Circulate these positive statements through your mind and feel your sincere commitment to them in your body. Think these commitments throughout the day to get them firmly anchored in your awareness.

DAY 207
Heeding the Messages

Earlier leaps put you in touch with actions and feelings you might be trying to avoid by getting sick or having an accident.

If your upper limits have already created physical pain and suffering in your life, you can stop a repeat performance by heeding the messages your pain brings. Pain is a signal you need to expand in life, rather than contract. When you shrink away from what your deeper self is trying to tell you, it only causes more pain.

Today's leap will help you directly address what you're trying to avoid, rather than let your unconscious mind provide more painful solutions.

YOUR LEAP FOR TODAY

The actions and feelings you're trying to avoid—sometimes through illnesses and injuries—are likely masking a powerful insight you're afraid to hear, things like it's time to move on from a job or a relationship, or to take some other action that will require you to leave your comfort zone.

To allow yourself to hear the message trying to get your attention, sit with this wonder question:

Hmmm, **what is the underlying positive (and perhaps scary) message I'm avoiding?**

Let the question easily circulate through your mind and body. Remember, any insights you find will help you move closer to living in your Genius Zone.

If you discover any messages, follow up with this important inquiry:

What's the first step I can take to honor this insight?

If you get an immediate answer, take action right away. If not, keep the question in the background of your awareness during your day and going forward.

DAY 208
How Are Wonder Questions
Different from Ordinary Questions?

Usually when we ask a question, it's an ordinary one and we want an answer right now. Is it likely to rain today? What time is it in Singapore? In the old days, we had to find out if it was going to rain by consulting the pain in our joints, and it never mattered what time it was in Singapore. Now, we get frustrated if we can't find what we're looking for in a few seconds.

Wonder questions inspire creative answers in a very different way. When we wonder about something, finding the answer is only part of the equation. The process of exploration is just as important. Wonder questions open up more space. Ordinary questions narrow things down. When you want to know the temperature, go for an ordinary question every time.

The ordinary question is like driving on a freeway to a destination.

A wonder question is like taking a scenic drive.

One is all "go, go, go, let's get there." The other is soaking up the beauty all around us and taking little byways just to see where they lead. Both good, but very different.

The value of wonder questions is the expansion they create in our mind and hearts. This relaxed state allows us to explore deeper dimensions of ourselves, bringing us wisdom, insight, and humor.

YOUR LEAP FOR TODAY

Think of something you'd like to know. It can be about anything—for example, why someone did something, how to solve a problem you face, or simply what you should have for dinner.

First, take the ordinary-question approach and, for a few minutes, focus intently on finding the answer. Bring your whole being to bear on getting what you're after.

Then close your eyes and notice how you feel in your body. Where do you feel the most energy—head, heart, throat, stomach?

Do you feel relaxed or anxious? Is your mind expanded or contracted? Make a mental note of the answers.

Now, approach the same question with wonder: *Hmmm*, I wonder why X did that. Or *Hmmm*, I wonder how to get that project done on time. Or *Hmmm*, I wonder what I should have for dinner. Let the wonder question simply resonate within you. It may lead you away from your original question, and that's okay. For a minute or two, just let it take you wherever it goes.

Then close your eyes and again notice how you feel in your body. Where do you feel the most energy—head, heart, throat, stomach? Do you feel relaxed or anxious? Is your mind expanded or contracted? Make a mental note of the answers.

For the rest of today, play with going back and forth between ordinary and wonder questions and see what you discover.

DAY 209
Appreciating the Wisdom of a Mentor

Earlier, I mentioned a great friend and mentor of mine, the late Jack Downing, MD. Jack had a gift for metaphor, and one in particular made a lifelong impression on me.

He said that many people erroneously think about their emotions as if there were two faucets, one marked "pain" and one marked "pleasure." People mistakenly think that the goal is to turn up the "pleasure" faucet and turn down the "pain" faucet. However, Jack said, the truth is there is only one faucet, marked "awareness." The goal is to become more aware of the whole range of your experience, including anger, joy, fear, grief, and love.

The principle behind the faucet metaphor has been of great benefit in my own life, as well as those I've shared it with: give yourself full permission to feel life's hurts as well as its joys. Happiness comes from letting yourself be aware of it all.

YOUR LEAP FOR TODAY

Here is a commitment statement that expresses the essence of Jack's "faucet" wisdom in practical form:

I commit to growing more aware of the full range of my experience.

Say the commitment in your mind and feel it in your body. Speak it out loud and savor the sound of the words. Bring it to mind as you go through your day.

DAY 210
You've Got a Friend . . . Twenty Thousand Times a Day

If you befriend your breathing, you have twenty thousand opportunities a day to benefit from this natural resource. There have been dozens of scientific studies on the power of breathing techniques to reduce anxiety, lower hypertension, improve athletic performance, and generate other positive outcomes. Even the ultra-conservative American Medical Association now features seminars on the use of breathing for healing maladies of body and mind. With so much information on breathing coming out, it can be a challenge sifting out what's truly useful in daily life. Today, we focus on what I consider to be an essential breath-awareness process.

Nature and millions of years of evolution have given us two main breathing patterns. Pattern #1 is when we're at ease. It's slow, about six to eight cycles a minute, and when we're in it, our bodies digest food, rest, and recharge for the next round of action.

Pattern #2 started back in the days when hyenas, wolves, and other predators often interrupted dinner. Within a split second, our breath speeds up to fifteen or more cycles a minute. Pattern #2 pumps adrenaline into our bloodstream, tightens our muscles, and stops us from digesting food so the energy can be used for escape or resistance. Both patterns are still alive in our bodies today, as the process below shows you.

YOUR LEAP FOR TODAY

The simplest way to know whether you're in pattern #1 or #2 is to notice your chest and belly. When you're in nature's stress pattern, your breathing will move your chest more than your belly. When you're at ease in pattern #1, your belly moves more than your chest. The speed of your breathing is another good way to tell. If you're breathing fifteen or more times a minute, you're in stress mode.

Incorporate breath awareness into today's activities. At rest and in action, tune in often to your breathing. Simply focus on whether your breathing is moving your chest or your belly. Use your breathing as a friend to tell you whether you're at ease or in arousal.

If you spot yourself in pattern #2, take a moment to wonder about what's got you agitated, then shift back to a slower breath that moves your belly.

DAY 211
ULPs Piggyback on Our Survival Wiring

The brain is like Velcro for negative experiences, and Teflon for positive ones.

—Rick Hanson, American author and neuroscientist

Because of our prehistoric survival wiring, our brains have an inborn tendency to pay more attention to the negative emotions and events in our lives. For example, millions of years of walking barefoot over rocky and sharp terrain has equipped us with hundreds of thousands of nerve endings on the soles of our feet.

Humans have been dealing with adversity of all sorts for a very long time, so it's no surprise we tend to pay more attention to painful rather than pleasant events.

One of our evolutionary tasks as humans now is to reverse that tendency consciously. We need to train ourselves to savor the positive and let go of the negative. Today's leap helps you do that.

YOUR LEAP FOR TODAY

Make a conscious decision to pay attention to all the ways things work out for you today and how much joy you experience.

Use this affirmation to set the stage:

I savor my positive feelings and celebrate when life goes well for me.

Circulate this positive idea in your mind and savor the feelings it produces in your body. Pause occasionally throughout the day to refresh the affirmation in your awareness.

DAY 212
Fun

I never did a day's work in my life. It was all fun.

—**Thomas Edison, American inventor and businessman**

As you make the leap to living in your Genius Zone, it's important to make having fun a priority. At various times izzzn my life, people have asked me to do things with them, such as skydiving, that didn't sound like fun to me.

I'm sure that many of the things I've done for fun, such as riding a bike in Tibet or taking peyote in the Mexican desert with the Huichol people, wouldn't be much fun for a lot of folks.

Now is a good time to home in more clearly on what's most fun for you, to enhance your FQ (fun quotient).

- -
YOUR LEAP FOR TODAY
- -

As I've told my audiences for years: genius is fun! Use today's wonder question to highlight the fun of your quest for genius.

Keep this question humming in the background of your mind:

Hmmm, how can I have the maximum amount of fun as I explore my genius?

If you have a partner or close friend, initiate a discussion with them about what's most fun for each of you and why. See if you can find some fun adventures to share.

DAY 213
Another Look at Integrity as Wholeness

Integrity sounds scary to some people, because they associate it with painful experiences of being caught out of integrity. With most of us, though, our problems with integrity come from how we look at it. If you see integrity only in moral terms, you tend to feel like a moral failure when you do something that violates your sense of integrity. Feeling bad, though, seldom leads to change.

As you learned in an earlier leap, there's a better way to understand integrity, one that goes back to the original meaning: integrity as wholeness. A violation of integrity, even a small one, takes us out of feeling whole. Wholeness is restored when we heal the gap in our integrity.

My life changed when my view of integrity changed, and I came to see it in terms of physics as well as morality. Instead of just feeling bad when I didn't tell the truth or failed to keep an agreement, I began to see how my integrity problems were actually Upper Limit Problems. I unconsciously used lies and broken agreements to dampen or stop the flow of positive energy inside me and in my relationships.

Why did I do that? I did it to prove an old limiting belief that I didn't deserve love and other good things in life. Once I shined the light of awareness on this ancient belief it faded away, leaving me free to feel more love and positive energy than I'd ever felt.

YOUR LEAP FOR TODAY

Revisit your understanding of integrity as wholeness with today's simple process. First, bundle the two main integrity problems—lying and breaking agreements—into that one entity I call "integrity glitches." Then use these affirmations to guide you:

I become more aware of integrity glitches every day.

I see my integrity glitches and restore wholeness through clear communication.

Entertain these affirmations in your mind now. Feel the truth of them in your body. Take them into your day and refresh them in your awareness from time to time. Notice if they give you a heightened awareness of integrity glitches around and in you.

DAY 214
The Art of Closing the Gap

The more clearly you can communicate with people, the more time and energy you have for your genius. One thing that really helps you communicate clearly is what I call "closing the gap." Closing the gap is when you notice something going on inside you—and say something about it rather than keeping it hidden within.

Closing the gap is when you start to walk away from a conversation without saying something important—then you catch yourself and return to the conversation to complete it.

Closing the gap frees up energy that could have been wasted thinking about the incompletion.

- -
YOUR LEAP FOR TODAY
- -

Take a moment to think back over the last week or two of important communications. How would you rate yourself on closing the gap? Did you communicate everything you needed to say, or did you carry away incompletions?

After you reflect on these questions, use this affirmation to guide your future interactions:

I communicate to satisfying completion in all my interactions.

Savor this conscious intention in your mind and feel it in your body. Keep it in the back of your mind as you move through the interactions of your day.

DAY 215
Closing the Gap on Positive Things

I like to close the gap on positive things, too. After a beach walk with a friend, I was walking toward my car and found myself thinking of how much I appreciated him. I closed the gap by hailing him down as he drove past me. "I just wanted to tell you how much I appreciate you and your listening ear." His face lit up and I got to feel the satisfaction that comes when you close the gap.

YOUR LEAP FOR TODAY

Focus on closing the gap in a positive way today. If you finish an interaction and realize you left something positive unsaid, say it—even if it means calling someone back, or retracing your steps to reopen a conversation with a coworker, cashier, server, friend, or family member. Savor the good feeling created by closing the gap.

DAY 216
Grandmother Wisdom

I was blessed to grow up with a grandmother next door. My mother was a busy career woman, so I spent the majority of my early years at my grandmother's house. I loved listening to her stories of the "old days" and I also thrived in her easygoing, steady presence. She was a great believer in keeping things simple, and one lesson she gave me on the subject became a keystone of the life wisdom I write about in my books.

Gran said that if you always told the truth, you never had to remember what you said. She also said that if you *didn't* tell the truth you'd eventually "trip over your own shoelaces." To her, telling the truth was not just a moral idea; it had an effect on your physical reality. It kept you from tripping over your own shoelaces.

- -
YOUR LEAP FOR TODAY
- -

Subjects related to integrity, such as telling the truth, are sometimes uncomfortable to look at in yourself. Things you find can trigger old guilt and shame, so do your best to explore these areas with a microscope rather than a judge's gavel.

Use these wonder questions to mount a friendly inquiry into truth telling in your life:

Hmmm, throughout my life, are there things I've avoided telling the truth about?

Hmmm, how could I tell the truth in such a way that everyone prospers from it?

These are questions to carry into daily activities such as journaling and talking with friends. Some of your discoveries may inspire you to connect with people in your past or present with the intent of clearing up old conversations where you weren't fully transparent. The important first step, though, is to acknowledge old transgressions and accept that you did the best you could at the time.

DAY 217
Keeping Agreements, Changing Agreements

Earlier in the year, we discussed how we humans use the breaking of agreements as a ULP, a way to stop the flow of positive energy. For example, you may know people, as I do, who habitually break time agreements by showing up late. It's a reliable way to create drama and interrupt good times.

A lot of drama can be prevented by learning to change agreements consciously. There are going to be times in just about everybody's life when it becomes impossible to keep an agreement. If that happens, changing it consciously is the solution. It usually just takes a quick phone call or an email, but I've been surprised at how often people fail to take these simple steps and create unnecessary drama.

YOUR LEAP FOR TODAY

Go through agreements you made for the next week or two. Review them all, including the places you said you were going to be and the times you said you'd be there.

Consider each one of them and ask yourself if it needs to be changed in any way. If so, make the change consciously by communicating with the relevant people.

DAY 218
ULP!: The Big Leap Attitude

Humor, playfulness, and lightheartedness are the best tools you have for dealing with your Upper Limit Problems. I have a friend who, when she makes a mistake or bumps up against a problem, instead of beating herself up or cursing, says, "Ruh-roh!" just like Scooby-Doo, her favorite childhood cartoon character. She told me that saying it always makes her smile.

Another example of meeting problems with humor—the hallmark of the Big Leap attitude—is one I mentioned in an earlier leap, our students' nickname for the Upper Limit Problem: ULP, to rhyme with "gulp."

If you pronounce it that way, "ULP!" it sounds like the word comic book characters use to mean, "Yikes!"—an upbeat recognition of the challenge they face. It lightens the mood considerably to refer to an ULP this way.

YOUR LEAP FOR TODAY

Find an expression that will help you stay cheerful when you recognize you're dealing with an ULP. It's a far more useful response than anger, regret, or discouragement.

Be creative. It doesn't matter what you use, as long as it works for you. Feel free to use "Ruh-roh!" or "ULP!" if they do the trick.

DAY 219
What's Your Story?

Limiting beliefs strung together create limiting stories. And the most limiting story you have is about why you can't live in your Genius Zone. That story seems especially convincing because we didn't come up with it—we were born into it.

As a child, you hear the bits and pieces that form your limiting story from your parents. They tell you cautionary tales about relatives who aimed too high in life with disastrous results, like abandoning their families or living in poverty or even going mad. These stories are meant to protect you—but end up keeping you stuck in your Competence and Excellence Zones.

YOUR LEAP FOR TODAY

Identify your family story of why you shouldn't access your genius. If you're having trouble coming up with it, think of the four hidden barriers and see if that jogs your memory.

Did someone in your family succeed and then lose it all because some hidden scandal came to light?

Did a relative's success cause them to become estranged from the rest of you?

Was your great-aunt's health ruined by the stress of managing her wealth?

Did someone in your family commit the crime of outshining their siblings?

Identifying a story is a major step in moving beyond it. If you find your story involves old, limiting experiences, use this affirmation:

I free myself from all my limiting stories and focus on my genius every day.

Get this positive idea established in your awareness and take it with you into your day.

DAY 220
That Was Then

Up until you stop believing your limiting stories, your adherence to your old story is unconscious. Now that you've brought your story to your conscious awareness, you may be tempted to give yourself a hard time for letting it control your life for so long. I'm here to ask you to resist that urge.

Like all of us, you didn't ask for your story—it was passed down to you, an inheritance, like the color of your eyes and the size of your feet. It is what it is. The important thing is that now you're doing something about it.

YOUR LEAP FOR TODAY

Here's a powerful exercise I've done in dozens of seminars. On a piece of paper, write down one descriptive sentence to represent each limiting story you found in yesterday's leap. For example, for one of mine I would write: "Being more successful than my family is disloyal."

Now, for each sentence, use one finger to point at the sentence on the paper and say out loud, "That was then." Then, using the same finger, touch your chest and say out loud, "This is now."

You may feel some resistance to doing this—thoughts like "This is stupid" or "This won't work" may come up. You're working with some deeply ingrained beliefs and that can cause the part of you that's invested in those limiting beliefs to try to stop this process. If it does, take a deep breath or two, then thank that part for trying to protect you, and just keep going.

Continue pointing back and forth at least ten times for each sentence.

This exercise has big consequences, well worth further reflection. I suggest getting out your journal, now or later, to write your thoughts and feelings.

DAY 221
Become Fascinated by Your Genius

As a kid, I was fascinated by coins. I had a small collection and loved nothing more than going to coin shops in search of rare specimens. Later, coins were replaced by a fascination with the stock market. Two weeks after high school graduation, I cashed my first paycheck as a furniture mover—twenty-seven dollars for two forty-hour weeks—and immediately went to Leesburg, Florida's only stock brokerage. I bought one share of stock for seventeen dollars. Size didn't matter, though. I was in the game, pursuing a fascination.

I'm a long way now from that coin-collecting kid, but I'm more fascinated than ever. When I began discovering my genius, I discovered the ultimate fascination. What could possibly be more fascinating than helping people (and myself) find their unique abilities and express their genius?

Now that you've spent time exploring your genius-limiting stories from the past, it's time to focus your fascination fully on your genius-expanding story.

YOUR LEAP FOR TODAY

Use the following statements to affirm your fascination with your genius:

I'm absolutely fascinated doing what I most love to do—all the time.

I'm absolutely fascinated with expressing my unique gifts in the world.

I'm absolutely fascinated with making my most inspired contribution to the world.

I'm absolutely fascinated with inspiring others to live in their Genius Zones.

Let these affirmations circulate through your mind. Feel the resonance of them in your body. When aimed in the direction of your genius, fascination can be a good companion on the journey.

DAY 222
The Art of Living

Art washes away from the soul the dust of everyday life.

—Pablo Picasso, Spanish artist

One of the many things I love and admire about my wife, Katie, is that, in her twenties, she made a conscious decision to create her life as a work of art. Not only did she make this bold intention, she succeeded! I see it every day in the way she dresses, the way she moves across a room, the jewelry she wears, the way she communicates with people—it's all imbued with an artist's essence, the expression of Katie's genius. Today's leap gives you a direct look at the aesthetics of your life.

- -
YOUR LEAP FOR TODAY
- -

Take a look around at the various aspects of your life: what you're wearing, the room around you, what you are doing in service of beauty today. Are all these elements in alignment with your particular genius? Would more beauty amplify the expression of your genius?

Wonder:

Hmmm, what could I do to make all this more aesthetically harmonious to me?

You may already have yourself surrounded by beauty. If so, take a moment to savor it. If not, spend some time now and later today wondering how you could add the element of art to your life.

DAY 223
Making Every Day Your Lucky Day

The greatest discovery of my generation is that human beings can alter their lives by altering their attitudes of mind.

—**William James, American philosopher and psychologist**

In our book *Conscious Luck*, Carol Kline and I invited readers to explore a new world: how to make yourself luckier by conscious actions you take. You can find all the details in the book, but for today, focus on a crucial first step. To explore a new world, you must first conceive that it's even possible.

I remember sitting with my high school girlfriend, listening to John F. Kennedy's inaugural address on the radio. There was an electric moment when he declared that we were going to put human beings on the moon by the end of the decade. I remember we looked at each other in surprise. Where did that come from? It was an unthinkable idea suddenly made thinkable.

That's how I felt when I realized we could change our luck by changing our minds. It's a big subject that we'll spend a few days this year exploring. Today's leap gives you a jump start.

YOUR LEAP FOR TODAY

Use this essential affirmation to open your mind wide to the new possibility. For the moment, simply focus on a single idea—that you can get luckier by the thoughts you create and the commitments you make.

I enjoy more and more good luck every day of my life.

Say the affirmation in your mind a few times, then speak it aloud. Circulate it through your awareness as you go through your day, savoring the idea of getting luckier by the minute.

DAY 224
Overcoming Alexithymia

Several thousand years ago, the Greeks coined the word "alexithymia" which describes a problem still plaguing us today. Alexithymia is difficulty identifying and expressing emotions.

In the course of your Big Leap Year, you'll come in contact, both in yourself and in other people, with the full range of feelings. Your ability to identify and work effectively with those feelings will help you move smoothly through situations that might otherwise trip you up. Today, and for the next few days, we'll explore key issues around the subject of your emotions.

YOUR LEAP FOR TODAY

Set the stage for deep learning about your emotions with this basic willingness statement:

I'm willing to feel and express all my emotions in ways that are friendly to myself and others.

Taking a stance of openness toward all your emotions, rather than resisting or ignoring them, gives you the maximum opportunity to learn about the full range of your feelings.

DAY 225
Emotions Bring Important Messages

If you understand the messages your feelings are bringing you, you're much less likely to tune out or ignore them. The three main feelings people struggle with are fear, anger, and sadness. Many people do not know how to identify when they are in the grip of those feelings, and because of that they're unable to express them effectively.

When you're scared, the message is that you are perceiving some sort of threat.

When you're sad, the message from your body is that you have experienced some kind of loss.

When you're angry, your body is signaling that you feel trespassed upon or violated in some way.

In many situations, all three of these occur at once. You feel sad if someone you care about dies, but you may also be angry about the circumstances and scared about the future. Because of the complicated nature of our emotional lives, any time you devote to learning about your feelings rewards you in your daily life.

YOUR LEAP FOR TODAY

Fear plays a major role in your ULPs. Things start going better, then up comes a fear and a limiting belief such as "I don't deserve to be happy and successful." You pull back to make the fear go away and your ULP wins.

Change this pattern with a new commitment:

I commit to using my fears as fuel for my journey to genius.

Say this commitment a few times in your mind and try it on in your body. By making this commitment, you change your relationship with fear. Instead of something to be resisted, your fear becomes something you can put to work for you.

DAY 226
Learning from Sadness

Sadness is a second feeling that plays a large role in your ULPs. As I pointed out in yesterday's leap, sadness is your body's way of responding to loss.

It doesn't have to be a big loss, such as the death of a loved one. Sadness can also be triggered by subtler losses, such as losing respect or esteem in social situations.

Many people say they feel the sensations of sadness in their chest and throat. Learning to identify your sadness signals can be instrumental in helping you avoid ULPs.

- -
YOUR LEAP FOR TODAY
- -

Take a moment to reflect on the losses in your life, both the major ones and subtler ones that can occur daily. Notice your body's signals as you think about your losses.

To assist, use this wonder question:

Hmmm, where do I feel my sadness in my body?

You may, like many people, experience your sadness in the heart and throat areas, or you may feel it in some different way. Notice how you experience your sadness, so that next time it occurs you can be more sensitive to it.

DAY 227
Transforming Anger

Anger is the third and often the most difficult emotion to deal with in daily life. Almost everyone has a stack of memories in which you or someone close to you displayed anger in ways they later regretted. It's to everyone's advantage, particularly yours, to find ways of dealing with anger that actually contribute to positive resolutions rather than blocking them.

Katie and I have seen hundreds of couples in relationship counseling, and almost all of them came in stuck in patterns of repetitive anger. In helping them move toward positive resolutions, we learned a fact about anger that changed our own life, as well as the lives of our clients: when you're angry, you're also sad and scared. When we could help couples talk about what they were sad and scared about, the repetitive anger pattern dissolved.

- -
YOUR LEAP FOR TODAY
- -

Think of one or two situations, recent or past, when your anger came out in a way that upset you or people around you.

Bring one of the situations to mind and ask these wonder questions:

Hmmm, when I'm angry, what am I also sad about?

Hmmm, when I'm angry, what am I also scared about?

Circulate both these questions through your mind a few times, creating a genuine wondering you can feel in your body. As you go through your day, be open to answers coming through in their own time and place.

DAY 228
More on Transforming Anger

John Sarno, MD, was a celebrated doctor at Rusk Rehabilitation in New York. In treating thousands of cases of chronic back pain and headache, he discovered a profound relationship between anger and body pain.

The muscles that tighten in the back and neck when we get back pain or headaches are also the muscles that tighten when we get angry. He found that only a tiny percentage of patients needed surgery for their back pain.

What they needed, and what Dr. Sarno taught for decades in his famous Tuesday night meetings, was how to notice when anger was tightening the muscles up the back to the neck. He showed people how to accept their anger and communicate about it in friendly ways.

YOUR LEAP FOR TODAY

Take a moment right now to tune in to your body and its sensations. Focus your attention on the muscles between your shoulder blades and on up into your neck.

These are the areas Dr. Sarno found that tighten up when we're even slightly angry. Map out the area by consciously tightening and releasing those muscles a few times.

As you move through your day, stay open to signals of tension in your back and neck. See if you can identify even small flickers of anger by tuning in to muscle tension in your back and neck muscles.

DAY 229
Transforming Anxiety

I remember asking one of my professors fifty years ago whether there was any difference between anxiety and fear. Practically speaking, he said, there's no difference. The only difference is that people find it easier to say, "I feel anxious," than "I feel scared."

Whether we call it fear or anxiety, we're usually referring to the same set of sensations: a speedy sense of agitation coupled with a slightly queasy feeling in our stomach area, or "butterflies." If it's more extreme, you feel sweaty palms and a narrowing of vision.

I've found that many people try to conceal their anxiety. For example, men who grew up in the forties and fifties of the last century, as I did, were exposed to countless versions of the "strong, silent type." The screen heroes were John Wayne, Gary Cooper, and other stoic stars of the day.

When I got into my teens, though, I discovered that the silent-guy act didn't work very well, especially in my relationships. Now, after a half century of emotional growth, I know that all of us need to be conversant with the full range of our feelings.

YOUR LEAP FOR TODAY

Tune in to your body and its many sensations. Focus in on the stomach area between your navel and your spine. Notice if you feel any of the racy-queasy sensations of anxiety or fear.

As you go through your day, tune in often to this zone. The more you learn about your fears and anxieties, the better you will be able to respond effectively to the world around you.

DAY 230
Hops and Leaps

Very often in life we move forward in hops rather than leaps.

Hops feel safer—and less scary because we don't land too far from where we started. We tend to hop along in our Competence and Excellence Zones. Hops can be difficult—like earning a degree or other comparable achievements—but aren't leaps unless they move you toward your Genius Zone.

Leaps feel riskier. They require more bravery and faith because we aren't familiar with where we'll land. Use today's leap to have a frank conversation with yourself about your hops and leaps.

- -
YOUR LEAP FOR TODAY
- -

Spend a few minutes thinking about how you're moving through life. Ask yourself these questions:

Are you *not* moving—staying in one place, too comfortable or too fearful to make any changes?

Are you testing each step before you take it, like a tightrope walker, wanting to move, but unwilling to take any chances?

Are you plodding along, simply putting one foot in front of the other?

Are you hopping, making progress within your Competence or Excellence Zones, but not really going for genius?

Are you taking leaps—actions that often land you in unknown territory?

Are you committed to and fearlessly moving in the direction of expressing your genius?

Inquiring into uncomfortable subjects the way these questions do can be difficult. Make it easier on yourself by being super friendly with yourself, free of self-criticism, while you explore these areas.

DAY 231
Exploring Rust-Out

Today, we go deeper into a state you're familiar with from earlier in the year: rust-out. If you limit yourself to anything less than leaps—especially the Big Leap—over time, you might find yourself in the state of rust-out.

Rust-out is burnout that happens in slow motion. The damage occurs gradually—like iron patio furniture left out in the weather for years—so you may not be aware of the extent of the rust until it becomes too obvious to ignore.

I became aware of my rust-out only after my genius finally got fed up with me hopping through my Excellence Zone. Once I discovered it, I became very sensitive to its unpleasant feeling in my body. I don't ever feel that anymore, and I haven't missed it a bit. Use today's leap to get your attention fully engaged with this slowly creeping problem.

- -
YOUR LEAP FOR TODAY
- -

Review your answers to yesterday's leap. They'll give you a good idea of whether you're free of rust, in danger of rusting out—or may have already developed some rusty patches.

The good news is rust-out is completely reversible! All you need to do is keep going on your journey to genius.

Use the following sentence to renew your commitment to living in your Genius Zone:

I commit to keep going through these pages, taking daily leaps that take me to my Genius Zone.

Take a few moments now to circulate the commitment through your mind. Say it out loud a few times to get the feel of it in your body. Pause occasionally throughout your days to refresh the commitment in your awareness.

DAY 232
More Steps on Your Journey to Genius

During this year, you've focused on recognizing and dissolving your Upper Limit Problems—a process that never ends but gets easier with practice.

You've also spent time identifying your unique strengths and talents and reflecting on what you most love to do, another important piece of the genius formula.

Whether you're plodding along in your Incompetence Zone, making steady, if unexciting, progress in your Competence Zone, or experiencing success in your Excellence Zone—the path is the same. Repeated and sincere self-inquiry are the steps to finding and expressing your genius.

YOUR LEAP FOR TODAY

The commitments you've made, the affirmations you've taken to heart, and the wondering you've done so far this year have had an impact on you. Asking the you of today questions you asked an earlier version of you may yield new and surprising answers.

Let these two foundational wonder questions float through your mind throughout the day:

Hmmm, what is my genius?

Hmmm, how can I bring forth my genius in ways that serve others and myself at the same time?

Wherever you are in your journey to genius, returning to these foundational questions keeps you on track. Use them liberally today and going forward.

DAY 233
Exploring Longing

As you learned in an earlier leap, what you deeply and truly want—what you long for in your heart—is connected to your genius. You may suppress your longing or dismiss it, but it will keep popping back up. Your genius can only be put off for so long.

If you welcome your longings as signposts pointing you in the direction of your genius, you'll be filled with excitement and hope.

If you consider your longings unattainable, you'll find yourself drooping in despair.

- -
YOUR LEAP FOR TODAY
- -

Find out how you feel about your longings by reflecting on this wonder question:

Hmmm, what do I long for?

Keep dropping this question into your heart and see what arises.

Also notice how you react to each longing you discover. Do you feel excited or pained by it?

Register your feelings about each longing and write them down.

DAY 234
The Essential Ingredient of Love

As you no doubt know in your bones by now, the big message of the Big Leap is this: do more of what you most love to do. In my experience, the more people focus on their unique gifts and skills—what they most love to do—the happier and more fulfilled they become. One reason living in your Genius Zone feels so good is the miracle ingredient of love.

Finding out what you most love to do doesn't happen all at once. It's like seeing more and more elements of a treasure box. When I first fell in love with Katie in 1980, it was like catching a glimpse of infinite treasures. The past forty-plus years have been a process of revealing those treasures one by one. One element may catch your eye at first, but then more brilliance comes to your attention as you explore the treasure further. Today's leap focuses on one brilliant aspect of your treasures.

YOUR LEAP FOR TODAY

When you're doing something you love, you often lose track of time. I remember occasions in childhood when I was playing so intently that I didn't hear my mother calling me for dinner until she raised her voice a few decibels.

Focus on this facet of your genius with a wonder question:

Hmmm, **what do I love doing so much that I forget about time?**

There's usually more than one thing that meets this criterion. Let your mind play with the question and reveal multiple facets of your genius.

DAY 235
Being Prepared

Chance favors the prepared mind.

—**Louis Pasteur, French microbiologist**

Are you ready for genius when it emerges? Dr. Pasteur noticed that impeccable preparation had a powerful effect on scientific outcomes. The same is true for genius. From years of teaching, I noticed that people who worked on their preparations diligently had more frequent visitations from their genius.

By preparations, I'm mainly talking about alignment in yourself:

You're aligned with your chosen life purpose and the emotions inside you.

You speak honestly and in resonance with what you feel inside.

You take responsibility for the events of your life, and you resist jockeying for the "victim" position in your interactions.

These are the kinds of preparations that invite the emergence of genius in your life.

YOUR LEAP FOR TODAY

Use today's wonder question to open up a conversation with yourself about your preparations:

Hmmm, how best can I prepare for the full expression of my genius?

Let the question resonate in your mind. Feel the wonder of it in your body and take it into your day. Pause now and then today to check in with your question.

DAY 236
Daily Practice

I read an inspiring interview thirty years ago with the twentieth century's greatest cellist, Pablo Casals. He was in his eighties at the time, and the interviewer asked if, given that he'd been the world's premier cello artist for decades, he still practiced. Casals said he only practiced three hours a day at that point, down from five or six hours earlier in his career.

I remember thinking at the time if there was anything I loved enough to still be practicing in my later years. The only two things I could think of were writing and expanding every day into more of my genius. And here I am, still happily doing both as I cruise through my seventies.

YOUR LEAP FOR TODAY

No matter what age you are, what do you love enough to be practicing every day in your elder years? (If you're already an elder, roll the clock forward five or ten years from where you are now.)

Turn it into a wonder question you can savor all day:

Hmmm, what do I love so much that I'd happily practice it for hours a day in my elder years?

Think of this question as an investment in your future well-being, a deposit in your savings account of good feeling.

DAY 237
Work That Doesn't Feel like Work

As you explored earlier in the year, one of the best ways to identify your Genius Zone is to notice how you feel toward the work you're doing at any given moment. When you're in your Genius Zone, work doesn't feel like "work." It has a flow to it. You can do it all day and not feel tired or stressed out.

When you're doing what you most love to do, when you're in the sweet spot of your genius, you engage with your work in a different way. It's not a job you're obligated to do; it's a fulfillment of your highest creative potential.

When you're doing that, you know inside that you're not just making a living. You're making a life. In today's leap, you'll revisit this aspect of identifying your genius.

YOUR LEAP FOR TODAY

Take a moment right now to think about the work you do. Scan through a day or two of whatever you consider your work. Include unpaid domestic employment and volunteer jobs.

Use this wonder question to illuminate your experience:

Hmmm, how much of my work time do I spend in an easeful flow of good feeling?

Ask yourself this question right now and come back to reflect on it as you go through your day. Let it be a guide to working easier rather than harder.

DAY 238
Doing More of What You Love To Do

I've always been fascinated by the spontaneous, unplanned support I've experienced over the years. My life has been incredibly enriched by chance meetings, being in the perfect place at the perfect time, and other events that no one could have predicted.

These events seem to happen more and more as I devote more and more of my life to expressing my genius, which means doing only things I love to do.

As I spent more of my time doing what I most loved to do, as if by magic, positive events happened with greater frequency.

Today's leap gives you a chance to revisit the dimension of love in your life. The wonder question below is one I keep in the background of my awareness all the time. Even after fifty years of discovering and expressing my genius, I occasionally catch myself slipping out of my Genius Zone and agreeing to do something I don't love to do. Practice really helps, though, because now I notice the drift right away instead of being oblivious to it until I am well into an ULP.

YOUR LEAP FOR TODAY

Doing more of what you love to do is also a process of doing less of what you don't love to do. *Hmmm* this wonder question a few times today to keep your focus on this crucial subject:

Hmmm, **are there things I do in my life that I don't absolutely love to do?**

Take a moment right now to contemplate the question. Be friendly with yourself as you do your wondering. If you discover anything, make note of it and get creative about eliminating it from your life.

DAY 239
Appreciating Your Genius

A study at the University of Washington by relationship researcher Dr. John Gottman showed that relationships thrive when there's a five-to-one or better ratio of positive appreciations to negative comments. Think of creativity and genius in the same way.

Since your relationship with your genius is one of the most important connections in your life, imagine how it could thrive if you increased your appreciation of it! Today's leap gives you a direct experience of appreciating the different facets of your genius.

YOUR LEAP FOR TODAY

There are many aspects to each person's genius. Circulate the following fill-in-the-blank sentences through your mind, using your creativity to complete the sentences:

One aspect of my genius I really appreciate is _____.
Another aspect of my genius I appreciate is _____.
Another aspect of my genius I appreciate is _____.
Another aspect of my genius I appreciate is _____.
Another aspect of my genius I appreciate is _____.

Sometimes it's not as easy to appreciate yourself and your own powers as it is to appreciate others. If it's challenging for you to name and appreciate your genius, spend some extra time later with this process.

Writing the sentences out can also help you get comfortable with appreciating the different aspects of your genius.

DAY 240
Integrity with Life Purpose

In earlier days we explored integrity from several different viewpoints such as speaking authentically and acknowledging emotions such as fear, sadness, and anger. Today we focus on a different dimension of integrity: being in alignment with your chosen life purpose.

In my own case, I didn't sit down and consciously figure out my life purpose until I was in my midthirties. However, it doesn't matter what age we are when we finally choose our purpose for being here. Whether you're a teenager or an elder, life takes on a special clarity when you know what you are choosing to focus on during your time on earth.

The purpose I chose for my life at thirty-four later found its way into *The Big Leap* in the form of the ultimate success mantra: "I expand in abundance, success, and love as I inspire others to do the same."

Once I sat down and put my focus on it, it only took me an hour or so to get clear on my life purpose. It's guided my life every day since, though, so it was definitely one of the best investments of time I've ever made.

YOUR LEAP FOR TODAY

You're welcome to use my purpose or a variation of it as your own. I can vouch for its positive results—more than four decades of good times! I also want you to put in some serious think time about creating your own purpose statement. Use your journal to reflect on and write about these wonder questions:

Hmmm, what are the essential things and experiences I want to create during my precious time on earth?

Hmmm, at my very best, what am I doing here?

These are big questions, and they produce life-changing answers. Even though you may have worked on your purpose in earlier days, do a deeper dive into it on this new day. I suggest reflecting on these questions until you can get your purpose refined into one sentence. In our seminars, I teach people to create a purpose they can say with one out-breath. Use that as a criterion for creating your own purpose statement.

DAY 241
Mining for Raw Material

The secret to success is to know something nobody else knows.

—Aristotle Onassis, Greek shipping tycoon

Everyone knows *something* nobody else knows. Since nobody has had exactly the life experience you've had, your perspective is one of a kind.

Unfortunately, because we're all encouraged from a young age by our parents and teachers to adopt a shared world view—so that life can be more manageable and orderly—we often lose sight of our individual perceptions and ideas. This robs us of the raw material necessary to make our unique contribution to the world. Today's leap gives you an opportunity to learn more about your distinctly personal impact on the world.

YOUR LEAP FOR TODAY

Taking the cue from Onassis's quote above, home in more closely on what your special input to the world is.

Float a wonder question through your consciousness right now:

Hmmm, **what do I know that allows me to offer a unique contribution to the world?**

It may seem odd to think that you know something nobody else knows, but I encourage you to keep looking inside until you find it. You are a unique person and have your own gifts to bring to the world. Use today's wonder question throughout the day to bring forth more of your inimitable contribution.

DAY 242
Transforming Jealousy and Envy

It's natural to feel jealousy (or its close cousin envy) when others win, or when we compare what we feel is our lesser life to someone's apparently wonderful one. Jealousy and envy can also be ULPs, permutations of fear that come up solely to bring our energy down.

Whenever you feel jealousy or envy, the best response is immediate compassion for yourself. Beating yourself up is just helping the ULP do its job of reducing your positive feelings.

Remind yourself that someone else winning only adds to the universal winning energy, making more available for everyone: their win makes it easier for you to win, too! Doing this turns the ULP into an opportunity to celebrate.

YOUR LEAP FOR TODAY

As you go through your day, be on the lookout for flashes of jealousy or twinges of envy. When you feel one, rather than feeling bad or grumbling at the person, take a few deep breaths and celebrate their good fortune.

If it's something you'd like for yourself, take a mental snapshot of it and say, "That's for me, too!"

DAY 243
Remember Who's Holding the Kite String

I was taking a walk on a breezy day and saw a couple of kids flying kites in the park. I was trying to imagine what the scene would look like if I'd never seen a kite: you're walking in a park and see two grinning kids staring up at two paper-covered wooden frames dipping and darting through the air. Then you take a closer look to see that the kites are attached to the kids by long strings. What looked like random flights in the air are being controlled from the ground.

Life is a lot like a kite, sometimes soaring, other times plummeting, often holding steady in one spot. If we don't realize we're holding the string, things can look very capricious indeed.

When you realize that you hold the key (or, in this case, the string) to good fortune, abundance, harmony, and love, life becomes a lot more interesting, exciting, and *fun*.

YOUR LEAP FOR TODAY

Take the kite analogy to heart and add that important dimension of fun to your quest for genius. Use this affirmation to get a fun mindset for your day:

I enjoy harmony, ease, and fun as I expand in genius every day.

Remember, nobody ever said genius has to be serious all the time.

It's easier on you and everyone around you if you have fun as you go about your quest for the Genius Zone.

DAY 244
Fascinations

Filed away in my mind is a story a friend told me thirty or more years ago, about driving along the highway occupying her mind with the mystery and magic of numbers. I found that intriguing and remember commenting to her about how differently our minds worked. My math skills topped out around long division, and I've generally avoided having anything to do with numbers. I certainly couldn't imagine voluntarily thinking about them.

However, the way she spoke about numbers brought the same glow to her face as I'd seen on other people as they talked about art or music. It told me that her appreciation of numbers was an expression of her genius, one of the places where she can connect to her deepest self.

- -
YOUR LEAP FOR TODAY
- -

Take ten minutes and explore your own fascinations. Sit down and get yourself centered with some easy, deep breaths.

Use two wonder questions to heighten your awareness of what really delights you:

Hmmm, what fascinates me most right now?

Hmmm, how can I use my fascination with _____ to nurture my deepest self?

Finding out what fascinates you is a guidepost to your genius. Keep these questions in the background of your awareness as you move through your day.

DAY 245
Your Own Personal Superpower

I first encountered the idea of a superpower in the comic books I devoured as a kid. Superman was big in my neighborhood, but my favorite was Captain Marvel. He couldn't fly like Superman, but he had something I thought was even cooler. He possessed a secret word—*"Shazam!"*—that he could employ when the chips were down. I grew up in a family of wordsmiths, so the idea of a magic power word really appealed to me.

Think of your genius as a superpower, one that has an extra-special quality: it doesn't rely on magic. You're always in charge of where you place your attention; you can choose to focus on bringing forth your genius and see the actual results in your life. To me, that's the best kind of magic.

YOUR LEAP FOR TODAY

In the spirit of comic-book heroes such as Superman, whose superpower lets him fly, use these fill-in-the-blank sentences to learn more about the superpowers your genius gives you:

The superpower of my genius allows me to _____.
My genius gives me the power to _____.
When I fully embrace my genius, I'm able to _____.

Circulate these ideas through your mind and contemplate them as you go through your day. To get the full value from the process, I also recommend journaling, using the sentences as a stimulus.

DAY 246
Conscious Planning

Intellectuals solve problems; geniuses prevent them.

—**Albert Einstein**

In any situation of life there are things you have control over and things you don't. It's essential to focus your energy on those things you have control over.

One thing you have control over now is the kind of conscious planning you do. Often, a moment of planning can prevent hours of frustration. Today's leap explores the planning function in your life.

YOUR LEAP FOR TODAY

Taking the hint from Einstein, circulate this wonder question through your mind every hour or two today:

Hmmm, what planning can I do that could make things go smoothly for me today?

As you go through your day be on the lookout for things you can do, often small, that could prevent problems and allow you to feel "in the flow."

DAY 247
When You Feel Off-Center

"Off-center" is what I call it when things don't feel exactly right inside me. You probably recognize the feeling, although you may call it "off-kilter" or something else. As my twentysomething assistant puts it, "You just feel weird." It's not like feeling ill, with a scratchy throat or intestinal cramps. It's subtler than that but you can still feel it.

There can be a lot of different causes for feeling off-center: something you ate, something somebody said to you, something you didn't say. Once you notice you're feeling off-center, you can sometimes restore your harmony quickly by saying the thing you didn't say or doing the thing you didn't do. Sometimes, though, you feel off-center and aren't sure why. Today's leap gives you a tool for those occasions.

YOUR LEAP FOR TODAY

When you feel off-center and the reason isn't clear, use it as an opportunity to go back to one of your fundamental commitments.

Pause and refresh this statement in your mind:

I commit to bringing forth more and more of my genius every day of my life.

The off-center feeling can be a good reminder to remember what your life is all about. You've chosen to make your life about the expression of your full genius. Celebrate that today if you drift into that off-center feeling.

DAY 248
Using the Ultimate Success Mantra in the Digital Age

In an earlier leap, I explained how I reminded myself to use the USM by putting sticky notes on my car dashboard. Today, you have a few more options to help you keep the USM front and center—your phone and computer!

YOUR LEAP FOR TODAY

Make a plan for reminding yourself electronically of the USM at different times throughout the day:

Set a smartphone reminder to ping you at least two or three times during the day with "**I expand in abundance, success, and love every day, as I inspire those around me to do the same**" as the message.

Make the USM your screensaver on your computer screen or the wallpaper on your phone's lock screen.

Have fun with it as you use your creativity.

Invite yourself to do whatever is necessary to make the USM a basic part of your reality—like driving on the correct side of the road or drinking when you're thirsty.

With time and practice, you won't have to think about it— "expanding in abundance, success, and love, and inspiring others to do the same" becomes automatic.

DAY 249
Wondering Versus Pondering

Once, when I was explaining to an audience the power of wonder questions, someone asked, "Is wondering the same as pondering?"

I thought for a moment, weighing how to answer, when a thought occurred to me. "Well," I said, "they have a similar meaning—to think deeply about something—but have completely different flavors. Look at the adjectives related to each one: ponderous, meaning weighty and cumbersome, versus wondrous, inspiring awe and delight."

Wonder is the mind at play. It has a light quality, but when applied to something you have a passion to know, it is a potent way to gain knowledge.

When you wonder about something, you often get many answers to your one wonder question. Each answer is a road worth exploring.

YOUR LEAP FOR TODAY

On a piece of paper, preferably in your journal, write the following wonder question in longhand:

Hmmm, what do I most passionately want to learn?

Write it out four times and then close your eyes and ask it again in your mind. Pause for two easy breaths, then ask the question again, silently in your mind. Repeat the question two or three more times, breathing in and out twice between each asking. Then open your eyes and grab your pen.

Keep your pen moving along the paper as you write down whatever comes into your mind for five full minutes. Remember, there is no right answer. Time the five minutes and don't stop early.

When you're done, review what you've written and see if anything jumps out at you as what you most passionately want to learn right now. You may want to learn about everything you've written, but pick one that feels the most right in this moment.

Each day, take time to wonder about that subject and see what surfaces.

DAY 250
Ease

You do not need to leave your room. Remain sitting at your table and listen. Do not even listen, simply wait, be quiet, still, and solitary. The world will freely offer itself to you to be unmasked, it has no choice, it will roll in ecstasy at your feet.

—**Franz Kafka**

Yes, you saw this same quotation unnecessary earlier in the year in a daily leap about stillness, but today I want to focus on a different part of it. I've always loved Kafka's phrase about the world rolling "in ecstasy at your feet." What a vivid image.

Rolling in ecstasy is an extreme form of ease that I want to cultivate. In fact, it's been one of the background intentions of my life's journey to date, the idea of creating my life in greater degrees of ease.

The Grand Canyon was created by millions of years of water looking for the easiest way to get where it was going. Let's take the hint and look for greater ease as we go through life.

YOUR LEAP FOR TODAY

One of the characteristics of living in your Genius Zone is a sense of ease.

Today, dedicate yourself to the study of ease.

For example:

How much of your day do you feel at ease?

What does ease feel like in your body?

Would it be possible for you to preserve and enhance that sense of ease as you go about your day?

DAY 251
The Power of No

In an earlier leap, I shared that at the start of my own quest for genius, I was surprised to learn how important it was to learn to say "no." Particularly, I had to learn how to say "no" to things that were not in my Genius Zone.

It wasn't easy. Like many of you, I didn't get much useful training in that particular skill. I often felt guilty when I said no, and tended to avoid saying it, resulting in my own inconvenience.

As I got better at it, I eventually concluded that staying in my Genius Zone required mastering the art of turning down things that were in my Excellence, Competence, or Incompetence Zones. Though you've already committed to using the "enlightened no," today's leap gives you a helpful tool.

YOUR LEAP FOR TODAY

Use this affirmation to refine your ability to say "no" to things that aren't in the sweet spot of your genius:

I say "no" with ease and grace to things that are not in my Genius Zone.

Today and going forward, bring this idea to mind frequently. It took me years to develop my ability to say a graceful and timely "no." Be generous and friendly with yourself as you go about mastering this skill.

DAY 252
Your Willingness to Receive

To enjoy more love, abundance, and creativity in your life, you need to take positive, productive actions. In other words, you need to *do* things. However, you also must learn to *be* a new way.

Your willingness to receive more love, abundance, and creativity is as important as anything you do. In one way it's even more important. When good things come our way, we need to have an inner structure that allows us to integrate them into our lives without stirring up Upper Limit Problems.

YOUR LEAP FOR TODAY

One of the best things about human consciousness is our ability to use conscious intentions to create change. Use the following intention to consciously expand your ability to receive more of the good things of life.

Today and every day I expand my capacity to enjoy more love, abundance, and creativity.

As you move through your day, bring this intention to mind and circulate it through your awareness.

DAY 253
Mastery

If people knew how hard I had to work to gain my mastery, it wouldn't seem so wonderful at all.

—Michelangelo, Italian sculptor, painter, and architect

"Mastery" is usually defined as having a great set of skills in an area, but I add another dimension to the definition. To me, masters are not only good at something, but they're able to transmit that mastery to others. There's a Zen saying: "Masters are not known for the number of students they have, but by the number of those students who become masters."

What is your experience and your definition of mastery? Today's leap gives you an opportunity to claim your own version of mastery, so you can best nurture it and put it to use.

YOUR LEAP FOR TODAY

Sit down with a favorite beverage and reflect on mastery. With your journal near to hand, reflect on these questions:

What do you consider yourself a master of?

How would you best like to express your mastery over the next ten to fifteen years?

Let your mind roam free over these questions. Write down your thoughts, feelings, and creative ideas. If you feel comfortable doing so, share your discoveries with a good listener in your life.

DAY 254
Getting Luckier

On an earlier day, we discussed the idea at the heart of *Conscious Luck,* that we can make ourselves luckier by consciously changing our beliefs about luck. One key limiting belief about luck is that some people are born lucky. That may or may not be true, but people sometimes use that belief to disqualify themselves from being lucky. In actuality, the quest for getting luckier is similar to the quest for your genius. If we can just get out of our own way, we discover a natural genius that lives within us.

In my view, we're all born lucky. There are approximately nine million species on our planet, half of them bugs; you and I got lucky enough to be members of the one species that can have a conversation about getting luckier. You already beat nine-million-to-one odds; now you just need to learn how to nurture and build on that good luck.

YOUR LEAP FOR TODAY

There's an affirmation I use to keep expanding my good luck every day. I didn't consider myself a lucky person until I decided to reinvent myself as one of the lucky ones. Now I think I'm the luckiest person I've ever met. Can you do that for yourself?

Use the following affirmation and keep your eye on the results:

I'm remarkably lucky and getting luckier by the day.

Get comfortable with this affirmation in your mind and body. Note the addition of the word "remarkably." It means that you have the kind of good luck that people remark on.

Bring your affirmation to your mind throughout your day and be on the lookout for instances of good luck.

DAY 255
Getting Unstuck

Everybody gets stuck now and then, for all sorts of reasons. A relationship goes sour, an old habit returns, weight stubbornly refuses to come off. No matter what the reason is, it doesn't feel good. In helping people get unstuck for the past fifty years, and from my work on myself, I've found two reliable keys to getting unstuck.

The first key you learned in an earlier leap: simply acknowledge you're stuck. When they're stuck, many people do more and more of what already isn't working. That creates noisy drama but no resolution. As soon as you can say, "Okay, I admit I'm stuck," you take the first step toward freedom.

The second key is to reaffirm your essential commitment. You'll have the opportunity to practice those two key moves in the process below.

YOUR LEAP FOR TODAY

Recall a time, recent or in the past, when you felt stuck. Notice the feelings and sensations of being stuck in a pattern, unable to get out of it. Feel it, acknowledge it, accept that you get stuck from time to time.

Next, reaffirm one of the foundational commitments of your Big Leap Year:

I commit to expanding my genius every day of my life.

Return to your fundamental commitments when you get stuck. It will help eliminate much of the unnecessary drama that occurs when we catch ourselves mired in a rut.

DAY 256
Transitions

It is when we are in transition that we are most completely alive.

—William Bridges, American author and speaker

In October, when the first hint of autumn is in the air and the leaves are beginning to fall, the squirrels in my yard begin to work over-time, scurrying around to bury nuts for the winter.

I watch them every year and appreciate their approach to tran-sitions: they don't resist the change. Instead, they get busy doing things in the present to benefit themselves a few months down the line. In today's leap, you'll have a chance to explore transitions in your own life.

YOUR LEAP FOR TODAY

Bring these wonder questions to mind several times during the day:

Hmmm, what are the biggest transitions and changes going on in my life?

Hmmm, how can I best participate in the transitions going on within me and around me?

Squirrels are locked into their genetic patterns for dealing with transitions. Human beings can be more creative. Spend a few min-utes journaling later about how you can respond to transitions in ways that further your journey to genius.

DAY 257
"Lazy Daze"

I was out walking one day and saw an old-fashioned RV drive by with the words "LAZY DAZE" emblazoned on its side. I didn't see the driver, but imagined an older couple, embarking on a well-deserved retirement trip; or a family, setting off on vacation to a nearby wilderness destination.

Continuing my walk, I reflected that being lazy is usually viewed as a negative trait, but not in retirement or on vacation. Then laziness is ease we have permission to feel. We allow ourselves to do what we love to do and simply enjoy being alive.

In our Competence or Excellence Zones, that ease is a big contrast to our normal state. We only mete it out for weekends or a couple of times a year or put it off for our golden years.

In the Genius Zone, ease and delight are constant features of our daily life.

YOUR LEAP FOR TODAY

Close your eyes and take a few deep breaths. Remember the feeling you had as a kid waking up on the first day of summer vacation, the summer stretching ahead of you, full of promise and fun. Or, if you can't relate to that, imagine being on the perfect vacation and allow your mind and body to fully relax.

Savor that feeling, letting it sink in. It's both a preview and a step on the path to living in your Genius Zone.

DAY 258
The Seasons of Life

In the depth of winter, I finally learned that within me there lay an invincible summer.

—Albert Camus, French philosopher and author

Do you have a favorite season? I love autumn, as does Katie. It's the season I often get some of my best creative work done and enjoy launching new things. You may be a spring or summer person, as I was growing up in Florida. Then I moved to New England, where autumn is glorious. Try as I might, though, I never got to love winter and now go to great lengths to avoid even the hint of it. I have friends, passionate skiers, who love winter and are sad in the spring to see the snow melt. No matter what season it is when you're reading this, take a few moments in today's leap to wonder about seasons in your life.

- -
YOUR LEAP FOR TODAY
- -

Float these wonder questions through your mind:

Hmmm, what is my favorite season and what do I most love about it?

Hmmm, what meanings do I attach to the changing of the seasons?

Hmmm, how can I be with the changing of the seasons to bring myself maximum joy?

Were you surprised by any of your responses? Your feelings and thoughts about seasons can change over time, as mine did. Did you learn anything about seasons that you can apply to your life today?

DAY 259
Handling Hurry: Part 1

Wherever I go in the world I see people in a hurry. I used to think people on Manhattan streets defined the concept of being hurried, but that was before I walked the streets of other cities such as Tokyo, London, and New Delhi. Even on a Saturday in Tokyo, the streets are teeming with businesspeople clutching briefcases. What is it about hurrying that seems so intrinsic to modern life? I had to confront my own issues with hurrying to find out how to eliminate it from my life.

I remember a vivid moment walking home after the last day of high school. My girlfriend, Alice, lived in the same direction and often walked part of the way with me. We hadn't been walking a minute before Alice paused and said there was something different about me. I asked her what it was, and she said, "It's the first time I've ever seen you not be in a hurry." When she said that, I realized she was absolutely right. I'd been in a hurry for as long as I could remember.

I've come a long way since then. Now, I see hurrying as a sign of declining mental health, a problem I've spent years clearing out of my life. I urge you to clear it out of yours, too, because there is no way to hurry yourself to happiness.

YOUR LEAP FOR TODAY

Hurrying is such an important issue that we will devote tomorrow to it, too. Right now, take a few moments to explore hurrying in yourself.

Here are several wonder questions I've used to illuminate this area:

Hmmm, in what situations do I feel most in a hurry?
Hmmm, when I'm in a hurry, where do I feel it in my body?
Hmmm, what am I afraid would happen if I didn't hurry?

Reflect on these now and keep them in the background as you go through your day. Be aware of your body sensations today to notice if you feel the signs of hurry.

DAY 260
Handling Hurry: Part 2

I didn't get hurry out of my life overnight. It took me years to get to the point where I felt like I was moving at a healthy pace. In yesterday's leap, I raised the question of why being in a hurry seems so natural to so many. For me to find a satisfying answer, I had to confront an uncomfortable awareness in myself. I realized that the real issue was what I could only call adrenaline addiction.

Being in a hurry kept my body in a chronic stress response, a sense of never quite getting to where I needed to be. As I hurried, I required a constant drip-drip-drip of adrenaline for fuel. Fifty years after I first turned the searchlight of awareness on my hurrying, science has now mapped out the addictive properties of adrenaline I had only suspected. Now we know that chronic stress, anxiety, and excess adrenaline take years off the human life-span.

Hurrying is certainly a health issue, but it also takes a toll on productivity. When we're in a hurry, we're in the grip of a delusion that going faster will make us more productive. In one study after another, science has proven that being in a hurry actually decreases efficiency and productivity. The extra adrenaline gives us the feeling that we're being more productive when we actually aren't.

YOUR LEAP FOR TODAY

To get the unpleasant effects of hurry out of your life, take a deeper look at the issue with these wonder questions:

Hmmm, when did I first notice being in a hurry in my life?

Hmmm, what is the ideal pace for me to move through my life?

Take a few moments now to contemplate the questions. Carry them with you through your day and pause to reflect on them, especially if you notice being in a hurry.

DAY 261
Is Time Your Friend?

Time is a big force in daily life, a presence that's sometimes in the foreground but always in the background. How we deal with the issue of time in our lives has a lot to do with how we feel from moment to moment. If time is your friend, you have an easier "time" of it than you do if you're wrestling with time all day. You let time serve you, rather than you serving time.

In an earlier exploration of this subject, you learned the difference between time slackers and time cops. Whichever one you lean toward, use today's leap to deepen your friendship with time.

YOUR LEAP FOR TODAY

Focus for a few moments on how you feel about time. First, think about a good friend in real life, someone you genuinely care about. Notice how you feel when you think of your good friend.

Then, make this commitment:

I commit to being good friends with time throughout every day of my life.

Sound out the commitment in your mind, then say it out loud a few times. Bring it to mind as you go through your day, especially if you start feeling in a hurry, pinched for time, bored, or any other negative feelings about time.

DAY 262
Another Take on Einstein Time

I received the following email from a student who had been struggling with the concept of Einstein Time. Her insight moved me deeply:

> Hi Gay, When I first read *The Big Leap*, I couldn't wrap my head around the Einstein Time chapter. There are only 24 hours in each day, so how can anyone create more time? Then I realized that you were pointing out that time has a subjective aspect too.
>
> In the person you love/hot stove analogy, an objective amount of time passes in each instance—an hour with the beloved, a minute with the hot stove—but it feels as if more or less time has gone by.
>
> So, I started paying attention to my subjective experience of time passing. When I had a project due in an hour, I felt stressed, the minutes slipping by creating a pressure in my chest. When I waited 30 minutes in the doctor's office, I felt antsy and bored, and time dragged. When I wasn't pressured or bored, I had a neutral experience of time. And when I was listening to music or caught up in a part of my job I enjoy, I felt a spaciousness and engagement that made me forget about time.
>
> I finally understand that although we can't control the objective aspect of time—there are still 24 hours in a day—we can control how we feel while it passes. I'm not able to do just my genius activities yet, but I've learned to monitor and adjust my subjective experience of time, so that it truly feels like I have more time in my day.

This is a great example of applying Einstein Time. To me, Einstein Time is not a lofty concept—it has a practical impact on your daily life. The feeling of having more time in your life affects every moment of your day.

- -

YOUR LEAP FOR TODAY

- -

Do you relate to my student's struggles and her paradigm shift? Today's activity will help you understand your present conception of time.

Spend today focusing on your subjective experience of time. Notice particularly if you go through cycles of being bored, impatient, or in a hurry.

Time is a big subject, ideal for journaling. Make time later for writing down your current thoughts and feelings about time's role in your life.

DAY 263
The Creative Value of Boredom

I grew up when "screens" were mesh-covered wooden frames that you put on your windows to keep out the bugs. I remember when the first family on my block got a TV set, but my conservative mother didn't get one of the newfangled devices until I was out of high school. When I got bored as a kid, I didn't have a screen in my hand to relieve it. Being bored was the catalyst for imagination, fun, and adventure.

When you don't allow yourself to be bored, you rob yourself of the opportunity to create something new and original from within. You miss the rich texture of all that's going on in your inner *and* outer worlds. And if you don't exercise your curiosity muscle, it gets weak, setting you up for more boredom in the future.

YOUR LEAP FOR TODAY

Starting today, when you feel the urge to reach for your phone to watch a video, play a game, or scroll through social media, take a deep breath, and reach for your journal or a pad of paper instead.

Use your moment of boredom to do some introspection. Write down how you're feeling.

Or look around you and write a description of what you see— the scenery, the people, the sounds, sights, and smells.

Write down any snatches of conversation you overhear. Be present to what's happening around you.

Or let your boredom be a springboard for free mind play. Jot down any ideas that surface that you want to remember.

DAY 264
A New Way to Celebrate

There is a space inside, in which all things are free to be as they are, to come into existence and pass away. That is the space I choose to celebrate every day.

—**Gay Hendricks, from a talk given at a seminar**

Before you can let something go in your life, you've got to be able to feel it, and ultimately love and celebrate it. What I've found is that it's often easier to feel—and ultimately love and celebrate—the space *around* something than it is to feel or celebrate the thing itself.

For example, suppose you want to let go of the problem of time urgency, rather than concentrating on the problem directly, widen your focus and feel the space around it and then love and celebrate that space. This will have the same result as if you loved the thing itself.

YOUR LEAP FOR TODAY

Take an issue you sometimes struggle with, or if one doesn't come to mind, use the one I mentioned above—time urgency—which almost all of us struggle with.

Put your attention on it, find out where you feel it in your body, and then love and celebrate the space around it as much as you can.

As you go through your day, remember to pause occasionally, and love the spaces around things inside you and outside, too.

DAY 265
Serenity

Before I ever heard the famous serenity prayer, I came across its essential wisdom in a two-thousand-year-old book by a philosopher named Epictetus. I was a keen Latin student and devoured everything I could on the Roman philosophers. That's where I first encountered a life-changing idea in the first line of Epictetus's book of sayings: "The secret of happiness is knowing there are some things you can control and some things you cannot."

When he taught that idea to small groups of students in Rome, he probably didn't imagine that they would eventually be on the lips of millions of 12-step participants each day.

I have many friends who have benefited from 12-step programs. I asked one of them whom I see almost every week how he used the core idea of the serenity prayer in his life.

He said, "I got my life back by letting go of the crazy idea I could control my drinking and putting my attention on whether I took a drink *today*." Two decades of sobriety later, Epictetus's wisdom is serving him every day.

YOUR LEAP FOR TODAY

Here is one of the key wonder questions I ask myself often in my quest to liberate my genius:

Hmmm, what am I expending energy trying to control that I don't actually have any control over?

I'm still using this question today, and I encourage you to make it part of your life going forward. Remember to be friendly to yourself in your wondering; it takes time to liberate ourselves from layers of misguided attempts to control ourselves and others.*

---

*If you'd like a great modern translation of Epictetus, see Sharon Lebell's book *The Art of Living*.

DAY 266
Procrastination: Part 1

An Indian friend once told me about a saying she'd often heard growing up: "Time eats intentions." Her parents would say this to her whenever she put off doing anything, like her homework or chores.

What the saying meant to me was when you put a task off, it drains your energy and momentum—and weakens your commitment to getting it done.

I know I've experienced that, and I bet you have, too. How many times have you procrastinated doing something and then find it somehow never happens? Today is an opportunity to get conscious about the things you're putting off.

YOUR LEAP FOR TODAY

Make a list of the actions and decisions that you want to do and make but are dragging your feet on. For example, setting up a meeting with someone, planning an event, or cleaning out a drawer or closet or room. Include agreements you've made with others but haven't yet followed through on. Be specific.

Resist the temptation to criticize yourself, instead be gentle and friendly with yourself as you write them all down. Becoming aware of your procrastinations is a key first step.

Keep your list handy. In tomorrow's leap, you'll be looking at the items on your list with an eye to how they relate to your genius.

DAY 267
Procrastination: Part 2

Procrastination falls into two categories.

On the negative side it can be an ULP: an act of self-sabotage, or the creation of an integrity glitch.

On the positive side: not being able to make yourself do something can be a wake-up call. It's your genius rebelling against spending one more minute in your Incompetence, Competence, or Excellence Zones. This kind of procrastination is a call from your genius to get going again on the journey.

YOUR LEAP FOR TODAY

Take out your list from yesterday's leap and read through it carefully.

After each item, close your eyes and ask yourself these questions:

Is procrastinating on this item a way to bring my energy down?

Is procrastinating an act of self-sabotage?

Is my procrastinating a wake-up call from my genius?

By asking these kinds of questions you explore your procrastination rather than avoiding it. Procrastination, like any other Upper Limit Problem, is best dealt with by being friendly and respectful toward yourself as you inquire into it.

DAY 268
Time Worries

Many people use time itself as an Upper Limit Problem. I was one of them; see if you recognize yourself when I describe the pattern. I would be going along just fine when suddenly I'd start looking at my watch and worrying about time. *Would I have time to finish what I was doing? Was my dentist appointment at 3 or 3:30?*

Until I started becoming more aware of my ULPs, I didn't realize how much time I'd spent worrying about time. Or how I'd used time worries to block the flow of positive energy in me.

I also noticed I'd done the same thing in my relationships. I'd be in the middle of a good conversation with someone when I'd look at my watch and say, "Oh, sorry, got to run." Whether it was at home or at work, I caught myself often using time as an ULP to block the flow of connection. Use today's leap to explore this issue in your life.

YOUR LEAP FOR TODAY

Do you let time worries interfere with your inner good feeling or your flow of connection with others?

Use the following affirmation to establish a more harmonious relationship with time:

I always enjoy plenty of time for feeling good and being connected to others.

Circulate this positive idea through your mind several times. Feel the meaning of it in your body.

As you move through your day, be on the lookout for time worries popping up in your mind. When that happens, take a moment to refresh the affirmation in your awareness.

DAY 269
Acknowledging Your Commitments

If you want to know what you're really committed to, look at the results you're producing. If you're happy with what you see, your commitments are in line with your intentions. If not, your unconscious commitments are probably hijacking your conscious agenda.

The power of your commitments is such that you create what you want most—whether it makes sense on a conscious level or not. The first step to bringing the commitments and intentions into harmony is to become fully aware of your unconscious commitments.

YOUR LEAP FOR TODAY

Take out a sheet of paper and write down the top three or four complaints you have about your life. For example, "I don't have enough money." "I weigh more than I want to." "My relationship with my romantic partner is difficult." "I'm in a boring job."

Now, turn each complaint into a commitment sentence. For example, "I'm committed to not having enough money." "I'm committed to not being healthier," and so on.

If you find it hard to state your unconscious commitments so bluntly, know that I did, too, along with just about everybody else I've ever worked with. It's important to do so, though, because until you're willing to take an unflinching look at your unconscious commitments, you remain in their grip.

The first step is to sit with them without judgment. Simply accept them as decisions you made in a "less evolved" state. You may even see payoffs for the unconscious commitments you have. You may find a new sense of self-understanding—"Oh, *that's* why I always do that. . . ."

Whatever your response, know that just the act of becoming

aware of your unconscious commitments loosens their negative grip on you.

Tomorrow's leap will take you through the next step: owning your power to choose new *conscious* commitments—to better health, richer relationships, and more abundance on every level of your life.

DAY 270
Owning Your Full Power

Acknowledge the awesome power that you already have—if you can create your life one way, you can create it another way.

Examining your unconscious commitments the way you did in yesterday's leap can be sobering, even upsetting, but it also shows you the power you have to create results.

Now, it's time to make conscious commitments so your full power can be used for making a home in your Genius Zone.

YOUR LEAP FOR TODAY

Start by reading the following statements, first silently and then out loud.

"I acknowledge that I am responsible for the results I experience."

"Through the power of my commitments, both unconscious and conscious, I've created my life as it is now."

"I now choose to use this power to create my life the way I consciously want it to be."

Now, take out a fresh piece of paper and write down any new commitments you want to make. For example, "I commit to creating financial abundance in my life." "I commit to being at my ideal weight." "I commit to having a harmonious and fulfilling relationship with my romantic partner," etc.

With time and practice, your new commitments will start to feel familiar and, more important, produce results that will move you far beyond your upper limits. Remember, it takes new seed for a new crop.

DAY 271
Space to Be

You must have a room, or a certain hour or so a day, where you don't know what was in the newspapers that morning, you don't know who your friends are, you don't know what you owe anybody, you don't know what anybody owes to you. This is a place where you can simply experience and bring forth what you are and what you might be.

—Joseph Campbell

When I first read that quote from the famed mythologist decades ago, I confess I really didn't know what he was talking about. Now, after years of meditation and working on my genius, I spend my days in that state.

The deep contact with the essence of myself nurtures my life as much as exercise, good eating, and good loving.

YOUR LEAP FOR TODAY

If you have ten minutes right now, sit down and do the following process. If not, find a specific ten minutes today to circulate this essential wonder question through your mind.

When you're comfortable and ready to begin, float this question through your mind every fifteen or twenty seconds.

Hmmm, who am I?

After you ask it in your mind, take a couple of easy breaths before repeating the question. The open space of your breathing gives your deeper mind time to bring forth creative answers.

Pause occasionally throughout the day to bring the question to life in your awareness.

DAY 272
The Importance of Full Ownership

A person stood up during the Q&A session after a lecture I gave on emotions. "You've been saying that we need to let ourselves feel our emotions deeply, but I'm confused. If I let myself feel my sadness deeply, won't that just make me more depressed?" She was voicing a common limiting belief about emotions. Often in childhood, we get punished for displays of anger, sadness, or fear. In response, we develop the belief that our emotions are dangerous and need to be concealed and lied about. This limiting belief makes us hold our emotions at arm's length, not allowing ourselves to give them the loving embrace that befriends them.

Emotions recycle until we acknowledge them and let ourselves feel them deeply. Full ownership of our emotions means to cease judging them and to accept them into the wholeness of yourself. Anything less sets up a war between us and emotions, a struggle that nobody wins. Today, you have the opportunity to learn more about the healing balm of full ownership.

YOUR LEAP FOR TODAY

Think for a moment about some of the core emotions human beings have: sadness, anger, fear, shame, excitement. Use this wonder question and related affirmations to illuminate this area:

Hmmm, of the major emotions I feel, which one or ones do I have most resistance to owning?

After you circulate the question through your mind a few times, use these affirmations to illuminate any resistance you still feel:

I own my anger and receive the messages it brings me.

I own my sadness and receive the messages it brings me.

I own my fear and receive the messages it brings me.

I own my shame and receive the messages it brings me.

As you say these affirmations, notice how your body responds. Notice if a particular affirmation stirs up tension or discomfort. That will give you insight into further work you can do on befriending those feelings.

DAY 273
The World of Relationship

Relationship is one of the essential areas we've explored often during your Big Leap Year. Today, and for the following two days, we make a deep dive into the world of our relationships.

In *The Big Leap* I showed how issues such as the Upper Limit Problem and genius apply to relationships. The first place I looked for answers was in my own love life. Like just about everybody else I knew, I had my share of relationship adventures (and disasters) in my teens and twenties. I had a brief but intensely painful marriage and a five-year on-again, off-again entanglement that lasted into my early thirties. Finally, I struck gold when I met Katie in 1980.

One thing I believe helped me find the gold was a question a friend asked me one day. I was complaining about the on-again, off-again girlfriend when he interrupted me. He said, "Have you ever figured out what you really want in a relationship?" After bristling a little, I had to admit that I hadn't.

Once I sat down and put my mind to it, it didn't even take an hour to sketch out the kind of love life I wanted. The three qualities I came up with were honesty, taking responsibility rather than blaming, and a partner who was as committed to her own creativity as I was to mine. Within a few months, I was in a relationship where all those dreams, plus a great many more, have been coming true for forty-plus years. It took me thirty years to figure out my relationship dream, but the outcome made it well worthwhile.

YOUR LEAP FOR TODAY

Are you willing to have your relationship dreams come true? If so, what are those dreams? Wherever you are in your close relationships at present, today's wonder question will help you clarify your goals and aspirations:

Hmmm, what are the three most important things I want to experience and achieve in my closest relationships?

Reflect on this question, then take time to sit down and generate answers. I suggest starting with three, although you may want to add more later.

Within a year of clarifying my goals I was in a relationship in which I had everything I'd put on my list. To this day that seems like a miracle to me. Now it's your turn. What relationship miracles can you create?

DAY 274
Deeper into the World of Relationship

Today we explore a paradox about relationships: the people you love and care about most are usually the people you have the biggest ULPs with.

As Katie and I point out in *Conscious Loving* and our other relationship books, when you love someone, you bring to light fears you didn't know you had. How you move through those previously hidden issues determines the quality of your relationship life.

- -
YOUR LEAP FOR TODAY
- -

Yesterday's leap invited you to home in on three big relationships goals. Today, you're invited to focus in even closer, singling out one area where you could use the biggest leap.

Use these wonder questions to illuminate this area for you:

Hmmm, where in my relationships could I use the biggest positive breakthrough?

Hmmm, what shift could I make that would give me a deeper experience of love in my life?

Reflect on these questions for a few moments now and bring them to mind as you move through your day. Focus on the questions and let the answers come in their own time.

You are now three-quarters of the way through your Your Big Leap Year! Congratulations on completing your third quarter of growth. Over the next few days, try to identify the ways that you feel different from and the same as the person who started this journey. If you've been journaling, take some time to read through your answers and notes from the past thirty-nine weeks. Take time also to celebrate your achievement, in whatever way makes sense for you.

DAY 275
Unconscious Relationship Commitments

In relationships, as with every other area of life, we get what we're committed to getting. Unfortunately, many of our commitments are unconscious and were put in place long before we could think for ourselves. Replacing those old unconscious commitments with new conscious ones is one of the ongoing challenges of relationship.

I remember the moment I first unearthed an old unconscious commitment that was causing pain in my love life. In 1973, I was dating a woman I'd been seeing for six months. I wasn't sure we were going to make it because we spent a lot of time criticizing each other. I complained about her being critical and focused on negative things. She complained that I had commitment issues and didn't talk about my feelings. We were both right, but we couldn't break through or break up. We just kept recycling the pattern. That is, until one magic day when I did something that set us both free.

The quick way to clear out an old unconscious intention is to claim it. On my magic day, I saw something that changed my life: based on the results I was producing, I was committed to having a woman in my life who criticized me. As soon as I owned the unconscious commitment, I could see the early-life origins of it. The details are in my books, but the short version is that I was conceived and gestated in a way that was the focus of a great deal of criticism and shame, particularly from my mother, her mother, and her sisters. No wonder I required a critical woman in my life. It was an ancient unconscious commitment.

YOUR LEAP FOR TODAY

Take the bold leap to claim an unconscious relationship commitment of your own. Think of one specific recurring pattern that causes pain in one or more of your relationships. Then, make the leap I did. I acknowledged, "I'm unconsciously committed to being criticized," and replaced it with "I commit now to being appreciated by the women in my life."

Use this fill-in-the-blank sentence:

Based on the results I'm creating, I'm unconsciously committed to _____. (Fill in the blank with "being criticized" or "being lied to" or whatever the pattern involves.)

Then, create a conscious commitment to the way you want to live and love now:

I commit to _____. (Fill in the blank with "being appreciated" or "being in a relationship where we're both absolutely honest" or whatever you desire.)

DAY 276
Kangaroos Have the Right Idea

For decades, hospitals have been encouraging parents to "kangaroo" their babies by holding the naked infant against the parent's own bare skin.

Although this practice has been used for millennia in indigenous societies, it only made a comeback in the Western world in the 1970s. There's a massive amount of research showing that skin-to-skin touch has many benefits, including improving bonding and the baby's health.

To improve bonding and the health of your relationship, make sure that both you and your partner get plenty of non-sexual touch.

YOUR LEAP FOR TODAY

If you're currently in a close relationship, go out of your way today to make physical contact with your partner: a warm hug, a squeeze of the hand, a shoulder massage, a quick kiss on the cheek in passing—anything that communicates your love and caring.

If you're not in a relationship right now, find other ways of making physical contact with people today, such as a warm handshake or a long hug.

DAY 277
Increasing Joy in Your Life

Poetry is life distilled.

—Gwendolyn Brooks, American poet

Poetry can do a lot of things to people. It can improve your imagination. It can take you to new places. It can give this incredible form of verbal pleasure.

—Billy Collins, American poet

I have favorite poems I return to often. Some, like Pablo Neruda's "Ode to the Watermelon" or Juan Ramón Jiménez's "The Final Journey," feel like old friends to me. I have favorite paintings I return to also—Rembrandt's self-portraits and van Gogh's *Starry Night* fill me with the same joy as my favorite poems.

Katie and I have also read poems to each other throughout the forty-plus years we've been together. There's always a book of poems on our bedside table, ready for us to open anytime, day or night. Shakespeare's sonnets are there, along with poetry books by Mary Oliver and Billy Collins.

YOUR LEAP FOR TODAY

Do you have favorite poems you appreciate in your life? If so, reread one or more of them today. If there are friends or family members who might appreciate it, read one of your favorite poems to someone special in your life.

If you're new to poetry or don't have any favorites, you're welcome to seek out some of mine—David Whyte and Sharon Olds are always great, as are the ancient mystical poets such as Rumi and Hafiz.

DAY 278
The Rule of Three in Relationships

The Rule of Three you learned about earlier in the year is a particularly useful piece of wisdom to apply to your relationships. In relationship seminars over the past forty years, we've introduced this idea to several thousand couples.

Here's one of our key discoveries: if you look carefully at relationship patterns that recycle three or more times, you will likely find there are only a few of them. However, those few cause most of the unpleasant dramas in your relationships. For that reason, any time you spend applying the Rule of Three to your own relationships will be well spent.

YOUR LEAP FOR TODAY

If you're single, think back to a significant relationship in your past. If you are currently in a committed relationship, focus on the last month or two.

With that in mind, ask yourself this wonder question:

Hmmm, what are unpleasant situations in my relationship that have happened three or more times?

Be honest with yourself and also friendly to yourself as you wonder about deep issues like this one. If you get the urge to criticize yourself for your past and present foibles, give yourself a lot of credit for even being willing to look into them.

Many people avoid exploring their repetitive relationship patterns for too long until crisis erupts or intimacy fades.

DAY 279
Sweaty Conversations

In my first session with a fifty-ish-year-old executive, it came to light that he had recently ended a six-month affair with another employee of his company. He asked my advice about whether he should tell his wife about it. I had my opinions but refrained from giving him direct advice. Instead, I asked him to give me the pros and cons of telling her or not telling. About a minute into doing that he abruptly stopped and said, "I've got to tell her."

We made a plan for doing so and I asked him to call me after the conversation. That evening he called me with the report. I said, "How did it go?"

"Sweaty," he said. "Sweaty but good." He said his wife was very upset but not inclined to break up over it. They had made arrangements to see a marriage counselor. I was pleased at that outcome, because I've always advocated the "honesty is the best policy" approach to revealing such transgressions. I'd borne witness to countless confessions from hundreds of couples in my office or seminars, and I'd learned, to my surprise, that resolution can come quickly when both people are honest with each other.

Sometimes a "sweaty" conversation is the most powerful, rapid way to restore harmony to yourself and your relationships. In my experience, both in my own life and professionally, I've found that the truth really does set us free, although it can sometimes make us sweat along the way.

YOUR LEAP FOR TODAY

Ask yourself this bold question:

Are there people in my past or present with whom I need to have a sweaty conversation?

It's always your choice whether to carry out the conversation or not, but let me encourage you to let the truth set you free. I've seen only good things come from being willing to bare, and bear, the truth.

DAY 280
Dance Therapy

If I can't dance, I don't want to be part of your revolution.

—Emma Goldman, early feminist and political activist

I was a latecomer to the power of conscious movement to facilitate healing and liberate creativity. The professors didn't teach that sort of thing at Stanford, the traditional institution where I got my doctoral training.

Then, I had the great good fortune to meet and marry Dr. Kathlyn Hendricks, one of the premier dance/movement therapists in the world. Until I met Katie, I'd barely heard of that branch of the healing arts. I didn't know there was a century-old field that used dance and other movement modalities to accomplish the same goals as talk therapy.

Living and working with a master dance/movement therapist for so many years has given me profound respect for her field and for the healing miracles I've seen her facilitate. I've learned so much from her about the value of body awareness and taking care of the precious vessel I occupy. As a result, I feel better and enjoy more activities in my seventies than I did in my fifties or sixties.

YOUR LEAP FOR TODAY

Whether you're a newcomer or a seasoned practitioner of body awareness, here's a process you can use throughout the day to get greater insight into your inner world:

Pause for a moment and bring your awareness to the sensations of your body. Do a quick scan of your inner body from your head down to your toes. Tune in and simply notice what you're feeling inside. Notice if there are any sensations—hunger, thirst; emotions such as anger, fear, or sadness—that could lead to productive actions.

As you go through your day, tune in and do your body scan

from time to time. Are you moving quickly? Slowly? Are you feeling one or more of the important emotions such as excitement, fear, and others? None of these aspects are right or wrong, good or bad. Greet your inner world like a good friend and it will give you good information.

DAY 281
Genius and Relationship

Our lives are defined in part by the company we keep. Today we'll take a close look at your relationships as they relate to your genius.

The essential question: Do your close relationships—specifically the five people closest to you—support your journey to genius? I suggest five people for a practical reason. In our seminars we found that three was too few to give a good picture of your relationship life, and seven was too many to focus on.

YOUR LEAP FOR TODAY

Make a list of the five living people you feel closest to in your life. Think of people who live at a distance, as well as those nearby. When you have your list made, reflect on each one of the people with the following wonder question:

Hmmm, to what extent does knowing _____ support me on my journey to my Genius Zone?

If you haven't talked to one or more of your five people about your quest for genius, wonder about this question:

Hmmm, why haven't I shared my passion for my genius with _____?

Be honest with yourself but also kind as you go about deep explorations such as this. If you tell all your five closest people about your genius journey, you can get more support from them than if they don't know about your passion for genius.

DAY 282
High-Firing

Long before I sat down and wrote *The Big Leap,* I'd spent years working with people, mainly business executives and professionals, on
the main ideas in the book. In helping people move beyond their
ULPs into the Genius Zone, I got very familiar with one ULP in particular: I found that people in the business and professional world
often upper-limited themselves by unconscious hiring and firing.

I found a nugget of gold in working with this problem, a tool
that people from every walk of life can use. I call it "high-firing."

Most of us have encountered a situation, whether it's with a
friend, an employee, or a babysitter, when we need to move a person out of our lives. High-firing is a way to do that so everybody
prospers. In high-firing, you first ask yourself, "*Hmmm,* what did I
overlook when I first hired _____ (or brought this person into my
life) that's now caused me to want to fire them?" You also ask yourself, "*Hmmm,* what is it about me that attracted them into my life?"

These questions help you keep from repeating the mistake again
with the next hire. They also mean you're taking responsibility for
manifesting that person in your life.

YOUR LEAP FOR TODAY

Take a bold moment to ask yourself two wonder questions that
illuminate this area:

Hmmm, who in my personal or work life do I need to separate
myself from in the service of my genius?

Hmmm, what was it about me that first drew them into my
life?

Questions such as these reach deeply into old, unconscious
parts of ourselves. Put special attention on maintaining an attitude
of loving acceptance of yourself as you explore these areas.

DAY 283
Opening More Space for Positive Energy

I was an avid runner and squash player up until my forties, when my knees started sending distress signals. Reluctantly, I decided to trade in my sneakers for golf shoes and also devote more of my exercise time to my bicycle.

For the last ten years I've also been doing resistance training three days a week. I've come to love the feeling of using my body thoroughly, breathing deeply, and feeling the exhilarating flow of blood and energy through my system.

For me, exercise is more than physical. It's about growing a nervous system that can accommodate larger and larger amounts of positive energy. For example, an hour of vigorous exercise will literally add a mile or two of new capillary space to the sixty thousand or so miles of it we carry in our bodies. It's no wonder we feel so good after an hour of exercise; we've actually grown our nervous system, so we have more room to feel!

YOUR LEAP FOR TODAY

Positive energy can be happiness, gifts you receive from others, uplifting things you say to people, and much more. Today's affirmation gives you a new way to focus your energy on what really matters.

I grow every day in my ability to enjoy more and more positive energy.

Say the affirmation in your mind a few times. Speak it aloud to get the feel of it in your body. Pause occasionally during your day to refresh it in your awareness.

DAY 284
Transforming Relationship Conflict

Your relationships will benefit from your understanding of the "drama triangle," a very common relationship dynamic first observed by Stephen Karpman, MD. My own relationships took a big leap forward when I grasped how it worked.

The drama triangle explains why relationship conflicts recycle and escalate. There are three roles in the drama triangle: victim, perpetrator, and rescuer.

As you know from an earlier leap, arguments start when one person claims the victim role: "If you'd stop doing _____ I'd be a lot happier." Nobody likes being cast as the perpetrator, so the other person claims the victim role, too: "Hold on a minute! It's your fault that _____ happens!" Each argument involves that race to occupy the victim position and make the other person the perpetrator.

Then, finally, after a few hours or days, somebody steps into the rescuer role and provides a temporary solution: "Aw, honey, let's forget this and go out for ice cream."

Once I understood the drama triangle, I found, to my chagrin, that I was very quick to put myself in the victim role when conflict came up. It took months, maybe even years, of awareness to get off the triangle. The first step is to become aware of it. Today's leap will enhance your insight into this troublesome dynamic.

YOUR LEAP FOR TODAY

Today's process would be a good one to do some journaling with, as it takes deep reflection to make the best use of it. Use this wonder question to stimulate the conversation with yourself.

Hmmm, in what relationship situations do I cast myself as the victim and the other person as the perpetrator?

You may not play out this dynamic very much or at all, but I was surprised and humbled to find out how much I did. May your exploration of this area bring you as much useful wisdom as it did for me.

DAY 285
The Practical Value of Oneness

I am part of such a whole. . . . I am intimately related to all the parts, which are of the same kind as myself. . . . If I remember these two things, I cannot be discontented with anything that arises from the whole, because I am connected to the whole.

—**Marcus Aurelius, Roman philosopher and statesman**

I came across that stunning piece of wisdom half a lifetime ago, and it has informed all my thinking since then. What can the words of a Roman emperor, written in a tent while at war with the barbarians, do for us in our daily lives two thousand years later? In my view, everything.

Think for a moment of our relations with other people. If we view them from a perspective of oneness, we see them as extensions of ourselves. If we don't, we view them truly as the "other," something outside and alien to ourselves.

The same is true for the inner world of our feelings. If we see them as emerging from the wholeness of ourselves, they are much easier to befriend than if we see them as caused by forces on the outside. Thousands of years ago, people thought their feelings were caused by outside forces such as gods and goddesses. Now, we recognize them as springing from forces inside us. When we can accept those forces as part of the oneness of ourselves, we can create serenity where before there was chaos.

YOUR LEAP FOR TODAY

Take a few moments right now to think about your life from the perspective of oneness. Use these wonder questions to open the conversation with yourself:

Hmmm, what feelings do I find difficult welcoming into the oneness of myself?

Hmmm, what people in my life do I have difficulty viewing as extensions of myself?

These are big questions, so give yourself plenty of time to let answers surface. Use the information you get to apply the wisdom of oneness to your life today and going forward.

DAY 286
What Does Genius Mean to You?

When you hear the word "genius," what comes up for you? When I was growing up, I always pictured Einstein; later it was Buckminster Fuller, Leonardo da Vinci, and Shakespeare. To me, genius is someone fabulously gifted who makes a meaningful contribution to the world.

At first, I held genius to be something rare, lofty, and virtually unattainable. It came as a revelation to me when I discovered that I and others had genius inside us. It is an extraordinary thing that is available to us ordinary people.

YOUR LEAP FOR TODAY

Over the course of this year, you've taken time to think about what you most love to do and how that intersects with your gifts, strengths, and talents. To continue refining the process of finding your own unique genius, simply float these wonder questions in your mind and heart as many times as you can throughout today:

Hmmm, what am I uniquely suited to do?

Hmmm, what is easy for me to do?

Hmmm, what do I love doing?

Circulate these questions through your awareness right now. Notice if your body reacts to them in an observable way: tension, relief, anxiety, excitement. As you move through your day, refresh these questions in your mind now and then. Stay focused on what you most love to do, what's easy and natural, and what you're uniquely suited to do.

THE
THIRD
CYCLE

- - - - - - - - - - - -

Repetition . . . leads to belief. And once
that belief becomes a deep conviction,
things begin to happen.

**—Muhammad Ali, American
professional boxer**

DAY 287
Trade in All Your Problems

Today, we take a deeper look at our old friend the Upper Limit Problem. You've probably experienced times when life was rolling along smoothly and then suddenly you got ambushed by a problem you couldn't possibly have predicted. I know I have. To make matters more complicated, the problems often come in twos and threes.

Fortunately, there's a way to simplify the often dizzying array of problems that beset us. Trade them all in for one overarching problem: how to feel good for longer and longer periods of time. As I worked with more people, I realized how many of our problems are really Upper Limit Problems, caused by our inability to let ourselves feel good inside and enjoy an easeful flow of connection with others.

I'm not saying that problems with money, people, and health aren't real. It's that they're often triggered and exacerbated by our unconscious programming to tamp down our positive energy. Keep your attitude of benign vigilance on expanding your ability to tolerate more positive energy, and watch your other problems disappear.

YOUR LEAP FOR TODAY

Transcending your upper limits will eliminate a huge percentage of problems that arise without having to address each one separately. Take a moment now to think about two or three current problems you're facing. Bring each to mind and consider it in light of the following affirmation:

I contribute to solving all my problems by expanding the flow of good feeling in my life.

Say the affirmation in your mind a few times. Speak it aloud to get the feel of it in your body. Pause occasionally during your day to refresh this powerful idea in your awareness.

DAY 288
The Three Inner Moves That Lead to Conscious Change

How do we get ourselves moving toward our consciously chosen goals? In working with people on Big Leaps for many decades now, I see that they go through three inner steps before change begins to happen.

Are there changes in your life you've been putting off? When I first started asking myself that question, I had plenty of things that needed changing. I was like an airplane sitting in a hangar. I couldn't get anywhere until I got on the runway, started moving, and reached lift-off speed. Later, I saw that all conscious change goes through the same stages as the airplane.

In practical terms, the first steps of conscious change begin inside:

I *want* to change.
I'm *willing* to change.
I *commit* to change.

Today's leap gives you an opportunity to explore the cycle of conscious change in your life.

- -
YOUR LEAP FOR TODAY
- -

Think of a change—large or small—that you want to make in your life but haven't acted on. Close your eyes, take a few deep breaths, and ask yourself, *Do I want to make this change?* Wait for the answer. Do you get a "yes"—a feeling of expansion? Or a "no"—a feeling of contraction? Make a mental note of your response.

Repeat the process for the following two questions: *Am I willing to make this change? Am I committed to making this change?*

If any of your answers are "no," you'll have an opportunity tomorrow to address those issues. Always remember to be friendly and gentle with yourself as you do these kinds of deep inner explorations. A little bit of loving acceptance of yourself goes a long way in your journey to genius.

DAY 289
Handling Inertia

Inertia comes from a Latin word that can mean "stuck," "lazy" and "sluggish." In plain English it translates as "I don't want to do it." Inertia is a powerful force that keeps you from making changes in your life.

In yesterday's leap, you did some internal exploring to discover what was keeping you from taking specific action toward a goal of yours. You may have found you were missing one, two, or all three of the steps of conscious change. Whatever you found, it's time to overcome your inertia and get back on track.

- -
YOUR LEAP FOR TODAY
- -

Revisit your answers to yesterday's questions. If you found resistance to one or more of the steps of conscious change, you're most likely hitting up against one of your hidden barriers to experiencing positive energy: fear of unworthiness, not wanting to outshine others, not wanting to be disloyal to or leave behind people in your world.

Take a few minutes to explore your feelings and see if you can pinpoint one or more of these old limiting beliefs. Later, do some journaling about this very large subject. Whatever emerges, be friendly and gentle with yourself in all your explorations.

DAY 290
Tilling and Tending the Soil

We've explored the important subject of willingness in earlier days; today we add an advanced dimension to it. In practical terms, the value of willingness in expressing your genius is like the value of good soil in growing a garden.

Before Katie and I planted our first garden, we hired a guy to come and till the soil. Before he started, our garden-to-be was a ten-by-twenty-foot rectangle full of rocks and weeds. When he was finished, the earth was dark, moist, and smooth—the perfect medium for growing vegetables and flowers.

Katie was a passionate gardener when I met her. I was anything but; I doubt if I'd ever given two seconds' thought to having a garden. It didn't take long to convert me, though. The joy of being able to go out to the garden for a sprig of fresh rosemary or a Persian lime is worth the tilling and tending it takes. Just like genius. Today's leap gives you a simple, familiar way to keep tilling and tending your inner garden.

- -
YOUR LEAP FOR TODAY
- -

Please take a moment now to check in with yourself on one of the fundamental questions I keep in the back of my mind all the time:

Am I willing to increase the amount of time every day that I feel good inside?

Feeling good is a natural, inner sense of well-being. It isn't dependent on outside influences such as ingesting substances or being entertained.

Asking this question goes straight to the heart of what we've been up to in our year together. If you're willing to experience more and more positive energy in your life, know you're right on track in your journey of genius.

DAY 291
Feeling Good Inside and Out

Yesterday, you reaffirmed your willingness to increase the amount of time every day you feel good inside. Today, you have the opportunity to reaffirm your dedication to extending the flow of good feeling in the external areas of your life.

YOUR LEAP FOR TODAY

As you go through your day today (and every day from here on out), keep this question in the background of your awareness:

Am I willing to increase the amount of time that my *whole life* goes well?

Your "whole life" means your relationships, your health, your work, and creative pursuits. You're asking yourself to be open to the experience of feeling good in "surround sound," in every possible dimension.

Remember to always be patient with yourself as you ask big questions. You've heard the old saying "Rome wasn't built in a day." Your genius isn't, either. It's built in one day after another of making conscious choices that move you steadily toward your goals.

DAY 292
Turning Too Good to Be True into Possibility

Alice laughed. "There's no use trying," she said. "One can't believe impossible things."

"I daresay you haven't had much practice," said the Queen. "When I was your age, I always did it for half an hour a day. Why, sometimes I've believed as many as six impossible things before breakfast."

—Lewis Carroll, from *Through the Looking Glass*

I've asked big questions to audiences all over the world. No matter whether I'm in Hamburg or Hollywood, Bombay or the Bronx, there's one question that always get a big reaction. I can predict what's going to happen when I invite people to ask themselves, "Am I willing to feel good and have my life go well *all the time*?" The room will erupt with protestations galore, such as "Nobody can feel good all the time!" The same audience who, when asked just a few minutes before, said they were willing to conceive of life going well *part* of the time, was now unwilling to imagine it going well *all* the time.

Asking that question plows straight into our collective deep-seated belief that you can't feel good and have your life go well *all the time*. It's a belief that comes from generations of people who struggled with adversity of every kind. Fortunately, in our long human experiment, we have lots of examples of people learning to change their beliefs as new evidence emerges.

The earth orbiting the sun? No way, said the authorities—until Galileo pointed it out.

People flying? Impossible, said the authorities—until two Wrights made them wrong.

Walking on the moon? Science fiction—until Armstrong took one giant leap for mankind.

Take some time to lean into the idea that what *seems* impossible might not be. I've given you a few examples of world-level scientific breakthroughs. There are many, many more in that category; think of cell phones, personal computers, and organ transplants. Look around you and see how many impossible things you take for granted that would blow the minds of our ancestors.

Then use this question to reflect on your own life:

Are there things I once didn't believe I could do—that I actually ended up doing?

It could be something small, like learning to drive or baking bread, or life-changing, like going to medical school or running the Boston Marathon. The point is to get in touch with the part of yourself that doesn't believe in "impossible things" and give it a little shake.

DAY 293
On the Way to Going All the Way

When I was a kid, I loved the *Dick Tracy* comic strip in the Sunday paper. The coolest part of Dick Tracy was his "two-way wrist radio," a clunky black gadget like a big wristwatch. Dick Tracy could speak into his wrist like a phone! It was outrageously cool because it was totally impossible. Or so we thought. Now, for a few hundred dollars, anybody can talk into their wrist.

Life in the Genius Zone is the daily practice of turning the impossible into the possible. Today's leap gives you a quick way to reaffirm your willingness to turn the extraordinary into the ordinary in your own life.

- -
YOUR LEAP FOR TODAY
- -

Wherever you are in your journey, use this wonder question to find out how willing you are to go all the way:

Hmmm, am I willing to feel good and have my life go well *all the time*?

Keep in mind that it's normal to feel some doubt or resistance from time to time. This wonder question is always useful for getting on track and staying there. Like Alice, get used to doing impossible things and watch the extraordinary become ordinary.

DAY 294
Increasing Your Velocity

Willingness and commitment increase your speed on the journey to genius. Every moment you allow yourself to enjoy more positive energy is a direct investment in your well-being. Every moment you dedicate (and rededicate) yourself to growing your flow of positive energy with others speeds you faster toward the ultimate goal, living full-time in your Genius Zone. Today's leap is one you can use at any stage of the journey to keep your vision on the ultimate goal.

YOUR LEAP FOR TODAY

Begin with a willingness statement:

I'm willing to live full-time in my Genius Zone, enjoying success in all areas of my life.

Say it a few times in your mind, then speak it aloud. Say it several times until you get the feeling of willingness in your body.

Next, use the following commitment statement to prepare you for action:

I commit to living full-time in my Genius Zone, enjoying success in all areas of my life.

Say it in your mind and out loud until you can feel a sense of genuine commitment in your body. Today and going forward in your life, keep your willingness and commitment alive in your consciousness by repeating this process whenever you like.

DAY 295
Committing to Good Feeling

As you know by now, letting yourself consciously enjoy the good feelings inside you is a direct way to transcend your Upper Limit Problems. Even after fifty years of living with Big Leap ideas, I still focus every day on cultivating a flow of positive energy inside me.

In my view, feeling organically good inside yourself is incredibly important to the rest of life. People who feel a flow of natural good feeling inside tend to make good decisions and treat others well.

By extending your ability to feel positive feelings inside, you expand your tolerance for things going well in your outer life. Use today's leap to prove this idea to yourself.

YOUR LEAP FOR TODAY

First, reestablish one of the basic commitments of *Your Big Leap Year*. Say the following sentence in your mind and aloud:

I commit to enjoying a flow of good feeling inside myself all the time.

With that commitment in your awareness, think of someone or something that brings a flow of good feeling to your body. Savor and nurture the good feeling with the intention of prolonging it. See how long you can enjoy the good feeling before it fades.

As you go through your day today, focus your awareness on cultivating longer periods of feeling organically good.

DAY 296
The Big Leap Two-Step: Dissolving ULPs and Cultivating Your Genius

Over the course of the last many months, you may have discovered you have little to no resistance to the idea of feeling good and having your life go well all the time. Or you may have found that those ideas sometimes trigger you, causing you to do the equivalent of slamming on the brakes.

Wherever you are on that continuum, know that the actual process of making the Big Leap always involves the same two things: dissolving your upper limits *and* making your home in the Genius Zone. What's unique to each of us is the order, frequency, and speed at which we do the Big Leap Two-Step.

Some people zoom out of the gate and then find themselves triggered later, facing a deeper level of ULPs, as they cultivate their genius. Others may find they take longer to reach escape velocity, but once they put their ULPs behind them, their ascent to the Genius Zone is strong and swift. There is an infinite number of possible variations. Today's leap gives you a chance to reflect on how the process is unfolding for you.

YOUR LEAP FOR TODAY

Take a few moments to reflect on where you are with the two steps of dissolving your ULPs and occupying your Genius Zone. Give yourself permission to accept whatever insight comes forth.

For example, you may feel excited about your journey so far. Let yourself savor that feeling, giving it permission to permeate every cell in your body.

Or perhaps you're in the midst of some resistance. Welcome those insights, too. Feeling negative about feeling negative never helps us grow.

Whatever your inquiries bring forth, always remember to be kind and generous to yourself as you go about learning these essential things.

DAY 297
The Lifelong Quest for Good Feeling

I spent a good chunk of my early life in school, from kindergarten through earning a PhD, but I was never offered a class on how to feel good inside. Also, I never encountered a class on how to have good relationships. To me, leaving those two areas out of our schooling is a form of educational malpractice.

It's different now than when I was in school; the junior high down the street from our house has mental health seminars and curriculum emphasis on cognitive and emotional well-being.

Fortunately, it's never too late to learn more about the fundamentals. Even though I've been keenly focused on internal and external well-being for decades, every day I discover new subtleties about the art of feeling good.

- -
YOUR LEAP FOR TODAY
- -

Today, take a few moments to compare your experience now with earlier in your Big Leap Year. Use the following wonder question to explore changes in your own tolerance for success and feeling good:

Hmmm, compared to earlier in the year, how much love, success, and abundance am I willing to allow in my life?

Float the question through your mind a few times. Notice the thoughts, feelings, and sensations it evokes. It takes courage to ask big questions, but it's worth it. Big questions lead to big rewards.

DAY 298
Consciously Advancing Your Thermostat

When I was first studying the Upper Limit Problem in myself, I lived in a prewar apartment building that was long on charm but short on things like functional heating. It had an elderly thermostat that you adjusted by pushing a little lever up and down. You had to do it carefully, because if you pushed it up too fast, a fearsome rattling and clonking would come from the basement. I remember chuckling one time when I set off the rattling, thinking, *That's exactly how the Upper Limit Problem works!* If we try to go too fast, our inner thermostat gets triggered and sends us an ULP to slow us down. I found the analogy helpful as I set about finding why my thermostat was set so low and how I could adjust it upward without the unpleasant rattle of an ULP.

YOUR LEAP FOR TODAY

Think about your current ability to receive love, abundance, and good feeling. In your mind's eye, picture yourself adjusting your thermostat to the just-right level for you.

Use the following conscious intention to guide you going forward:

Every day and in every way, I grow my ability to enjoy love, abundance, and good feeling.

Say it a few times in your mind and out loud to get the feel of the affirmation. Circulate it through your awareness often as you move through your day.

DAY 299
Joy Is an Art

Know that joy is rarer, more difficult, and more beautiful than sadness. Once you make this all-important discovery, you must embrace joy as a moral obligation.

—André Gide, French author

If you think of joy as an art form that can be practiced, you can then look at how, where, and how often you are practicing.

The great guitarist David Bromberg says it takes three hours of practice a day "to get my fingers to do what my brain is thinking." Pablo Picasso painted almost 150,000 works of art and was painting right up until the day he died at ninety-one.

We all need to ask ourselves: Are we putting in as much time practicing the art of joy as great artists spend on their work?

YOUR LEAP FOR TODAY

Reflect on these wonder questions to illuminate your practice of feeling joy in your life:

Hmmm, how can I experience the maximum amount of joy as I go through my life?

Hmmm, what can I do every day to assist others in feeling more joyful?

In your journey to genius, you are in a process of learning how to cultivate good feeling in you for longer and longer periods of time. Joy is a special type of good feeling and can be cultivated as well.

At the same time, we have many opportunities to contribute to other people's joy. Who wants to live in a world with more joy in it? Count me in!

DAY 300
Deep Appreciation

I make a distinction between gratitude and appreciation. Gratitude is something you feel; appreciation is something you do. I've found that both are essential for a happy life. I love the experience of gratitude, the openhearted, expansive feeling in my chest. I also love the acts of appreciation, such as the moment yesterday when I said to Katie, "I'm so grateful I get to be married to you."

Appreciation has two other meanings that are relevant to our daily lives. When something appreciates, it gets more valuable over time. If you dedicate yourself to finding your genius, your whole life becomes an appreciating asset. You get more valuable by the day.

A second meaning of appreciation is to become sensitively aware. If you stand before a Rembrandt and appreciate it, you're paying a subtler and more sustained attention than if you simply strolled past and gave it a glance.

YOUR LEAP FOR TODAY

Use these affirmations to deepen your relationship with gratitude and appreciation:

I enjoy the feeling of gratitude more and more every day.

I express my appreciation for the people and things I care about in my life.

Circulate these statements through your mind and say them out loud a few times. Going through your day, pause occasionally to refresh these affirmations in your awareness.

DAY 301
More Focus on Appreciation

There is a type of therapy called *Naikan* that originated in Japan. The word itself means "reflection," but the therapy uses a special type of reflection. The focus is on what people have done for you and what you have done for people. For example, one of the exercises is to calculate how many of your dishes your parent(s) washed when you were a child. I only did a few sessions of it many years ago, but I found it very useful in increasing my appreciation of the people in my past and present.

To me, living in gratitude and appreciation is a sound daily investment in your genius. If you go through the world with gratitude in your heart and appreciation on your lips, you're likely to have more time and energy for your genius. Why? Gratitude and appreciation create a positive flow inside you and in your relationships that's congenial to genius.

YOUR LEAP FOR TODAY

I tell my students, "Appreciate as much as you can from wherever you are." If you're feeling stuck, appreciate yourself for recognizing it. If you're colossally stuck, appreciate yourself for just breathing and being human. There's always something you can appreciate; begin with the simplest you can think of and work up from there.

Examples:

I appreciate the air I'm breathing right now.

I appreciate my heart beating and the blood flowing through me.

I appreciate being alive on earth in a human body.

I appreciate _____ for the way they love me.

Appreciate as many things and people as you can until you feel a flow of good feeling inside yourself. As you go through your day, look for opportunities to express your appreciation of the people and events that come your way.

DAY 302
Dealing with Big Infusions of Positive Energy

Whenever you have a big wave of positive energy in your life, whether it's an infusion of money or recognition or love, be on the lookout for an ULP to follow. Big infusions often stir up old fears about your worthiness.

For example, I got a call one weekend from a former client I hadn't heard from in a year. He was having a panic attack—about the last thing I expected. When I'd worked with him, he was a mega-millionaire investor, known for his steady hand in big acquisitions. Now, he was gulping for breath and telling me he felt like he was about to pass out. I worked with him for ten minutes or so to get his breathing stabilized enough to tell me what was going on.

What had triggered the first and only panic attack of his life? When he told me, it melted my heart. At age fifty-five, this titan of the business world had fallen in love for the first time. The specific trigger for the panic was three words that came out of his mouth to the woman he'd been seeing for a year. He said "I love you" to her for the first time, then went home and felt a rush of anxiety like nothing he'd ever experienced. His declaration of love had triggered an old fear: "Do I deserve to feel this happy?"

The story ends well; he got through his ULP and they're many years into a happy marriage. The larger point of the story, though, is one we all need to know: really good things can sometimes trigger really big ULPs. Today's leap shows you a new way to deal with gusts of good fortune.

YOUR LEAP FOR TODAY

Take a few moments now to review several good things that have happened to you in your life. Go back as far as you like. Do you recognize any ULPs that happened just after?

Being in touch with ways you responded to past good fortune can help you enjoy big wins in the future without following it with an ULP.

Use this affirmation to guide you in the future:

I enjoy big wins in my life and celebrate afterward with more good feeling.

Savor the idea in your mind and feel it in your body. Keep it in the background of your awareness as you move through your day.

DAY 303
Focusing on Loving Yourself

One of my first books, *Learning to Love Yourself*, came out more than forty years ago but is still selling steadily in the twenty-first century. It's an author's dream for a book to be touching people so long after its conception.

I think the reason is because human beings are having just as many challenges in giving ourselves loving acceptance as we had when I first wrote about it in 1980. The negative messages we internalize about ourselves growing up leave behind traces that continue to influence us as adults.

Whether you're fourteen, forty-eight, or eighty-four, any moment you devote to learning to love yourself pays off boundlessly in the form of good feeling and smoother flow in your outer life.

YOUR LEAP FOR TODAY

Pause right now for a pure moment of loving yourself. Think of someone you love deeply, and when you have that feeling resonating in your body, love yourself just as deeply. Feel deep love and unconditional positive regard for yourself.

You can expect some back talk from your mind when you do deep, profound things like loving yourself. Back talk sounds like "How can I love myself when I've done _____?" or "That's ridiculous." Expand your loving acceptance to welcome those and other bits of mind-stuff.

Loving yourself is often a new skill that takes practice before your mind fully accepts that you're lovable.

DAY 304
Upper Limit Problems: Shame Edition

Guilt is feeling bad about things you've *done*.
Shame is feeling bad about *who you are*.

The thing about shame—one of the more common emotional barriers to your genius—is that it's so often hidden. The energy of shame lodges in your body and becomes an invisible but very real negative influence on your life. You carry it around with you year after year and get so accustomed to the weight of it that it feels normal and natural.

Shame distorts your feelings of worthiness, and when you feel unworthy, ULPs get triggered. That's when you start to sabotage your success and progress toward your genius. To free yourself from shame, I suggest you take an unusual step: identify where you feel shame in your body and work with it on that level.

- -
YOUR LEAP FOR TODAY
- -

For this leap, you'll need to have a pen and paper handy. Then find a place where you can sit comfortably and undisturbed. Read through the exercise before you start it. Take two or three deep, slow breaths, close your eyes, and silently ask yourself this question:

Where do I feel shame in my body?

Let your awareness flow through your body scanning for sensations. Many people feel shame in their buttocks or back of the legs where, as kids, they were struck. Or you might feel something in the pelvic area due to feelings of shame around sex. Others feel a heaviness in their hearts or throats.

Simply notice any areas of your body that contain the feeling of shame. Then take a few more deep breaths and open your eyes. On your paper, write down the areas of your body where you felt shame. Describe the sensations you felt and your thoughts about them.

That's all you need to do today. In tomorrow's leap, you'll be revisiting those areas of your body to transform them into free space for experiencing more and more positive energy.

DAY 305
Transforming Shame

Yesterday, you located areas in your body where you carry shame. Today, you're going to practice a shame-transforming process that will help you introduce new awareness into those previously unexplored areas. As part of today's action, you'll have the opportunity to do a self-paced version of the process I've taught to many clients and seminar participants.

YOUR LEAP FOR TODAY

Find a place to sit or lie down where you won't be disturbed for about ten minutes. Take your list from yesterday and review the places in your body where you located feelings of shame. Now, close your eyes, take a few deep, slow breaths to settle yourself, and let your awareness go to one of the areas on your list. Notice any tension or tingling and let yourself feel it thoroughly.

Keep breathing into that area for about twenty seconds—about three deep, slow breaths—or until you feel a greater sense of ease and openness in the area.

Now, imagine the open space filling with light, as if it's pouring into the space that was occupied by shame. Continue taking slow, easy breaths. Take as much time as you like to savor the feeling of ease and light.

Repeat this process for any other places you found yesterday: feel the sensation of shame in your body, breathe into it until it releases into openness, and then fill that space with light.

When you feel complete, take a few more slow breaths and, keeping your eyes closed, gently start wiggling your fingers and toes, stretching your neck, your arms, and your legs. When you're ready, open your eyes. Notice any feelings of lightness or ease still present as you transition into your normal activity.

DAY 306
The Big Leap Attitude Mantra

Forming new habits requires conscious action. You need to be on the lookout for your old programming, gently interrupt it, and intentionally replace it with the desired behavior. In time, you develop what I call the "Big Leap attitude." It's a spirit of wonder, curiosity, commitment, and inspired action. When you feel these qualities flowing inside you and working for you outside in the world, you're going through life with the Big Leap attitude.

If you have a habit of beating yourself up when you find flaws or faults in yourself, you'll want to take special care to cultivate the Big Leap attitude of wonder and play.

Today's leap gives you a fundamental intention to use to put the new attitude into your day.

YOUR LEAP FOR TODAY

To bring the playful qualities of wonder and curiosity into your awareness along with commitment and action, use the following mantra:

I commit to transcending my Upper Limit Problems, discovering my genius, and having a good time all the while.

Say it a few times in your mind and speak it aloud. To add a fun dimension to the process, write the mantra on brightly colored sticky notes and add them to the ones you already have in places where you'll see them throughout the day. Move them all to different locations each week to renew their impact.

DAY 307
Inspired Laziness

Deep summer is when laziness finds respectability.
—Sam Keen, American author

A common ULP is not taking time for yourself. This is usually related to the hidden barrier of not feeling worthy.

To reverse this limiting tendency, do something every day to cultivate what I call "inspired laziness." It's different from ordinary laziness, when you're trying to avoid doing something you don't want to do.

With inspired laziness, your goal is to create some time to do as little as possible. Even a few minutes of inspired laziness can give you time to relax and deeply recharge for the next stage of the journey.

YOUR LEAP FOR TODAY

Take ten minutes right now or designate time in your calendar for later. When it's time, begin with this wonder question:

Hmmm, how can I spend the next ten minutes consciously doing absolutely nothing?

After you've done your ten minutes of "absolute nothing," notice if your body and mind feel recharged. If so, you may want to adopt one or more periods of inspired laziness in your day.

DAY 308
Celebrating You

I celebrate myself, and sing myself.

—**Walt Whitman, American poet and essayist**

To counter the hidden barrier of feeling fundamentally flawed, dedicate this day to celebration—of you! Most of us are a great deal more skilled at celebrating others than we are at celebrating ourselves. It may feel difficult to focus your celebration on yourself, but it's important to get beyond this prejudice against self-appreciation. Today is a special day to celebrate the best things about you.

YOUR LEAP FOR TODAY

Take a few moments right now to think of the best things about the life you've created. Use these wonder questions to illuminate this area:

Hmmm, what do I most love about my life right now?

Hmmm, what do I most love and celebrate about myself right now?

To take these questions into the practical realities of your life, find some new way of celebrating yourself today. Use your creativity to devise a celebration ritual you haven't done before.

DAY 309
Exploring Limiting Beliefs

In earlier leaps, you worked with the most frequently encountered limiting belief: the inner conviction that you are flawed in some way. Because of this flaw, you believe you don't deserve a full measure of love and success.

The second most common limiting belief we've explored is the unconscious conviction I call the "fear of outshining." You keep your own talents hidden or only partially expressed because you think others deserve praise and recognition more. This pattern often starts in a family where there's a "golden boy" or "golden girl" and you aren't it. Because of that early programming, you hold yourself back from being the star of your own life.

- -
YOUR LEAP FOR TODAY
- -

In all my years of working with the fears underneath Upper Limit Problems, I've encountered many versions of the fear of outshining. Here is a wonder question to illuminate this area of your inner world:

Hmmm, do I hold myself back so that others can shine?

Be honest but also friendly with yourself when you wonder about deep subjects like this one. Embrace all your discoveries with loving acceptance.

DAY 310
Upper Limits and Outshining: Part 1

The fear of outshining was a big one in my life. I grew up with an older brother who was the classic "golden boy." He was good-looking, an A student, Eagle Scout, and class president.

I was fat, a smart but apathetic student, socially inept, and whatever the opposite of Eagle Scout is. It was a small town, so when I came along eight years behind Mike, I had many of the same teachers all the way through senior year. I was often compared to Mike, usually accompanied by a sad shake of the teacher's head.

I was so intimidated by Mike's brilliance that for years I didn't even try. When I realized I did possess some talents after all, I was careful not to excel too much. I didn't want to outshine my brother's golden reputation. I survived and ultimately thrived, but it took a lot of work in my twenties and thirties to get that old story out of my life.

Here's how to handle outshining in your life now. First, here's what *not* to do. When you find yourself shining and up comes the fear that you might be *outshining,* don't tone down your genius to fit the old script. Toning down your genius looks like making mistakes or losing your focus or getting distracted.

Instead, go ahead and let yourself shine. Step into your genius. I finally did it at age thirty-four, but if I'd had this guidebook, I could have done it a lot sooner!

YOUR LEAP FOR TODAY

Take a moment to reflect over your past, looking for instances when you've toned yourself down to keep from outshining others. Recall any specific names of people who were part of those moments.

With those memories in mind, take a new stand with this affirmation:

I love letting my genius shine through all my challenges.

Circulate this new positive idea in your mind and let it resonate in your body. Keep it in the background of your awareness as you move through the day, reminding you to let your light keep growing as you deal with what life brings you.

DAY 311
Upper Limits and Outshining: Part 2

In yesterday's leap, we looked at one type of ULP: toning down your light so it won't outshine others. There's a second response that is equally prevalent: you let your light shine but don't let yourself enjoy it.

Instead, you develop guilt, shame, and health issues so people will know you're suffering despite your success. It's why kings don't walk down the street with a big grin on their faces, shouting out, "Wow, I've got it made. I'm rich, live in a palace, wear cool clothes, and everybody does what I tell them to do!" Instead, they're instructed early on to adopt a grave look on their faces, except when a dutiful smile is called for.

The antidote to dampening your enjoyment is to amplify it. I happened to grow up in a family with eight generations of Southern Protestants behind it. One look at the old photos when I was a kid told me these were not cheery folks.

I've heard the same basic story from people with Jewish, Hindu, and Islamic backgrounds. The basic message is not to let yourself feel too good. If you let on you're feeling too good, other people won't like it. Today's leap gives you a way to replace that old programming.

YOUR LEAP FOR TODAY

Use the following affirmation to create a new openness in yourself to enjoy your good feelings, free of the fear that they will make others feel bad.

I enjoy my good feelings and inspire others to feel their good feelings.

Savor this positive idea in your mind and body. Take it with you into your day to inspire you, and others, to enjoy your good feelings more and more each day.

DAY 312
Transitions, Worry, and Creativity

Making the Big Leap to your full genius is a big transition—you're leaving behind the familiar limitations of your comfort zone as you soar beyond your upper limits into exciting but unknown heights.

As you go through these and other transitions in your life, remember to pay close attention to fundamentals: breathing, working out, eating vibrant food, enjoying time with family and friends. It's natural for transitions to stir up fear, which provides the fuel for worry thoughts and ULPs.

Creative thinking doesn't come out of fear; the kind of creative thoughts that move you toward your genius draw from a deeper fuel source, the natural creative flow of the universe itself. It will serve your present and future path to genius if you learn to know whether your thoughts are serving your old fears or your creativity. Today's leap gives you a simple way to do that.

YOUR LEAP FOR TODAY

Write yourself several notes that read:

Notice the difference between my creative thoughts and my worry thoughts.

Post them around on places you're likely to look during the day: bathroom mirror, dashboard, computer screen. When you catch sight of one, take a moment to be aware of your thoughts.

The more you can shine the light of your attention on them, the better you can dismiss worry thoughts and focus on the creative.

DAY 313
Seeing Through Worry

If worry is a constant companion for you, you may resist seeing it as an upper-limit symptom. You may be convinced that *your* worries are different—that they're real and necessary. That was certainly my attitude toward my worries when I first started working on my ULPs.

I found worrying a difficult habit to break. If you're like me and most of the chronic worriers I've worked with, you may even start worrying about what would happen if you *stopped* worrying. Today's leap gives you a new way to put your worries to rest.

YOUR LEAP FOR TODAY

Human beings have been worrying for a long time. You came by your attachment to worry honestly, because worry played an important role at one stage of human evolution. Cave worriers were the ones who survived long enough to reproduce.

But now, we've moved to a new stage of evolution beyond simply surviving to making the Big Leap into our Genius Zone.

Allowing ourselves to enjoy love, abundance, and all forms of positive energy without sabotaging ourselves is humanity's next step.

Use these affirmations to help you shift to this new perspective:

I'm contributing to the evolution of humanity by experiencing more positive energy for longer periods of time.

I'm helping humanity evolve by moving into the Genius Zone.

Seeing a habit like worry in its evolutionary context helps us by giving us perspective and helping us feel more benign toward our worrying. Like anything that bugs you, the more you accept and love it the less it interferes with your enjoyment of life.

DAY 314
The Spiral of Growth

As we've discussed earlier in the year, dealing with your hidden barriers and ULPs is not usually linear—you don't handle a barrier once and never see it again.

Growth is more like a spiral—a barrier may come up repeatedly, but each time it does, you address it with a more expanded version of yourself. Today, we take a deeper look at an ULP you'll recognize from earlier in your work.

- -
YOUR LEAP FOR TODAY
- -

Earlier, you did a Daily Leap about learning to recognize your worry thoughts as an Upper Limit Problem. You made a list of your worry thoughts and evaluated if they were real or just there to bring your energy down.

Bring the you of today to do that leap again. Make a new list of your current worry thoughts. Going through each one, ask yourself:

Is it a real possibility?

Is there any action I can take right now to make a difference?

Notice two other things: To the best of your knowledge, do you have as many worry thoughts as the last time you did this exercise? Also, is it easier to let go of your worry thoughts now than when you did this the first time?

There are no right or wrong answers to questions like these. As you work on them, be patient and friendly with yourself. Take time to celebrate your daily progress to your genius.

DAY 315
Dropping the Ball in a Good Way

From this hour, I ordain myself loos'd of limits and imaginary lines.

—Walt Whitman

Remember earlier in the year when I asked you to imagine dropping a ball to illustrate letting go? Today I'd like you to do an advanced version, preferably with an actual ball.

First, let me tell you where this idea came from. A client came to me with a recycling experience of regret: each month, she met for a planning session with other leaders in her company. After every meeting, she'd be plagued with thoughts that she'd talked too much or dominated the meeting.

When I asked her to do the same exercise you did yesterday, she realized that the feeling of being "too much" was a familiar one. She'd always been at the top of her class and extremely articulate, so she'd often felt that she'd be rejected if she outshone others.

It was illuminating for her to understand this, but her next question was, "How do I let it go?" There was a tennis ball on a shelf in my office, so I gave it to her and asked her to squeeze the ball hard for about ten seconds. After ten seconds I said, "Now drop it." She let go of the ball and let it bounce on the floor. I asked her, "How did you do that?" She blinked and said, "I just let go of it."

YOUR LEAP FOR TODAY

Get two tennis balls or a suitable substitute. A couple of wadded-up balls of paper will do just fine. Hold them in your hands and squeeze as tightly as you can. Hold the tension for ten seconds, then say to yourself, "Drop it." Let go and let the balls drop. Take a moment to savor the feeling of letting go.

Repeat the exercise two more times: squeeze the balls, feel the tension, say "Drop it," and let go. Savor the feeling of ease and relief when you let go.

As you go through your day, keep the feeling alive by pausing occasionally to make a fist, give it a squeeze, then whisper "Drop it" to yourself and let go of the tension.

DAY 316
Criticism and Blame Reality Check

Earlier this year, you examined how criticism and blame are almost always upper-limit symptoms. Unfortunately, when you fall into an upper-limit trance, you, like most of us, tend to forget this and become convinced that your criticism and blame are justified—even necessary. Today's leap provides a reality check, reinforcing your understanding of how your upper limits operate.

- -
YOUR LEAP FOR TODAY
- -

Take a few minutes to reflect on any recent critical or blaming statements you've made. Include any critical or blaming thoughts you've had, including self-criticism and self-blame. As you review them, separate them into one of two categories:

Category 1: Real things you plan to do something about

Category 2: All the others

I predict you'll be surprised by the number of items that are in category 2. I know I was when I first did this process myself. I ultimately came to see that criticism and blame were ULPs that slowed my progress down. Find out what happens as you get more and more skilled at letting go of criticism and blame.

DAY 317
Are You Still Deflecting?

Early in my quest for genius, I caught myself in a pattern that definitely wasn't serving my genius. I realized that much of the time I deflected positive energy that came my way. Someone would thank me for something and I'd say, "Oh, it was nothing," rather than a simple "You're welcome." If a golf buddy said, "Nice shot," I'd say, "It's about time," or some other negative comment. As I caught on to my own "deflector" at work, I also began to notice that almost everyone had their own version of the deflector. Almost nobody seemed to know how to take a compliment.

As you know, this pattern has larger implications. It speaks to our overall unwillingness to let ourselves enjoy positive energy.

Ideally, when someone gives us a compliment, the generous thing to do would be to feel it deeply inside yourself and then deliver a heartfelt "Thank you!" That's generous to yourself and to the person who gave you the compliment because it lets them know you received it and appreciated it. Today's leap gives you practice in the art of receiving positive energy rather than deflecting it.

YOUR LEAP FOR TODAY

In our seminars we use a simple process to help people learn to enjoy more and more positive energy. It's a great one to do with a partner so, if possible, get a friend or family member to do it with you.

First, make a list of the five best things you can think of about yourself. Examples: I'm a good dad, I'm in excellent health, I love where I live.

If you're doing this activity solo, say one to yourself, then take three easy breaths to let your body register it. Say the next one, take three easy breaths, and so on through all five.

If you're doing the process with a partner, have the person speak each one to you: "You're a good dad." Each time, take three easy breaths after you hear each one of your "best things," then say a heartfelt "Thank you." The sequence is: receive, breathe, thank. As you go through your day, be on the lookout for positive energy you can receive and appreciate.

DAY 318
Growing Your Receiver

Here's an odd paradox I've noticed from working with people from every type of background. Many people of compassion and goodwill have a great deal of trouble extending that compassion and goodwill to themselves. In fact, some of the most giving people I've ever met were also some of the stingiest when it came to letting themselves receive appreciation. I found I had my own version of the problem and dedicated myself to growing a bigger capacity to receive.

I used a direct way to break the habit of underappreciating myself. It's an affirmation I share with you below, designed to grow your overall willingness to receive more of life's essentials such as love, abundance, and creativity.

YOUR LEAP FOR TODAY

Use this affirmation to include yourself in your generous giving of compassion and goodwill:

I grow every day in my ability to receive love, abundance, and creativity in my life.

Say the affirmation in your mind and out loud. Get the feeling of it in your body. Feel free to add or substitute other words that fit your situation more exactly.

DAY 319
Body Wisdom

Breathe deeply, until sweet air extinguishes the burn of fear in
your lungs and every breath is a beautiful refusal to become
anything less than infinite.

—D. Antoinette Foy, American poet

Over the past forty years I've taught emotional literacy to thousands of people, from professionals and graduate students to elementary kids. One thing I always tell my students is how to deal
with fear and other emotions: your breath is your best friend.

Feelings such as fear, anger, and sadness are directly connected
to breathing. The problem is that people hold their breath when
they are trying to hide their feelings.

Earlier, I pointed out that Nature has equipped us with two essential breathing patterns: one for stress and one for ease. When
you're feeling tense, your breathing often goes faster, shallower, and
high up in your chest. When you're at ease, your breathing is slow
and flowing. Knowing the difference between the two can be very
helpful in staying centered and at ease through your day.

YOUR LEAP FOR TODAY

Take a few easy, slow breaths and notice how you feel in your body.
Then, do what we humans do when we're scared: take rapid, shal-
low "stress" breaths high in your chest. Notice how you feel.

As you go through your day, keep your breathing in your
awareness. Note if it feels easeful and flowing or short and choppy.
Notice the situations in which your breathing goes into stress
mode. Find out if you can be in these situations without going into
distressed breathing.

DAY 320
Keep Your Creativity Blooming

Your genius is your natural creativity in full bloom. Think of your creativity as a garden that needs daily attention to bring out its natural beauty. In today's leap we focus on things you can do to get the most out of your garden.

Human beings are immensely creative. We got here through thousands of generations of people who were using their creativity to make their lives better. We inherited an amazingly creative nervous system; our task is to learn to use it to the maximum. Often, though, people get so caught up in thinking about the past and worrying about the future that they don't have time or energy to use their creativity today.

YOUR LEAP FOR TODAY

Take a few moments now to reflect on your creativity and how to employ it right now.

Use these wonder questions to illuminate this area:

Hmmm, how can I best make use of my creativity today?

Hmmm, how can I bring forth my maximum creativity every day?

Savor these questions, then open your awareness to receiving answers from your deeper self. Put your heart behind the questions and the answers will spontaneously appear when the time is right.

DAY 321
The Possible Health Benefits of Benign Vigilance

When I started viewing my illnesses and injuries as possible upper-limit symptoms, a funny thing happened—I got healthier.

For example, the moment I noticed I had a tickle in my throat or the sniffles coming on, I immediately scanned my life to see if getting sick might be an ULP triggered by an influx of positive energy. I did the same thing if I tripped, bit my tongue, had a near miss on my bike, or did some other self-injurious thing. After my scan, whatever I found, I always took a few moments to locate something positive in my life and fully savor it.

Sometimes just catching my upper limits in the act was enough to nip my illness or a bigger injury in the bud. And the savoring practice always expanded my capacity to feel good for longer and longer periods of time.

YOUR LEAP FOR TODAY

As you go through your day today, be aware of the warning signs of illness or notice if you're having "one of those days." We've all had them—days when you race around, drop and spill things, bump into people and furniture, and generally have more energy than awareness.

If you notice feeling "off" in any way, take a moment right away to scan for positive events that might be triggering your upper limits. Then, no matter what you find, just take another minute to practice savoring something good in your life.

DAY 322
Flow-Breakers

At this stage of my life, I've had more than fifty years of studying the Upper Limit Problem in myself and other people. In previous days, we've explored the cause of ULPs from several different perspectives. Today, think of your ULPs in a simple, practical way: they're anything you do that breaks the flow of good feeling inside yourself or between you and others.

One of the first things I learned about my own ULPs was how quickly the flow of good feeling would disappear if I didn't tell the truth. It didn't have to be a big truth, either.

I remember a moment in the checkout line at the market. The cashier dropped his soda can and spilled it on his shoes. He groaned and said, "One of those days, huh?" Out of sympathy I agreed with him, although I was actually having a great day. When I walked out to my car, I realized I wasn't feeling good inside. Even a trivial, sympathetic lie had interrupted the flow.

YOUR LEAP FOR TODAY

Today and going forward, get in the habit of observing your interactions with others while also being aware of your inner flow of good feeling. Increased awareness will allow you to stay in the flow for longer and longer periods of time.

Use this commitment to heighten your awareness of moments when you say things that interrupt your flow:

I commit to being sensitively aware of how my communications affect the flow of good feeling inside me.

Take a few moments right now to entertain the commitment in your mind and feel it in your body. Carry it with you into your day and bring it into your consciousness from time to time.

DAY 323
Genuine Peace of Mind

In our seminars, I teach a principle that has important consequences in every area of life: genuine peace of mind comes from total participation.

When I say "total participation," I mean it in two main ways. The first involves our inner life. To feel happy and balanced as we go through the day, it's essential to be aware of and in harmony with our emotions. To participate with your emotions means to allow yourself to feel them and communicate about them in effective ways.

Second, in the outside world of other people, total participation means to live in a state of completion, where there's nothing left unsaid or undone. For example, if there's an important project you're not working on actively and passionately, you probably are not going to feel genuine peace of mind.

In the same way, if there's a leftover communication that keeps running through your mind, genuine peace of mind only comes through delivering it to the relevant person in a way that produces completion.

YOUR LEAP FOR TODAY

Take a look today at any factors that might be in the way of experiencing genuine peace of mind.

Use these wonder questions to make a friendly inquiry into this key area of life.

Hmmm, are there any emotions that I resist letting myself feel?

Hmmm, are there any people in my life with whom I have incomplete communications?

If you become aware of feelings you habitually avoid or communications that have been left unsaid, make a conscious choice to participate fully with your feelings and communicate with people until you feel at peace.

DAY 324
When Truth Meets Fear

You've probably been in situations where you're aware of your feelings but unwilling to share them with the other person. It may be because you're afraid of hurting someone's feelings or making them angry. Sometimes we hide our truths simply because we're scared of being vulnerable.

The problem, which you've met in earlier leaps, is that withholding the truth may feel better in the moment, but over time it has a huge cost—far more destructive than the negative response you're avoiding. It stops the flow of connection with yourself and with the other person.

A first step in overcoming your fear of speaking the microscopic truth is to share that fear. "I'm scared to tell you how I really feel, because I'm afraid you'll _____ (be hurt, be angry, leave me—you fill in the blank). That small act of revealing your fear primes the pump for further honesty.

In our seminars, we say that any time is the right time for telling the truth, with one exception: don't speak a potentially alarming truth while you or the other person is operating equipment, such as a car. Although it always gets a laugh, it's based on many stories from couples therapy, such as the husband who chose to reveal an affair while his wife was making his green smoothie in the blender. I'll let you imagine the outcome.

- -
YOUR LEAP FOR TODAY
- -

Reflect on any current conflicts or on any situations in which you're withholding the truth from the other person. For each one, write down your microscopic truth about what's going on *and* your fears about sharing it. For example, "I've been afraid to tell you this, but I am actively looking for another job."

Then comes the question of whether to communicate your withheld truth to the other people. Consider each situation on its own. By now you know I'm a hearty advocate for sharing our truths (except for the blender caveat described above). However, you are the absolute and only judge of whether it's right for you in each particular situation. It's been my experience that sharing even the most uncomfortable truths really works according to the old saying: the truth will set you free. What will your experience be?

DAY 325
Agreements and Your Body's Wisdom

One of the most common integrity glitches is broken agreements, which you explored in an earlier leap.

Whether you agree to something that you know you can't do from the outset, or over time the agreement becomes unsustainable, the outcome is the same: when you don't honor your promises, you create a gap in your own wholeness.

This glitch in your integrity has a negative effect on your energy, which is why it's such an effective way to upper-limit yourself.

It's useful to learn 1) how to recognize when an agreement no longer feels right *before* you break it, 2) to express and listen to all the feelings involved, and then 3) renegotiate a clear new agreement.

YOUR LEAP FOR TODAY

In today's leap, you're going to use a special process for identifying which of your current agreements are no longer in alignment with your integrity. Your body feelings are an excellent guide. When you're out of integrity in any way, there's a "jangling" sensation at your center.

Close your eyes and, one by one, mentally review all the agreements you have at present. As you go through each one, scan your body for any sensations. If you feel any jangle, make a mental note of the problematic agreement, and jot it down on your paper when you're done.

In tomorrow's leap, we'll explore how to make new agreements.

DAY 326
Making Agreements That Work for You: Part 1

When you break an agreement or feel that you need to, the only path back to integrity is to acknowledge what's going on and make a new agreement. Having to own up to a broken agreement or asking to renegotiate a current one might feel uncomfortable in the moment, but I guarantee that the effortless, joyful flow of living in integrity will be worth it.

Acknowledging your lapse is best done with a sincere apology and making reparations or amends, if necessary.

Coming up with a new agreement starts by listening to the needs and feelings of everyone involved, and then working together to craft a win-win arrangement going forward.

YOUR LEAP FOR TODAY

If yesterday's leap made it clear you need to make new agreements, today, prepare for the "sweaty ten-minute conversations" you'll need to have to kick off the process. That means taking time to get clear about all your feelings so you can share them in their entirety, without withholding.

To easily explore all the nooks and crannies of your feelings about each situation, float these wonder questions through your mind and heart:

Hmmm, what do I feel when I think about honoring this agreement? (Anger? Sadness? Fear?)

Hmmm, what's causing that feeling?

Hmmm, which part(s) of honoring this agreement feels wrong for me?

Big questions call for deep exploration. Float them through your awareness right now and take them into your day. Journaling is always useful in clarifying your thoughts and feelings about deep questions.

DAY 327
Making Agreements That Work for You: Part 2

One of the best ways to know if agreements are in integrity for you is to use your whole-body wisdom. Earlier, you used this wisdom to decide which of your agreements were no longer right for you.

But your body also has clear "yes" signals that will guide you if you learn to recognize them. Today's leap will help you do just that.

YOUR LEAP FOR TODAY

Experiment today by observing how your body reacts to different scenarios in your mind.

What happens in your body when you think about some person or activity or food you don't like? What sensations do you have?

What happens in your body when you think about a dear friend or doing something you enjoy or your favorite food? What sensations do you have?

Learn to identify the "jangles" and "ahhhs" that signal a negative or positive response.

Your body's wisdom can often reveal more truth than your rational mind.

DAY 328
Putting It All Together

Now that you know how to recognize your whole-body "yes" and "no" signals, you can use them to make new agreements to replace broken ones—and for a whole host of other decisions.

From choosing what to have for lunch to where to go on vacation to which city to live in, when you pair your body wisdom with your commonsense evaluation, it will keep you humming along in integrity.

YOUR LEAP FOR TODAY

Science tells us that the left side of your brain runs your right hand and vice versa. Use that awareness to get both sides of your brain working for you. Write the following statement two times—once with your dominant hand and once with your nondominant hand:

I commit to using my whole-body "yes" and "no" signals to make conscious choices every day.

Now, hold your pen with both hands and write out the commitment. Notice how you feel inside as you write it each way. Circulate the commitment through your mind and speak it out loud a few times. Pause occasionally during your day to refresh it in your awareness.

DAY 329
Keeping an Eye Out for Integrity Glitches

Be who you are and say what you feel, because those who mind don't matter, and those who matter don't mind.

—Bernard M. Baruch, American financier and statesman

When you're living in your Genius Zone, you're living in a rare, special form of integrity. For people to feel fully in integrity, it's more than telling the truth and keeping your agreements. We also need to be sensitive to our relationship to our genius.

When we're in harmony with genius we move through life with a flowing ease. When ULPs interrupt the flow, it's a good time to look at where you might be out of integrity—are you failing to tell a truth or keep an agreement? Integrity glitches stop you from taking action to live your genius.

Whatever the nature of the glitch, they can all get handled with consciousness and clear communication. Today's leap gives you a way to bring your awareness to this important life skill.

YOUR LEAP FOR TODAY

Tonight, before you go to sleep, review your day. Go through how you spent your time and the people with whom you interacted. Were there any instances when you didn't express what you truly felt? Perhaps you told someone you were fine when you weren't or said you agreed with someone when you didn't.

Go back through one or more of those interactions and complete the conversation in your imagination. Say the thing you didn't say or apologize for an agreement you didn't keep. I've done this exercise many times in my own life and can vouch for the good night's sleep I get afterward.

Know that planting that seed will be the basis of more results down the road.

DAY 330
Doing What It Takes

Although our upper limits have a lot of different ways to keep us down, the steps to dissolve them are simple and don't require a lot of time. You just have to recognize when you're upper-limiting yourself and then take immediate action to halt or reverse the negative direction in which you're heading.

For example, it only takes one or two seconds to determine whether your worry thoughts are about something real that you can affect. If you find they're only there to bring your energy down, it takes just another few seconds to drop them mid-thought.

It's the same for everything you've learned so far. The challenge is to do the short tasks over and over, for as long as it takes.

All you need is a keen interest in your own growth, the right attitude, and a commitment to the process.

If you're reading this book, it's clear you have a keen interest in growing. And if you've made it this far, you've got the right attitude. Today's leap allows you to focus on the third ingredient: commitment.

YOUR LEAP FOR TODAY

Living in your Genius Zone doesn't happen overnight so today you're going to commit—to recommitting.

Repeat the following statements a few times out loud, then in your mind.

I recommit to my genius whenever I notice I've gotten off-track.

I recommit as often as it takes to dissolve my ULPs and live in my Genius Zone.

Finish by writing them down—once with your dominant hand, once with your nondominant hand, and once holding the pen with the fingers of both hands.

DAY 331
Focus Again on the Excellence Zone

This year you've spent a good bit of time wondering about your activities in the Excellence Zone—the things you do very well. Those activities usually make you a good living, and you get a lot of recognition, maybe even awards, for doing them. Life in your Excellence Zone feels dependable and steady. The people in your life who count on you are invested in you being there. In seminars, I call the Excellence Zone the "EZ," because it's easy to get stuck there.

I never felt fully satisfied until I left the Excellence Zone behind and stepped into my Genius Zone. I want everyone to feel the joy and sense of liberation that come from transcending the familiar and living in the exciting new world of your genius.

YOUR LEAP FOR TODAY

Do another quick inventory of your Excellence Zone, the things you do really well. Make a list of them and then review them one by one. Use these questions:

How do I feel when I do this activity?

Do I feel a sense of expansion or contraction?

Do I feel excited or emotionally flat?

Do I enjoy the whole process of doing this activity or just finishing it?

There may be activities in your Excellence Zone that are also in your Genius Zone. This process will help you distinguish how much of your time you're still spending in your Excellence Zone.

DAY 332
Associations with Genius

In teaching Big Leap ideas over the years, I've found that some people have negative associations with the idea of genius. For example, one of my clients had a "mad genius" type of person in his family, an uncle who was extremely creative but also had personal baggage such as alcoholism, a history of domestic abuse, and a prickly personality.

I didn't know about any of this when I first talked to my client about his own genius. He made a face and said, "I don't want anything to do with my genius." When he told me about his uncle, I understood his negative impression of genius.

Today's leap invites you to go beyond any negative associations you may have had with the idea of genius.

YOUR LEAP FOR TODAY

Use this affirmation to develop a 100 percent positive attitude about your genius:

I love my genius and welcome it gratefully into my life.

Circulate the affirmation through your mind several times in your own tone of voice, then say it out loud a few more times. Get comfortable with the idea of loving and welcoming your genius instead of resisting it for any reason. Carry the affirmation with you and reflect on it now and then throughout your day.

DAY 333
At Home in Your Genius Zone

When you're in your Genius Zone, you spend your time doing activities you're uniquely suited to do. Not only do these activities draw on your inborn gifts and strengths, you also truly love to do them.

All throughout this year, you've been zeroing in on your Genius Zone activities—identifying what they are and committing to spending more and more of your time doing them—as you move steadily toward a life filled entirely with their magic. Today's leap asks you a bold question and invites an even bolder commitment.

YOUR LEAP FOR TODAY

Now that you've focused on your genius for a while, would you be willing to live in your Genius Zone full-time? If so, use the following affirmation to guide you:

I live and thrive in my Genius Zone every day.

Say the affirmation in your mind and out loud until you feel comfortable with it. Carry it in the background of your awareness and repeat it frequently as you move through your day.

DAY 334
Heeding the Call of Genius

The path to the Genius Zone is always available to us, but because of our upper-limit programming, we get sidetracked into detours and cul-de-sacs. Your inner GPS keeps trying to reroute you back to your Genius Zone with the inner promptings I've named "calls to genius."

Unfortunately, due to the power of old programming, most of us ignore the first calls. As time goes by, these unheeded calls become like an unanswered phone that keeps ringing. If the call to genius is resisted too long, the messages escalate and are often accompanied by anxiety, depression, illness, accidents, and unhappy relationships.

When you answer the call of genius, your life goes through a genuine Big Leap. You start being aware of your ULPs and coming to terms with the underlying fears. As a result, you experience fewer and fewer eruptions of old programming. You grow your ability to feel good inside and maintain a flow of easeful connection in your relationships.

YOUR LEAP FOR TODAY

Even if you've been heeding the call of genius for a while, renew your commitment today with a simple, specific action. If you've been wavering in your commitment to your genius, today's leap will get you reoriented.

Today, schedule time (even ten or fifteen minutes is fine) for doing something you truly love to do. Savor each moment; each one is an investment in your genius.

DAY 335
The Joy of Contribution

The first dimension of the Genius Zone is love—doing what you most love to do. The second dimension is contribution.

In my experience, life is at its best when you are doing something you love to do while also making a positive contribution to the world around you. Contribution is not easy to quantify, but I came up with a practical definition: As a result of my work, will people wake up in the morning feeling that their lives have more value?

Given the nature of your work, your definition of contribution may be different. No matter what you do, though, it's always a good idea to be thinking of how your work is making someone's life better.

YOUR LEAP FOR TODAY

Focus on contribution today, starting with this wonder question:

Hmmm, how does the work I do make people's lives more valuable?

Be honest with yourself but also friendly. When I first started asking this question, it revealed answers that made me uncomfortable. I had to admit that a lot of what I did made no sort of meaningful contribution to anyone. I remedied that lack by making a deeper commitment to my genius and to finding practical applications for it. May your discoveries do the same for you.

DAY 336
A Key to Your Genius

Earlier in *Your Big Leap Year*, we explored ways you can know you're in your Genius Zone. Today we add a new dimension to one of the main ways.

In *The Big Leap*, I discussed one of the best and most practical ways I know of to tell when you're working at your highest potential: notice what work you do that doesn't seem like work.

In other words, pay careful attention to how much effort you're putting into your activities. Notice when you're doing things that have an effortless flow to them.

YOUR LEAP FOR TODAY

Take a moment to review the last few days of your work, however you define it. Ask yourself how much of your work feels like "work" versus how much has an easy flow to it that doesn't feel like "work" at all.

Whether you find that the majority of your work feels like work, or it flows easily, renew your commitment to keep moving in the direction of your full genius. For today, use this affirmation to help establish a new positive way of working:

I enjoy my work so much it doesn't feel like I'm working at all.

Say this positive idea several times in your mind. Feel it in your body and say it aloud several times. As you move through your day, be aware of whether you're in an easy flow or using excess effort to do your work.

DAY 337
My Hut! My Hut!

If, in the leaps you've done so far this year, you found that you're primarily living in your Competence and/or Excellence Zones, you may be feeling a mixture of things—excited, but also slightly anxious about making the Big Leap. Comfort zones, even though limiting, are familiar, safe, and, by definition, comfortable.

So, if you're feeling attached to the way things are or hesitant about rocking the boat, you're not alone. We humans have been resisting change since the dawn of time.

In India, there's a story about a poor woodcutter who one day, while working in the forest, finds a treasure chest full of jewels and gold. With his newfound wealth, he builds himself a magnificent palace. But when the day comes to move into the palace, he stands looking at his shabby old hut and begins to cry, "My hut! My hut! How can I leave my hut?" With his back to the beautiful new home that's ready and waiting, he's overcome by the pull of his familiar surroundings.

- -
YOUR LEAP FOR TODAY
- -

On the path to your genius, the best way to overcome the "My hut! My hut!" syndrome is to be friendly with yourself but keep your gaze focused on the spectacular life awaiting you in your Genius Zone.

Use these wonder questions to gaze into your future life living your genius:

Hmmm, how will it feel to do what I most love to do all the time?

Hmmm, how will it feel to live my soul's purpose?

Hmmm, how will it feel to contribute the gifts I was born to give?

Let the questions resonate in your mind. Feel a genuine sense of wondering about them in your body. Pause occasionally in your day to wonder about them as you go through your activities.

DAY 338
Deeper into the Genius Zone

As you've no doubt noticed, most people don't live in their Genius Zone. They go along in a daily routine, sometimes unhappy or even reasonably happy, but *not* living the life they were truly born for.

You are clearly not one of those people. You seek a life where you make your unique contributions and spend your days doing what you most love to do.

Today's leap shows you how to turn on the power of your imagination to fine-tune the details of your home in the Genius Zone.

- -
YOUR LEAP FOR TODAY
- -

Take a few minutes now to sit quietly and let your thoughts settle. Consciously summon a vision of the life you want to live. Let any images come, along with words and ideas. Let it all flow through you, clearing a path for your genius to move into physical reality.

When you're finished, reflect and journal in response to these questions:

In my genius life, what do I spend the hours of my day doing?

In my genius life, who are the people I spend my hours with?

If you enjoy sketching, draw some pictures, or find photos that match the ideas and images you experienced. Place them where you can see them every day and pause occasionally to savor them in your mind and body.

DAY 339
Exploring Your Goals

Have you ever seen a horse pushing a buggy? Probably not.

I haven't, either, and there's a good reason why. Horses, like humans, have muscles that are better equipped to pull rather than push. There's a metaphor in the buggy example, too: it's much more powerful to be pulled toward the future by a conscious goal than it is to be pushed from the past by your programming.

Working with a large and varied array of people over the past half century, I've found that human beings have the capacity to accomplish three to five big goals in their lives. As I say in seminars, "You can have anything, but you can't have everything."

When I was a teenager, I wanted to be a race-car driver, an astronaut, the author of the "great American novel," run a four-minute mile, and a few other things I've forgotten. As we mature, though, we usually realize that we have to refine our focus on a few big things. What are your big goals right now in your life?

- -
YOUR LEAP FOR TODAY
- -

Goals change along with the growth in your life. Take a moment now to reflect on your current life goals. Use these fill-in-the-blank sentences to highlight this area of your life:

My most important life goal right now is _____.
My second most important life goal right now is _____.
My third most important life goal right now is _____.
My fourth most important life goal right now is _____.
My fifth most important life goal right now is _____.

This type of deep reflection deserves plenty of time. I encourage you to journal about this activity and discuss it with family and friends.

DAY 340
Heart Energy

One of my mentors, Jack Downing, MD, gave me a piece of wisdom early in my career that I've treasured ever since. "When we get the power of our minds lined up with the energy of our hearts, we are unstoppable." By "energy of our hearts" he meant the passion we can bring to life when we're doing what we most love to do.

Jack was the first role model for me of a principle that would change my life profoundly: find what you most love to do and you'll never work a day in your life.

He started in traditional medicine, found a home in psychiatry, but then left it behind because of its focus on pharmaceuticals. Finally, in the sixties he found his passion in the new fields of Gestalt therapy, Rolfing, and dance/movement therapy. When I met him around 1970, he impressed me as one of the only truly happy people I'd ever met.

YOUR LEAP FOR TODAY

Affirm your commitment today to bringing your heart's energy into harmony with the power of your mind. Think of one of your most important goals and get it clearly established in your mind.

Then, tune in to your heart energy by focusing your awareness on your chest in the region of your heart. Feel the connection between the energy of your heart and the goal in your mind.

As you move through your day, pause occasionally to feel the connection between your mind and your heart's energy.

DAY 341
Conscious Commitment

As you start to walk the path, the way appears.

—Rumi, thirteenth-century Persian poet

One of the big themes in *The Big Leap* is the power of conscious commitment and positive intentions. When you form a new positive intention, such as a commitment to liberate your genius, you create forward movement in your life in more than one way.

In working with more than twenty thousand individuals, couples, and executives, I've come to believe that when you make a sincere commitment to your genius, the world around you supports it. New possibilities emerge and you connect with people who can help you along the way.

YOUR LEAP FOR TODAY

Use this affirmation to invite support for your journey to the full expression of your genius:

I receive massive support from the world around me on the way to my Genius Zone.

Bring the affirmation to life in your mind by saying it several times. When you have it established in your mind, tune in to your body and feel the affirmation. Repeat often throughout the day.

DAY 342
Making the Most of Wonder

Once I discovered the power of wonder, I was off and running. I turned my new superpower of wonder on all the things that vexed me about my life. I found that wonder was like sunlight for my mind. It shined on things I hadn't been aware of and helped me clear up old patterns I was stuck in.

To get the full value out of wonder, think of a wonder question like you might think of flying a kite. To have the maximum fun, you have to let it dance free, diving and swooping in the wind currents.

To make the most of wonder, let your questions dance free without being in a hurry for answers. Answers often come later in surprising ways, sometimes even in dreams.

- -
YOUR LEAP FOR TODAY
- -

Take a moment right now to entertain a wonder question in a new way. Here's the question:

Hmmm, I wonder what aspects of my genius have yet to be discovered?

Repeat the question three to five times in your mind, each time taking several deep, slow breaths before you repeat it again. Giving your question "breathing room" helps you let the question float free in space rather than immediately seeking answers.

DAY 343
More About Intentions

In *The Big Leap* and its sequel, *The Genius Zone,* I discussed the value of having a central intention to which you can orient yourself. We've discussed how conscious and unconscious intentions work in earlier days. Today, take a deeper excursion into the subject of intentions, with an eye toward learning to employ them more powerfully.

Practically speaking, an intention is the first flow of energy toward a goal. Imagine you're reading in a comfortable chair when you suddenly notice your throat is dry. At the same time, you picture yourself drinking a glass of water and spot your water glass across the room. You have an intention to get the glass and have a drink, but before you get up another intention surfaces: the old urge to stay in your comfort zone, to sink deeper into the chair and put up with being thirsty. Back and forth go the battle of intentions until you finally get up. Or not.

That's why it's important to keep feeding your genius every day. It's a way of keeping one step ahead of our old, unconscious urges for the comfortable and familiar. The solution I use is to keep affirming my intention to live in my Genius Zone, as today's leap shows you.

YOUR LEAP FOR TODAY

Set a conscious intention for how you'd like your day to go. You can make up your own or try this one of mine that I use often:

I consciously intend for everything I do today to contribute to the full expression of my genius.

After you've said it several times, notice how your body is receiving the information. Does the intention feel harmonious to you in your body? The more you can embody the intention, the faster it manifests.

DAY 344
The Automatic Pilot

The autopilot on a plane embodies a fascinating paradox: it gets you to the destination by being wrong most of the time.

Once the pilot sets the coordinates, the autopilot starts doing one major thing—correcting. The plane drifts to the left and the autopilot says, "Correct to the right." Ten seconds later, the plane is drifting to the right and the autopilot nudges it back toward center. The actual time the plane is exactly on target is minimal compared to the time it spends off-center. The autopilot's superpower is self-correction.

One of the goals of your Big Leap Year is to put your central intention on autopilot so it gives you nudges of self-correction when you drift off course.

- -
YOUR LEAP FOR TODAY
- -

Use the ultimate success mantra you learned earlier to do this process. Run it through your mind several times:

I expand in love, creativity, and abundance as I inspire others to do the same.

Tune in to your body and get the sense of the intention established in your chest, belly, and other parts of you. In your daily life, tune in often to ask yourself: "In this moment, am I practicing my central intention?" Remember always, the goal is to become more aware, not to criticize yourself for what you discover.

DAY 345
The Automatic Pilot: Part 2

The genius of the autopilot on an airplane is that it can self-correct all day long without getting upset. Imagine if two humans had the autopilot's job. It wouldn't be long before somebody said, "Do you have to be right all the time?" It's usually self-criticism that gets in the way of self-correction.

In our seminars, we teach a phrase that eliminates the criticism from self-correction: "Catch the drift and make the shift." Many people, when they catch themselves drifting off-purpose, respond with judgment, blame, and criticism and fail to do the one thing that will actually help—making a shift.

- -
YOUR LEAP FOR TODAY
- -

Here is a commitment you can make to remove judgment, blame, and criticism from your self-awareness:

I commit to growing more aware while liberating myself from judgment, blame, and criticism.

Criticism, blame, and judgment are unnecessary to your growth. What's important is to catch the drift and make the shift. Learning to do that without self-criticism speeds up your progress toward your Genius Zone.

DAY 346
Plot Twist

Many times in my life I've run up against a hard "no"—from women I wanted to date or from authority figures of various kinds.

It was never fun, but looking back, I can see that 99 percent of the time the "no" pushed me in a new and better direction. Now, I think of those rejections and roadblocks as enlightened "noes" from the universe—a "no" that steers you to a better thing. Now, when I get a "no" about something, I automatically wonder what better thing I'm being steered toward.

I encourage you to view the frustrations and snafus of daily life in the same way. Instead of retreating in rejection when you get a "no," stay open about what "yes" might be in your future.

YOUR LEAP FOR TODAY

Today, if something doesn't go the way you planned or wanted, try thinking or saying these words: "Plot twist!" It's a great way to remind yourself that it just might be an enlightened "no" from the universe.

Even if it's not, saying those two silly words will lighten your mood and help you deal with whatever needs your attention with more ease and grace.

DAY 347
Traveling to Inner Space

Beyond the edge of the world there's a space where emptiness and substance neatly overlap, where past and future form a continuous, endless loop. And, hovering about, there are signs no one has ever read, chords no one has ever heard.

—Haruki Murakami, from *Kafka on the Shore*

In my opinion, crafted after fifty years of personal exploration, inner space is the greatest travel adventure available to us. Although I've traveled to dozens of places around the world, my inner journeys stand out as turning points of my life.

Particularly, I've found the act of consciously tuning in to the feeling of space inside to be infinitely rewarding. The more I do it, the more creative I get and the better I feel. The Murakami quotation actually holds true in real life.

YOUR LEAP FOR TODAY

Pause right now to tune in for ten seconds to your experience of space in your body. It's there, beyond all your thoughts and feelings, but we typically don't pay much attention to it.

Now, give your attention to inner space. Feel it, breathe into it, celebrate it.

As you go through your day, tune in now and then to refresh your awareness of your inner space.

DAY 348
Big-Picture Creativity

Human beings got to where we are by millions, perhaps billions, of creative leaps, large and small. For example, somebody had the impulse to see what fish tasted like when you put it on a fire. Before then it was all sushi, all the time.

Somebody first came up with the idea of giving a polished stone to signify affection for another cave dweller. A few thousand years of marketing and design creativity later, millions of people wear a polished rock or two on their bodies.

We've looked at creativity from many different perspectives in *Your Big Leap Year*. Today's leap give you a big-picture view of this crucial element of life.

YOUR LEAP FOR TODAY

Float the following wonder questions through your mind several times:

Hmmm, **what are my current thoughts and feelings about my creativity?**

Hmmm, **how can my creativity serve me and others at the same time?**

Hmmm, **how can I best invite the creativity of those around me?**

Use these questions as seeds for further reflection as you go through your day. Creativity is so important to life that any moment you spend exploring it is useful.

DAY 349
Einstein Time Check-In

How are you doing with the idea of Einstein Time? Although there have been quite a few leaps about it this year, becoming the source of time can be challenging. If you're still working on it, don't worry. Making the switch from Newtonian Time to Einstein Time simply takes practice.

In Newtonian Time, there's only so much of it and it's getting scarcer by the moment. The Newtonian model pits you against time and creates a feeling of time pressure and scarcity.

Once you accept that you're in charge of your experience of time—making it either stressful or enjoyable—you have a superpower. When you find yourself feeling in a hurry or struggling with time in any way, you have a place to come back home to, the spacious world of Einstein Time. Today's leap allows you to see where you are in the process.

YOUR LEAP FOR TODAY

Check in with yourself to see which time model you're operating in.

Using a scale from one to five, where one means "never" and five means "always," answer the following questions:

How often do I feel stressed and overwhelmed?
How often do I feel relaxed and creative?
How often do I feel I don't have enough time?
How often do I complain about not having enough time?
How often do I feel gratitude and appreciation?
How often do I feel fascinated and engaged?
How often do I feel bored?
How often do I notice that time seems to fly by because I'm enjoying what I'm doing?

Your answers—whatever they are—are perfect because they help you become more aware of any adjustments you need to make to transition fully to Einstein Time. Feedback is vital for making progress. Use your answers in a friendly way to fine-tune your experience of time.

DAY 350
Transcending Your Time Persona

Earlier in the year, you identified your time persona as either time cop or time slacker—two ends of the spectrum for managing your experience of time.

To review, time cops are constantly aware of time and strict about adhering to its dictates—and expect others to do the same.

Time slackers rebel against the tyranny of time, blowing off deadlines and time commitments—or at least stretching them to their limits—whenever possible.

Most people are one or the other, but there are situational time cops and time slackers: strict at work and rebellious at home, or vice versa.

Whichever one you are, when you switch to Einstein Time, you transcend your time persona. You have a totally different relationship with time since you're in charge of how you experience it.

YOUR LEAP FOR TODAY

To transcend your time persona, use the following affirmations:

I am the source of my experience of time.

I can make as much time as I need or want.

Say them both out loud a few times, then think them—just dropping them into your inner space—as many times as you can throughout the day.

Your mind may still resist these ideas—your old programming can run deep—but just keep repeating the affirmations easily and lightly, the same way you lower yourself slowly into a hot bath, letting your body become used to the higher temperature and eventually relaxing into it.

DAY 351
Time Scarcity

Imagine stopping people in the street and asking, "Is there plenty of time to do all the things you want to do?" How many would say they had all the time they needed? My guess is that the number of "yeses" would hover near zero. Time scarcity is a belief so widely shared that many people don't even think of it as a belief. It's just the way it is.

I've reached several conclusions about time based on working with a lot of busy people over the years. One of them is: there's never enough time to do all the things you really don't want to do anyway.

There's tendency in life to distract ourselves from our genius by getting involved in more and more activities that don't serve it. There's only one permanent solution to time scarcity: taking full, joyful responsibility for creating the amount of time to do the things you most want to do. At the same time, make a dedicated effort to decrease the amount of time you do things you don't want to do. As you get more "love to do" activities going, your sense of time scarcity gradually disappears.

YOUR LEAP FOR TODAY

Use this commitment statement to take a stand for your genius:

I commit to creating all the time I need to do all the things I love to do.

Repeat the commitment a few times in your mind. Say it out loud and feel it in your body. Reflect on it as you move through your day. Every moment is made better with an attitude of time generosity in yourself.

DAY 352
Letting Go of the Past and the Future

In my book *The Genius Zone*, I show how the past and the future have a crucial factor in common: both of them are outside our control. In the case of the past, the fact that we can't control it is pretty obvious. It already happened. However, that doesn't stop us from bringing the past to mind frequently, bringing grief and shame to life in our bodies years after the event.

The future is less obvious. If I say at a lecture, "We can't control the future," hands will go up in the room: "Wait a minute, what about planning?" It's true that we can influence the future with planning and rehearsal, but when the actual event finally occurs, all bets are off.

In tomorrow's leap, I'll give you a vivid example of how I learned this truth the hard way. Today's leap gives you a new attitude to take toward present, past, and future.

YOUR LEAP FOR TODAY

Focus today on one common element of the past and the future, the fact that neither one of them are within your conscious control. Use these affirmations to get clear on this important idea:

I relax and let go of trying to control the past and the future.

I plan for future events and use my creativity to engage with what happens.

I focus on things I can do in the present that contribute to the future I want to create.

Circulate these ideas through your mind and say them out loud a few times. Bring them to mind several times as you go through your day.

DAY 353
Learning the Hard Way

In yesterday's leap, we explored the issue of control, particularly our inability to control the past or the future. Here's a story of the "hard way" of learning this simple truth.

I was giving a talk in the early eighties on my just-published book, *Learning to Love Yourself*. I was new to giving such talks and had done extensive preparations. In fact, I had three pages of typed notes for a half-hour talk! There were perhaps fifty people in the room, and things were humming along just fine for the first fifteen minutes.

Suddenly a woman in the front row jumped up, started screaming unintelligible things, and hurled her purse at me. She stormed out of the room, still yelling things I couldn't understand. When we recovered our collective breath, I asked the audience if anyone knew her or why she might have become upset. Nobody did, so I sent one of my friends who was at the lecture to go after her and help if he could. The class voted to proceed and so we did.

It turned out she was known to the authorities for similar public outbursts related to her mental health. That helped me not take it personally, but it also taught me how careful planning doesn't always guarantee the outcome we expect.

- -
YOUR LEAP FOR TODAY
- -

Focus on how you relate to the future. Particularly, think of the paradox of the future: How can we best influence something we actually have no control over? Use today's wonder question to open up this conversation with your deep creativity:

Hmmm, how can I let go of controlling the future and open myself to the best possible outcome?

Say it a few times mentally and then out loud until you feel comfortable with the question. Then, go about your day and into the future with a readiness to embrace positive solutions.

DAY 354
Wondering Big

Over the course of this year, I've talked a lot about wonder. For me, wonder is just as important a tool as a compass for steering your way through life. Once you learn to use this marvelous instrument, when you come to a place where you have a choice or decision to make, you'll find that wonder is the direct pathway to the most creative and expanded aspects of yourself.

Einstein, in one of his notebooks, wrote about wondering about something every day for twenty-seven years until he figured it out. That's some powerfully committed wonder.

I believe that if more people wondered on a regular basis about the many challenges we face as humans, eventually we'd find wildly creative solutions to even the most intransigent of the world's problems.

YOUR LEAP FOR TODAY

Pick something BIG to wonder about—for example, how to create world peace, or how to stop climate change, or how to deal with systemic racism. It doesn't matter what the subject is as long as it's important to you. Then, starting today, wonder about it every day by asking yourself this question:

Hmmm, I wonder how to _____ (fill in the blank).

When you wonder, even about something big like how to eliminate hunger in the world, you don't need to put any pressure on yourself. Just let your wonder tumble through you, bringing to light whatever it does.

DAY 355
Wonder: The Antidote to Unconscious Commitment

Today we focus on an important issue we've explored in earlier days: until we create a successful conscious commitment to something, we are ruled by our unconscious commitments to it. For example, fifty years ago I was obese, but I sabotaged one diet after another. Eventually, I had to admit that my unconscious commitment to being fat was greater than my conscious desire to slim down.

That turned out to be a crucial insight because it led me to ask what I now call a wonder question. It was a miracle—one moment of wonder unlocked a pattern that had kept me in its grip for years: *Hmmm*, why might I be committed to staying fat? In a flash, I saw how my obesity had gotten me massive attention from my family, even though the attention was often in the form of criticism and exasperation. If I lost weight, would I still get the attention?

Being fat was familiar to me; being slim was in a scary, unknown zone. I persisted through these and other Upper Limit Problems, though, and within a year lost over one hundred pounds that I've happily kept off ever since.

YOUR LEAP FOR TODAY

Positive change happens more rapidly when you acknowledge your unconscious commitments. Focus for a moment, as I did with my obesity, on some pattern in your life that's been resistant to change. For example, say you want to overcome shyness, but it hasn't gotten better in spite of things you've tried. Claim the unconscious commitment with this statement:

Based on the results, I seem to be unconsciously committed to staying shy. (Replace "staying shy" with your own personal example: staying unhealthy, staying single, staying stuck in a job.)

Then, turn your statement into a wonder question:

Hmmm, why might I be committed to staying shy? (Insert your own example instead of "staying shy," as in "*Hmmm*, why might I be committed to staying unhealthy, staying single, etc.")

Today and going forward, use these questions when you encounter any kind of recurring unpleasant issue in your life. A timely question can always help: "*Hmmm*, why am I committed to creating this issue over and over in my life?"

DAY 356
An Experiment in Receiving

Here's an enlightening one-day experiment I've asked many students to perform. It can also be a lot of fun. The instructions are below, but in general, I invite you to get aligned with a specific wonder question, then track the results for one day.

It often leads to surprising increases in the amount of positive energy you experience during the day. Ready to give it a try?

- -
YOUR LEAP FOR TODAY
- -

Take a few minutes to get thoroughly aligned, body and mind, with this wonder question:

Hmmm, how much appreciation and other positive energy can I allow myself to receive today?

Savor the question in your mind and feel the wonder of it in your body. As you go through your day, be on the lookout for results, especially in the form of appreciation from unexpected sources.

DAY 357
Culling Your Contacts—Again

It's been more than six months since you first looked through your contacts, a process inspired by a ritual I learned from Katie, who does it at least once a year. After watching her do it a few times, I got inspired to do it, too. I was amazed at the positive feelings it liberated. What is this magic action? Every now and then, she goes through her closet and culls out anything she doesn't love to wear.

When I did it, it felt odd to be asking, "Do I love wearing this?" I don't think I'd given ten seconds' thought in my life to whether or not I loved wearing something. I was astonished to find I was still wearing things I didn't even like to wear ten years ago. I loaded up the whole back seat with a giant bundle and took it down to the thrift shop. I can still feel that sense of liberation in my body. Later, I got inspired to do the same thing with my contacts list.

Before I kept my contacts on a computer or phone, I wrote them on little cards and stuck them on a gadget called a Rolodex. I've been teaching today's process so long I used to call it "Riffing your Rolodex." Looking at each of the two hundred or so names in my Rolodex, I asked myself, "Do I love communicating with this person?" In some cases, the answer was "no," but it was a service person I needed to keep handy.

However, I was able to clear about seventy-five people out of my list, including some who were no longer among the living. I had the same sense of liberation I did after clearing out my clothes. Plus, when I saw the names of people I loved to communicate with, I was inspired to reach out to them. Today's process takes you into this new dimension.

YOUR LEAP FOR TODAY

Once again, go through your contacts list on your phone or wherever you keep it. Find the people you love to communicate with and the ones you need to keep for practical reasons. Cull the rest out and trash them. Notice the feelings in your body afterward. Do you feel that sense of liberation I did?

Now, take this process into a positive conclusion. Pick out one or more people that you haven't talked to in a while, people who have passed your "love to communicate with" test. Call them and express your affection for them. Notice how you feel afterward, and if you like the feeling, make some more calls.

Culling your contacts is such an important process, I encourage you to repeat it often.

DAY 358
Your Relationship with Creativity

In *The Big Leap* and its sequel, *The Genius Zone,* I invited readers to think of their creativity as a living force in their lives. If you think of your creativity as a crucial resource, you are much more likely to devote time and energy to cultivating it.

I consider creativity so important in my own life that I treat it like a mate. Even though I've been married to Katie more than half my life, I put attention and time into our relationship every day. It's a living, growing entity that thrives with regular nurturing and tending. That's exactly the same way I feel about creativity. What is the role of creativity in your life right now? Find out below.

YOUR LEAP FOR TODAY

Take a moment to think of your relationship with creativity. Specifically, think of your relationship with creativity in the past week.

Use the following wonder question to inquire into this area:

Hmmm, how much time each day for the past week did I devote to expressing my creativity?

Be gentle with yourself when you ask big questions like that. There can be a tendency to get critical of yourself, especially if the answer is lower than you'd like. Do your best to be honest and friendly in all your moments of self-awareness.

DAY 359
Relationship Patterns

In one of the largest studies ever done on relationships, John Cuber and Peggy Harroff followed 437 people in long-term marriages. They found that only one out of five couples had what might be called a "vital relationship," defined as a relationship in which both people felt satisfied and excited by each other.

Four out of five couples fell into three categories. One group was in relationships described as "devitalized," where they stayed together as companions long after passion had disappeared. A second group was called "passive-congenial"; they'd never felt passionate about each other and stayed together as friends. The third group was called "conflict-habituated"; these couples fought a lot and sustained the marriage through the adrenaline released by their battles.

YOUR LEAP FOR TODAY

Do a clear-eyed but openhearted survey of your closest relationships, now and in the past. Ask yourself if any of the three unsatisfying relationship patterns are familiar to you, either in your own relationships or in what you saw around you growing up.

If you discover traces of devitalized, conflict-habituated, or passive-congenial relationships in your world, past or present, have some friendly conversations with yourself about moving toward greater vitality.

DAY 360
Committing to the Unknown

We've explored the element of luck in earlier days, specifically the art of consciously improving your luck. Since luck is such an important part of anyone's life, I encourage you to focus on it frequently in your life going forward. Today's process gives you a new and expanded look at this subject.

All the most significant commitments in our lives involve making a vow to something we have no idea if we can do. For example, every year people embark on new marriages or committed relationships by saying vows to each other. When Katie and I said our vows to each other in 1981, we committed to creating a relationship that ran on positive energy, free of blame and criticism. We also made other commitments, such as one to speak with absolute honesty and listen with generosity to the other. Neither one of us had ever been in such a relationship before, so naturally we had no idea if we could do the things we vowed to do. That's the magic of commitment. It can pull capabilities from us that we only suspect we have.

Do you have the hidden capability of being the luckiest person you've ever known? The only way I know of to find out is to make a heartfelt commitment to it and watch the results.

- -
YOUR LEAP FOR TODAY
- -

Take the bold step of making a commitment to being the luckiest person you've ever met. Of course, you have no idea if you can pull this off. None of us do.

Use this commitment statement to open up a new world to explore:

I commit to becoming the luckiest person I've ever met.

Take a few moments to get this commitment established in your mind and body. It's a bold idea, so give it the attention it deserves.

Imagine people looking at you and thinking, "That's the luckiest person I've ever met!" Own it, let yourself feel it, and carry it on through your day.

DAY 361
Ending Power Struggles in Relationship

Remember this piece of relationship wisdom from earlier in the year—money problems aren't about money, and sex problems aren't about sex? The point I was making, that problems are seldom what we think they are, is so important that we'll take a deeper look at it today.

According to research, couples mainly fight about what I call the "big four": chores, children, money, and sex. In each of those subjects, there are always deeper issues that are keeping the surface problems from resolving. When the deeper issue is addressed, the problem stops recycling.

Often the underlying issue is a power struggle about who's "boss" in the relationship. In power-struggle relationships, much energy is spent fighting about who's right and who's wrong. Sex, money, and other common issues such as chores and parenting are simply the venues in which the power struggles are acted out.

Power struggles are always driven by fear; when people are willing to explore the fear beneath the struggle—whether it's about money, sex, kids, or the dishes—the surface issue can often be resolved quickly.

What are those fears that cause power struggles to recycle? Today's leap gives you an opportunity to find out. (Not everybody has power struggles in their relationships, so if today's leap doesn't fit for you, use one of the Bonus Leaps.)

- -
YOUR LEAP FOR TODAY
- -

Take a moment to reflect on your current and past closest relationships. Use the following wonder questions to facilitate your awareness:

Hmmm, in my closest relationship now, do we have recycling power struggles about sex, money, children, or chores?

Hmmm, beneath the surface issues, what am I really scared about?

Bring those questions to life in your mind and body. Let your wondering extend into your day as you pause occasionally to bring the questions to mind.

DAY 362
Breath Presence

We are here and it is now. Further than that, all human knowledge is moonshine.

—H. L. Mencken, American journalist and critic

Our upper limits keep us focused on the past and future, which robs us of the opportunity to make necessary changes in the present. That's why I'm so passionate about healthy breathing. There is no better way to anchor yourself in the present moment than to take a conscious breath. Every mindful breath you take brings you into the here and now, which is the only place you can truly access your creativity.

When you get your breathing working in harmony with nature, you automatically open up creative space inside yourself. Keeping your belly relaxed is important, because only that will give your diaphragm room to move down through its full range of motion with your in-breath.

When an in-breath comes, your belly should relax to receive it. Holding your belly muscles tight prevents full reception of the in-breath.

YOUR LEAP FOR TODAY

The importance of keeping your stomach muscles relaxed cannot be overemphasized. To heighten awareness, start by tightening and relaxing your belly muscles several times. After you've tensed and released your stomach muscles a few times, add your breathing to the process. Let yourself take deep, easy breaths while keeping your belly muscles as relaxed as you possibly can.

Throughout your day, be aware of whether your belly muscles tighten in response to things that occur. Note the negative effect of tight belly muscles on your breathing.

When you notice tension in your stomach muscles, relax and let your breathing deepen and become easy again.

DAY 363
Spiritual and Mystical Experiences

I've been a daily meditator for more than fifty years now, and with every passing year I love and appreciate it more. The reason I love meditation so much is that it brings the spiritual experience into life every day. I find a direct connection to the mystical is just as nurturing as fresh air, exercise, and good breathing.

Whatever the path, through meditation, prayer, yoga, or other practices, I think we need to feel our spiritual essence on a regular basis to feel completely satisfied in life. Communing with your deepest spiritual self is a direct investment you can make every day in bringing your genius to light.

YOUR LEAP FOR TODAY

First, reflect on this wonder question:

Hmmm, what are two or three spiritual or mystical experiences that have shaped my life?

Then this one:

Hmmm, what could I do to open myself to an abundance of benign mystical experiences on a regular basis?

Savor these questions now and float them through your awareness as you go through your day.

DAY 364
Activism

Sacred activism is the fusion of the mystic's passion for God with the activist's passion for justice—creating a third fire, which is the burning sacred heart that longs to help, preserve, and nurture every living thing.

—Andrew Harvey, British author and religious scholar

Even though I was on college campuses from 1968 to 1974, a peak time of activism around the Vietnam War, I was pretty much oblivious to it for two reasons. First, I was consumed by a passion for the profession I was training for, counseling and clinical psychology. Also, I'd grown up in a political family—Mom was the mayor and my aunt a speechwriter for a senator. I heard political conversations around me every day, and by the time I got to my rebellious teen years I'd turned my back on the whole enterprise.

I didn't awaken an interest in the political world until my thirties. Now, I feel like I've found a balance between my commitment to exploring the inner world and my desire to make the world a better place through activism.

YOUR LEAP FOR TODAY

What are your current thoughts and feelings about activism? Today's leap gives you an opportunity to explore this area of life. Use these questions to stimulate a conversation with yourself.

What is my current level of activism?

What is my experience of Andrew Harvey's description of the "burning sacred heart that longs to help, preserve, and nurture every living thing"?

Where would my activism be most usefully focused?

Since politics, ecology, and human rights issues are so much a part of the world, it can be helpful to know where you stand and how you want to be involved.

DAY 365
Make the Big Leap Together

There was a time when a lot of my friendships consisted mainly of listening to each other complain and trading victim stories. The saying "misery loves company" was certainly true for me. I woke up to this problem in my twenties and did some major housecleaning in my friendship network.

I went through an even bigger housecleaning when I became aware of my Upper Limit Problems and saw how some of my friends were holding me back. I realized that spending time with people who were still caught in the grip of their upper limits (and worse, wanted me to stay there with them) wasn't a good idea. I began looking for people who understood my vision.

I was lucky enough to find quite a few (including my partner, Katie) who were happy to join forces and provide support for one another. We also kept each other conscious by giving our permission for the others in our group to gently call us out on our upper-limit symptoms.

YOUR LEAP FOR TODAY

Find at least three people to form a Big Leap support group or alliance. It can be a virtual or in-person group. You can meet formally once a week or once a month, or it can be a more informal connection—like a WhatsApp group, where you check in every day or every week.

Whatever type of group you choose, be sure to spend time reminding one another of your goal to feel the maximum love, abundance, and success possible. Share your victories and help each other through any challenges that arise. I think you'll be impressed and delighted by the power of a shared intention.

Congratulations! You have completed your Big Leap Year. Over the next few days, try to identify the ways that you feel different from and the same as the person who started this journey. If you've been journaling, take some time to read through your answers and notes from the past fifty-two weeks. Take some time to reflect on the ways you will bring everything you've learned into the next phase of your life, and then . . . it's time to celebrate this amazing achievement!

BONUS
LEAPS

-- -- -- -- -- -- -- --

In the course of *Your Big Leap Year*, you'll
probably come across content that doesn't
fit for you. (Or if it's a calendar Leap Year,
you'll need one more Daily Leap!) If that
happens, use these Bonus Leaps to fill in.
That way, you won't disturb your momentum. Each Bonus Leap has a piece of foundational wisdom and an affirmation that's
always useful.

BONUS LEAP 1
Natural Genius

You have within you a natural genius, an essential part of you that can be brought forth, nurtured, and expressed. Keep this key concept in the background of everything you learn in your Big Leap Year.

Your genius is a combination of what you most love to do and what makes your best contribution to the world. With practice, you can craft an entire life in your Genius Zone.

- -
YOUR LEAP FOR TODAY
- -

Use this essential commitment statement to make every moment of your life a deepening relationship with your natural genius:

I commit to doing what I most love to do and what makes my best contribution to the world around me.

Circulate the affirmation through your mind several times and feel the idea in your body. Dedicate yourself to it, body and soul. As you move through your day today, refresh it in your mind and feel it in your body again and again.

BONUS LEAP 2
Expanding Time

There's always plenty of time to learn how to create more time. That's because if you have an intention to create more time, your mind will get busy figuring out how to do it. In working on my genius over the past forty-plus years, my own relationship to time has changed so profoundly that I barely recognize the way I used to be.

In my twenties, I always felt like I was in a hurry and couldn't catch up. There was never enough time. Then Einstein Time dawned on me, and I stopped being the victim of time. The idea that I could make the time I needed to do the things I really loved was revolutionary and compelling. The payoff was equally compelling: I haven't been in a hurry since then.

- -
YOUR LEAP FOR TODAY
- -

Wherever you are in your relationship with time, take a few moments right now to develop a friendlier connection to this big subject. Use this affirmation to open a new space of possibility in your time consciousness:

I enjoy all the time I need to express more and more of my genius every day.

Say the affirmation in your mind and let yourself savor it in your body. Throughout your day, bring this idea to mind and pause to celebrate its power to change your relationship to time.

BONUS LEAP 3
Savor Savoring

One of the most important accelerators you can use in your Big Leap practice is the act of savoring.

Savoring is to gratitude what a deep, soul-stirring kiss is to a peck on the cheek.

Savoring is letting the feeling of gratefulness soak in until it's a whole-body/being experience.

Savoring counteracts your inborn survival tendency to notice the negative in life more than the positive. It helps the positive register more fully in your deepest self.

As I got better at savoring the moments in my life, I experienced an enhanced connection to my genius. I hope it will do the same for you.

YOUR LEAP FOR TODAY

Look around you and find something or someone to appreciate and feel gratitude for. Take a deep breath or two, and let the feeling of thankfulness, appreciation, awe, pleasure, or love settle into every part of your being.

Stay with the deepening until you get a whole-body smile. Consciously experience the pleasure of that feeling. Soak it in.

Repeat as often as necessary to make savoring your default response.

BONUS LEAP 4
The Big Leap Response

Though your upper-limit symptoms may vary, your response is always the same: switch your focus to expanding your capacity for positive energy.

When you don't get caught up wrestling with each ULP symptom, you're free to address the universal underlying cause.

- -
YOUR LEAP FOR TODAY
- -

Today, if you find yourself suffering, unhappy, or in pain, take a moment to reflect on this question: Could this be me upper-limiting myself?

It may be obvious—perhaps you just had an uptick in the areas of connection, intimacy, career, creativity, or money, and you've gone beyond your capacity for feeling good, triggering your upper limits. Or you may not see a direct connection.

In either case, in that moment, allow your whole being to experience more good feeling. Consciously fill the container of your mind and heart with all the love, happiness, and abundance you can. Savor the warmth and sweetness you feel inside. With each inhale, add a little more good feeling, and with each exhale, relax your body a tiny bit more.

This will help dissolve your current ULPs and prevent future ones.

BONUS LEAP 5
The Antidote to Relationship ULPs

In many of the leaps, you explored the inner flow of good feeling. Today, shift your focus to the flow of loving connection in your closest relationships. When I first focused on this area in myself, it was early in the eighties and a couple of years into my relationship with Katie. The two people closest to me at the time were Katie and my teenage daughter, then in boarding school in New England.

As I began to focus on the flow of connection between Katie and me, I noticed certain patterns that repeated themselves. We would get along just fine for a few days, then something would happen to interrupt the flow. Sometimes it was a critical remark leading to an argument, but other times it was something external like a plumbing emergency. Eventually, we just came to regard them all as Upper Limit Problems and started shining the light of awareness on them. It took a few months, but we eventually cleared ourselves of the pattern.

YOUR LEAP FOR TODAY

Pick one of your closest relationships to focus on. Use this commitment to extend the amount of time you experience the flow of loving connection:

I commit to feeling a flow of loving connection with _____ for longer and longer periods of time each day.

Say the commitment to yourself and aloud several times. Bring it to life in your awareness often as you go through your day. Going forward, notice the effects of your commitment on your close relationships.

GRATITUDE AND FAREWELL

As we come to the end of *Your Big Leap Year,* I want to express my deepest gratitude to you for your participation in the journey. I celebrate you for making the choice to go on an adventure that I believe to be genuinely heroic.

Joseph Campbell studied the myths of cultures all over the world and found a common structure for the hero's journey. At first, the person is living an everyday life but has grown dissatisfied with a mundane existence. Then, the person is awakened by a call to adventure and sees the possibility of a new world. In the third stage, the hero crosses over into that new world and leaves the old life behind. In the new world, the hero is confronted by one challenge after another that test character, commitment, and creativity. Heroes who pass the tests enter a fifth stage Campbell called "master of two worlds." You are able to function successfully in the material world while fully embracing your spiritual essence.

The *Star Wars* movies are all based on Campbell's stages of the hero's journey. Luke Skywalker's adventure begins when his world is blown up, sending him on a cross-galaxy quest to surmount all manner of challenges. Can you relate to that? I know I can. Fifty years ago, I was living a dreary existence, overweight, unhappy at home and work, puffing my health away on two to three packs of cigarettes a day. Then I caught a glimpse of a new world and chose to step into it. Within a year I created an entirely new life, one hundred pounds lighter, free of addictions, and liberated from the even heavier burdens of a stressful job and a painful relationship.

Now you know how I did it. You've been exploring that new world with me for the past year. Neither of us know where the future will take us, but wherever you go, know that I'm over here in my life on the same wondrous journey as you.

Three hundred and sixty-five days ago, we started this journey in a spirit of gratitude. Let's close in that same spirit.

Take this moment to celebrate yourself for the hero's journey you've been on. You were called to the adventure of bringing your genius to the world around you. You responded and are doing the work necessary to master the new world. That makes you a hero in my book.

Celebrate yourself for the investments you've made in your genius. You are worth celebrating, and I want you to remember to do it often in all your days to come.

Wherever you go, may your adventure be as full of wonder, creativity, abundance, and love as mine has been.

ACKNOWLEDGMENTS

I'm grateful to the many colleagues I've had the pleasure of discussing human transformation with over the years. Chief among them is David Hubbard, MD, whose company I've enjoyed for more than fifty years. He has been invaluable in grounding my ideas in supportive scientific research. I also want to salute the late Dr. Dwight Webb, who mentored me in the early stages of my career.

I'm incredibly grateful for the thousands of students in our classes, first in my twenty-one years teaching graduate students at University of Colorado, and later through our Hendricks Institute programs for professionals. Interacting with keen minds for the past half-century has been one of the greatest gifts of my life.

I'm also blessed with a circle of friends around the world with whom I discuss all my ideas. Jim Exon, Jim Selman, Kenny Loggins, Geneen Roth, Sophie Chiche, Meinrad Milz, MD, and Katrin Bieber, MD.

Lastly, I'm grateful once again for the editorial genius of Carol Kline, who brings clarity and congeniality to every project we work on together.

ABOUT THE AUTHOR

GAY HENDRICKS has been a leader in the fields of relationship transformation and body-mind therapies for more than forty-five years.

After earning his PhD in counseling psychology from Stanford University, Gay served as professor of counseling psychology at the University of Colorado for twenty-one years, then went on to found the Hendricks Institute, which offers seminars in North America, Asia, and Europe. Throughout his career, he has coached more than eight hundred executives, including the top management at firms such as Dell, Hewlett-Packard, Motorola, and KLM.

Dr. Hendricks has written more than forty books, including bestsellers such as *Five Wishes*, *The Big Leap*, and *Conscious Loving* (coauthored with his mate for more than forty years, Dr. Kathlyn Hendricks), the last two used as primary texts in universities around the world.

In 2003, Gay co-founded the Spiritual Cinema Circle, which distributes inspirational movies and conscious entertainment to subscribers in seventy-plus countries. Gay has offered seminars worldwide and appeared on more than five hundred radio and television shows, including *The Oprah Winfrey Show*, CNN, CNBC, *48 Hours*, and others. In recent years, his passion has been writing mystery novels.

DON'T MISS MORE FROM
GAY HENDRICKS

"Those intrigued by how mental visualization and intentionality can lead to a 'more abundant' life will love this."
—PUBLISHERS WEEKLY

"*Conscious Luck* takes everything you know about luck…and turns it on its head! This is an engaging, mind-blowing, and ultimately practical guide to creating more luck in your life. I highly recommend it!"
—MARCI SHIMOFF, #1 *New York Times* bestselling author, *Happy for No Reason* and *Chicken Soup for the Woman's Soul*

"The inner intelligence of the body is the ultimate and supreme genius. Gay shows how to connect with this inner intelligence and discover the secrets to healing, love, intuition, and insight."
—DEEPAK CHOPRA

ST. MARTIN'S
ESSENTIALS